Praise for *I Lived to*

"*I Lived to Tell the World* is a beautiful and searing gift of memory and reckoning. With this anthology of stories told by genocide survivors, Elizabeth Mehren offers stunning narrative and analysis in league with other unforgettable books that at once plumb the depths of human cruelty and soar to the highest levels of resilience and joy, among them *The Diary of Anne Frank*, *A Problem from Hell* by Samantha Power, and *We Wish to Inform You That Tomorrow We Will Be Killed With Our Families* by Philip Gourevitch. I can't wait to share these stories with my global health and journalism graduate students."

—JENNIFER BEARD, Department of Global Health, Boston University School of Public Health

"Drawing on vivid accounts and poignant anecdotes, this book demonstrates how storytelling is an indispensable tool in revealing truths. Seamlessly weaving personal experiences with global issues, it is a testament to the profound impact of narratives in challenging injustice and fostering action. It shows how the tenacious pursuit of truth-telling not only opens doors to accountability but also serves as a beacon of hope in a world shrouded in misinformation."

—GEETA ANAND, Dean, Graduate School of Journalism, UC Berkeley, and Pulitzer Prize-winning author and journalist

"It is common to look at the world's most horrifying man-made tragedies—war, genocide, mass persecution—through a magnifying glass, driving home the scale of the crime. In this powerful book, Elizabeth Mehren uses a microscope instead, zeroing in on the actual human beings who have been the victims of these tragedies, and the amazing courage and resilience that marks their refusal to let the horrors they've suffered define them. You'll find many people to cheer for in these pages."

—MICKEY EDWARDS, retired member of Congress and co-author of *Congress: The First Branch*

"*I Lived to Tell the World* is a book of incredible power, containing stories of courage beyond measure and perseverance beyond imagining. It is also a book that challenges us all to never forget the words of the great Elie Wiesel, who said, 'I swore never to be silent whenever and wherever human beings endure suffering and humiliation.'"
—KERRY TYMCHUK, executive director, Oregon Historical Society

"A phenomenal book! Pick it up!"
—RUFUS WILLIAMS, host of "The Morning Show With Rufus Williams," WVON-AM radio, Chicago

I LIVED TO TELL THE WORLD

Stories from Survivors of Holocaust, Genocide, and the Atrocities of War

ELIZABETH MEHREN

with a foreword by Timothy Longman

Oregon State University Press Corvallis
The Immigrant Story Portland

Oregon State University Press in Corvallis, Oregon, is located within the traditional homelands of the Mary's River or Ampinefu Band of Kalapuya. Following the Willamette Valley Treaty of 1855, Kalapuya people were forcibly removed to reservations in Western Oregon. Today, living descendants of these people are a part of the Confederated Tribes of Grand Ronde Community of Oregon (grandronde.org) and the Confederated Tribes of the Siletz Indians (ctsi.nsn.us).

Library of Congress Cataloging-in-Publication Data
Names: Mehren, Elizabeth, author.
Title: I lived to tell the world : stories from survivors of Holocaust, genocide, and the atrocities of war / Elizabeth Mehren ; with a foreword by Timothy Longman
Description: Corvallis : Oregon State University Press, [2024] | Includes bibliographical references.
Identifiers: LCCN 2024000998 | ISBN 9781962645072 (paperback ; alk. paper) | ISBN 9781962645089 (ebook)
Subjects: LCSH: Genocide survivors—United States—Case studies. | Holocaust survivors—United States—Case studies. | War victims—United States—Case studies. | Victims of political violence—United States—Case studies. | Genocide. | Holocaust, Jewish (1939-1945)
Classification: LCC HV6322.7 .M437 2024 | DDC 362.88/5092273—dc23/eng/20240203
LC record available at https://lccn.loc.gov/2024000998

∞ This paper meets the requirements of ANSI/NISO Z39.48-1992 (Permanence of Paper).

First published in 2024 by Oregon State University Press
in cooperation with The Immigrant Story
Second printing 2024
Printed in the United States of America

The Immigrant Story (TIS) is a volunteer-run nonprofit founded in 2017 whose mission is to foster empathy and build a more inclusive community by sharing thoughtful narratives of immigrants and refugees who often overcame tremendous odds to reach the United States. TIS combines nuanced storytelling with subtle performance art to share high-quality programs with the community. TIS public arts programming includes live events, exhibitions, podcasts, oral history preservation efforts, and development of public school curriculum.
www.theimmigrantstory.org

Oregon State University Press
121 The Valley Library
Corvallis OR 97331-4501
541-737-3166 • fax 541-737-3170
www.osupress.oregonstate.edu

This book is dedicated to those who have survived unthinkable human cruelty.

I believe firmly and profoundly that whoever listens to a witness becomes a witness, so those who hear us, those who read us must continue to bear witness for us. Until now, they're doing it with us. At a certain point in time, they will do it for all of us.

—Elie Wiesel

Contents

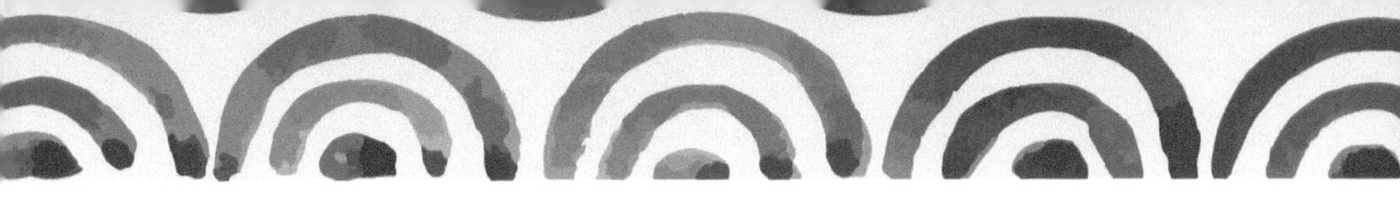

Foreword

My friend Espérance lost almost everything in the 1994 genocide against the Tutsi in Rwanda. She became a friend when I lived in Rwanda in 1992 and 1993, and when I returned to the country in 1995 as a human rights researcher, I relocated her, and she told me her story.

During the genocide, Espérance was held captive for more than a month and repeatedly raped, and then she spent another two months in hiding, fearing for her life. When she emerged from hiding at the end of the genocide in July 1994, she found that her parents and grandparents, all of her brothers and sisters, and all of her aunts and uncles had been murdered.

In fact, in her entire extended family of more than two hundred people, only she and two young second cousins had survived.

Espérance suffered greatly, and she might have spent the rest of her life mourning her losses. But of course, she did not. Like so many people who have survived the horrors of genocide and mass atrocity, Espérance picked up the pieces of her shattered past and set out to create a new life. She moved with her two cousins to Rwanda's capital city, Kigali, found a good job, and enrolled her cousins in school. She eventually traveled abroad to earn a college degree, then came back to Rwanda to take a position working to provide opportunity to the underprivileged.

The word "genocide" evokes almost unthinkable horror and suffering. In fact, when Polish lawyer Raphael Lemkin coined the word during the Second World War, he hoped to focus international attention on the specific horrors that genocide involves. In the face of the Holocaust, Lemkin hoped to raise awareness about the uniquely horrible nature of this crime that seeks to exterminate a people based simply on their identity.

As Alain Destexhe, the head of Doctors Without Borders, explained in *Rwanda and Genocide in the Twentieth Century* (New York University Press, 1995), "Genocide is distinguishable from all other crimes by the motivation behind it. Genocide is a crime on a different scale to all other crimes against humanity and implies an intention to completely exterminate the chosen group. Genocide is therefore both the gravest and greatest of the crimes against humanity."

Genocide has taken millions of lives over the past century. Even after the calls for "never again" in the aftermath of the Holocaust, the horrors of genocide have swept across Indonesia, Cambodia, Iraq, Rwanda, Bosnia, and Darfur. In just the past decade, the Yazidi people of Iraq and the Rohingya people of Myanmar have faced violent attempts to exterminate them, while the Chinese persecution of the Uyghur people looks increasingly like genocide.

Although journalists, activists, and others have sought to raise the alarm about genocidal violence in these cases, the international community has failed to act, allowing "never again" to happen again and again.

The international community's consistent failure to respond to genocide and other mass atrocities may be driven in part by the sense of fatalism and hopelessness that the focus on genocide's horrors encourages. The individual human suffering becomes lost in scenes of vast destruction and reports of the large numbers of dead and displaced. The numbers themselves are numbing, leaving a sense that nothing can be done.

What may be missing from international consciousness is the human face of these tragedies, the stories of individuals who have suffered and, like my friend Espérance, found ways not only to survive but to build new lives. If only people could understand the humanity that genocide destroys and see not the numbing numbers but the individual faces of those who have been lost and those who have survived, they might be more willing to act.

This collection, thus, plays an important part in promoting understanding of genocide and mass atrocity. Reading the stories of individuals who have lost their families, experienced violence themselves, and been forced out of their countries brings a human face to the horrors of genocide.

But significantly, these are also stories of survival and resilience. Those who courageously tell their stories in this book lived through the horrors they recount and then went on to make a new life for themselves in the United States. They have learned English, found jobs, married, and had children. The richness and productivity of their lives demonstrates just how much the world has lost through the deaths of so many thousands of their compatriots to genocide.

This book makes another important contribution to changing popular attitudes. At a time when sympathy for immigrants in the United States has waned, the stories of these individuals from such diverse backgrounds and how they have adapted so well to this country help to dispel the idea that immigrants are a source of crime and social problems. These immigrants have become active in their communities and contributed to our society in significant ways that call for sympathy rather than hostility.

To hear these stories of suffering and survival, then, is to see the humanity at stake when genocide takes place. These stories push us to act to stop genocide when it is happening and to show compassion for those who survive.

What we ultimately learn from these immigrant stories is that the people who fall victim to genocide are not so different from us. In the end, we learn that genocide is not merely an attack on strangers in faraway lands but an attack on us all and our common humanity.

Timothy Longman

TIMOTHY LONGMAN, professor of international relations and political science at Boston University, is director of BU's Institute on Culture, Religion and World Affairs and for eight years was director of BU's African studies program. He is the author of *Memory and Justice in Post-Genocide Rwanda* and *Christianity and Genocide in Rwanda*, both published by Cambridge University Press.

Introduction

Deep in the southeast of India, in the small village where I grew up, stories were what held our little community together. Our village, surrounded by rice paddy fields with thousands of temples, had no more than one thousand people in it. During the summer months when our school was not in session, grand festivals at these temples led to a culminating day of celebration. Devotees gathered. Vendors sold rainbow-hued candy. Teenage girls, some from our school and others from big cities nearby, wore colorful new silk half sarees. There were even some young men drinking local toddy and arrack. To me, as a small child, they seemed loud and scary.

Everyone in the village was involved in preparing for these festivals, which marked the celebration of a successful harvest and a time to give prayers for the upcoming season. Villagers erected a makeshift stage in the middle of the street and raised enough money to bring a locally known theater company from another nearby town to enact epic stories. As a young boy, growing up without television or a nearby theater to watch movies, these were the biggest shows I had ever seen. They were operatic, with an eight-piece band complete with a pedal harmonium and percussion instruments. Without mics, the actors sang at the top of their lungs to give voice to their stories, bringing them to life.

I remember going to see these plays with my grandmother. By then my grandfather had died, but my grandmother, though widowed, loved to get out and take part in these festivities. The plays would start after dinner, so she would take me and find a front row seat. We sat on the street, surrounded by friends and family from the village. By day in our village, the sun blazed relentlessly, but at night, the air was finally cooling off. Before us, the stories unfolded, accompanied by rhythmic music and dance. If I dozed off, my grandmother would wake me so I wouldn't miss an exciting scene. Year after year, harvest after harvest, we stayed up till the wee hours, watching and listening to these old stories coming to life.

Even as a very small boy, I found each story beautiful. I was mesmerized by the language and the storytelling itself. Even now, I remember the pictures that those stories created in my mind as a child and how they comforted me.

From these stories I learned important life lessons. I learned that truth matters, that you should be humble, serve others, and stand up for the values you know are right.

I also saw how the stories brought communities together and drew people closer.

Meanwhile, as I was growing up, events on the other side of the world were happening that would change my life and draw me across the globe. In the United States, people were protesting against the status quo, taking to the streets and the courts to insist on change. The anti-Vietnam war movement, women's liberation, and the civil rights movement challenged and helped transform US society.

One important element of this ferment, the civil rights movement, led to a nationwide push to remove racial discrimination from US law on many fronts, including immigration. President Lyndon Baines Johnson signed into law the Immigration and Naturalization Act of 1965, just a year after the landmark Civil Rights Act of 1964 became law. The immigration bill ended the system, in place since the 1920s, of having national quotas that favored migration from northern and western European countries. Instead, the new law gave preference to immigrants with skills judged useful to the United States and to reuniting families of individuals already in the United States. This change enabled migration from non-European countries. Higher education in the United States opened its doors to students from around the world, offering opportunities to further develop skills and, in many cases, to take jobs in the United States.

I was one of those students. In 1980, as a young man, I left my home in India and came to the United States as a graduate student in physics at Purdue University in Indiana.

I was wide-eyed and hopeful. I was comfortably settling down, and I was starting to realize my American dream. One Friday night, along with a couple of friends, I went to a local bar to celebrate the end of a long week and enjoy a happy hour together.

That evening, while I was standing in line for the rest room, a guy came out of nowhere, angry and yelling racial slurs. He hit me in the face before I even saw it coming. My face was bleeding, my glasses lay broken on the floor, and I was shaken to my core. Nobody came up and asked if I was OK. I was ashamed and didn't want my friends to see me getting beaten up. I went into the restroom and put napkins on my face to stop the bleeding on my nose. Then I went back to the table and asked my friends to give me a ride home.

It was by no means my only experience with anti-immigrant bias. But I never talked about that incident again, and each time someone called me a terrible name or judged me on the basis of my dark brown skin, I swallowed it.

I stayed silent until February 2017, when two Indian engineers went to a bar in Kansas for their own happy hour to watch a basketball game and get a drink after work. Suddenly, another customer came over to their table and shouted at them. "What kind of visa are you on?" he asked. "Are you illegals?"

Then he pulled out a gun and started shooting at them, yelling, "Get out of my country, you terrorists."

By the end of that day, one Indian, Srinivas Kuchibhotla, lay dead as a result of that incident. Two others, including a good Samaritan who came to help them, were injured.

When that shooting happened in Kansas, my own experience from almost forty years earlier came flooding back to me. Firearms were less widespread in the early 1980s than they are today, but if the man in that Indiana bar had had a gun, he might well have shot me. My life could have ended then. The Kansas story could have been my story. Right away, I knew I had to do something.

But I felt like I was just one guy in Portland, Oregon. What could I do to help address an increasingly toxic national conversation about immigration?

What I knew was that stories have power. Stories bring communities together. Stories create empathy and compassion. They inspire and encourage and show the way. A story can reveal history and present facts. Stories can reduce or even reverse stereotypes. Stories can make us laugh and cry. Stories can help us to confront difficult truths.

So, what I could do was to tell stories.

The very next day I registered the domain theimmigrantstory.org, taught myself how to create a website, and began to collect stories about immigrants. I wanted to humanize us. A common theme among immigrants is that America is the land of possibilities. This is something I believe in, too. Even today, I still believe that if you put your mind to it, you can make almost anything happen in this country. And what I want to make happen is for people to realize that immigrants are not "others." They are people just like themselves. At The Immigrant Story, we like to say that we tell stories to change the world.

My first interview was with a young Bhutanese woman who was born in a refugee camp in Nepal. Her family had landed there after the government of Bhutan conducted ethnic cleansing to remove all those who looked like South Asians from Bhutan, even though they had been born there and lived there for generations. As a novice at interviewing, I didn't take notes, but just recorded the conversation on a cell phone.

That interview opened my heart. Sumitra was a survivor. She talked about the trauma she and her parents had experienced for the twenty years they had lived in the refugee camp, without a country of their own. My next few interviews were with several other young women, all survivors of genocides and wars in Somalia, Iraq, and Burma. Spending time with these young people was my introduction to this topic of genocide.

Hearing their stories was transformative. When they offered first-hand testimony to what they had been through, I became a witness to these events, and I could not turn away. These young people told me how their parents and families had survived something that seems beyond the capacity of humans to endure, almost beyond imagining. And yet they had also made lives for themselves, created homes here in Oregon, and given back to their communities.

Ever since those first interviews with the young survivors of war and genocide, I have found myself drawn to these stories. On the one hand, I want to understand them, understand how people, just like me, yet clearly not just like me, have survived these atrocities. Also, I felt that, by listening, I had taken on an obligation. They had trusted me with their stories, and I had to do something with that gift.

Through no grand master plan—but simply because they were compelling narratives—these stories about survivors of wars and genocides were among the earliest pieces we published on our website. Later, when the Oregon Jewish Museum and Center for Holocaust Education asked us to create an exhibit, I decided it should be about survivors of war and genocides. It seemed like an appropriate place for these stories to be heard. The very first story that appears in this book is Elizabeth Mehren's profile of Les and Eva Aigner, published on October 11, 2018, with the headline "Miracles, Memories and a Message."

During our interview with Les and Eva Aigner, they told us that at one time there were forty Holocaust survivors here in Portland, speaking out and telling their stories. But now only three were left. So that's what this book does; it preserves the stories that would otherwise be lost. Sadly, with the death of Les Aigner, that number has now shrunk to two.

For many years, the Aigners did not speak out. Both held jobs, and they lived a productive life. They sent two children to college and saw them marry and have children. They defined themselves as Americans, not as victims of the largest mass killing in human history. But as the chorus of Holocaust deniers grew louder and more strident, many Holocaust survivors, like the Aigners, made it their mission to tell and retell their stories. Their purpose was to deliver the message that what happened to them should "never again" happen to anyone.

Tragically, however, the ideal of "never again" has gotten lost, and instead there are wars erupting "again and again."

In the seventy-five years since the Nazi Holocaust, many more wars and genocides have taken place. But the survivors have rarely talked about them to a world already saturated in violence and tragedy. Those who live through these events know in a visceral way that they must "never again" happen, but it is easy for the rest of us to forget, to look away from such atrocities, or to accept that they are inevitable.

In fact, although the Holocaust has been examined in detail, most of the genocides since then have been less noticed by the world at large. One reason is that, instead of paying attention and considering the causes and impact of current events, many of us have an addiction to the novelty offered by the media, which often fosters a habit of constantly looking for the next shocking news. As soon as each crisis hits the front page or blasts across the screen of our phone or laptop, we move on to the next one. It's fashionable to talk only about the latest disaster, the crisis of the day.

But our tragic mistakes, as well as the grand triumphs of our history, must be faced so that we can learn from them and not repeat our blunders. Unless we collectively remember our history, we forget how much war we human beings have brought upon ourselves in less than a century.

I Lived to Tell the World brings together stories of some of these major wars and genocides since the Holocaust. We have now interviewed sixty survivors of wars and genocides. Out of all those, we chose just fourteen for this book. We selected stories of people who lived in the midst of war and who now live in Oregon. They are not merely survivors but people who have moved on from the tragedies they have faced.

We tried to achieve both geographic and geopolitical diversity, but we simply could not locate subjects living in Oregon who have survived some of the conflicts. For example, Central America is not represented in this volume, and we regret that absence. We rejected several stories because we could not verify key details. In the end, we looked for and selected strong, honest stories whose facts we could verify. We tried to find a variety of voices: men, women, couples and in the case of several subjects, child survivors (or survivors who were children at the time).

From the outset, our intention was to assure the authenticity of the voices we were presenting. We were not seeking an arm's-length perspective. We also wanted to be absolutely certain we got our facts right about events that took place far away, and in some cases, long ago. We wanted the tone to be clear and appropriate. And so we decided to make these interviews a collaborative process. Our subjects were given the opportunity to review their stories. We welcomed their input and in almost all cases accommodated the changes they requested. We understood that this was a deviation from standard journalistic practice. But what we were aiming for with these stories was not conventional journalism. It was authentic reporting, thorough historical and contextual research, painstaking fact-checking, and deep respect for the experiences of our subjects, as they lived them.

Finally, each recorded interview, which is a vital part of Oregon history, is archived at the Oregon Historical Society for anyone to access.

Elizabeth Mehren came to The Immigrant Story after a rich career as an award-winning reporter and editor for the *Los Angeles Times*, *The Washington Post*, and other publications. She spent a decade as a professor of journalism at Boston University's College of Communication and has authored or co-authored four previous books. For this book, she conducted and wrote up all the interviews. In addition, she conducted extensive research to understand each conflict. Often, she consulted with academic experts, government officials, authors, and individuals who lived through the same or comparable experiences in order to assure full accuracy and context. She has worked hard to present these complex stories, along with their historical background, in a concise and engaging way. She writes with deep compassion supported by a skill with words that comes from her years as a journalist.

Reading these stories, perhaps we all wonder where we would find the strength to survive such challenges as they have faced. But what these stories tell me is that human beings, people like me, are capable of immense—often surprising—strength, courage, and resilience. Even though my problems are so much smaller than what they endured, I can learn from them. I can follow their lead to become stronger and more resilient. These stories give me hope, hope for humanity, and hope for myself.

So *I Lived to Tell the World* is a call to action for all of us. The subjects have done their part by telling their stories. It is up to us to do the next part: to listen to their words and do our best to act on what we have learned. We owe it to them to stand up against the injustices we see and hear and to confront what is sometimes even more damaging, indifference to injustice. Individually and together, we can engage with the world around us and help to work toward a future in which what happened to these storytellers and their families does not happen again.

Sankar Raman, board president,
with Nancy E. Dollahite, The Immigrant Story

CHAPTER 1

So Much to Tell the World

"Rwanda, Bosnia, Myanmar, Sudan . . ."

That was nonagenarian Les Aigner, back in 2018, sitting in his cozy living room in Tualatin, Oregon, as he pondered the frightful fact that even in a new century—the twenty-first—mass killings based solely on racial, religious, or ethnic hatred continued.

And that was before Russia launched its genocidal war against Ukraine, targeting ethnic minorities, destroying entire cities, and killing countless thousands—and before the United Nations High Commission for Human Rights concluded in a 2022 report that "serious human rights violations have been committed" by China in its treatment of Uyghurs and other mostly Muslim minorities in Xinjiang Province.

For Aigner and his wife Eva, genocide was personal. Les was just fifteen years old when he was packed into a train and shipped off to Auschwitz, the first of four Nazi concentration camps where he was confined during World War II. He was so naive when he arrived at Auschwitz that he thought the vaporous clouds spewing from the camp's smokestacks came from a bakery, not a crematorium. His wife Eva, also a Hungarian Jew, spent the final years of the war in squalid conditions in Budapest's hideously crowded Jewish ghetto. With her mother and sister, she foraged for food in filthy, rat-infested conditions. As Hitler's forces faced defeat in that war's final days, only a genuine miracle saved Eva and her sister from being shot alongside the Danube River by Nazi soldiers determined to eradicate the Jewish presence in Europe. Les, for his part, weighed just seventy-five pounds when he was liberated from Dachau, the slave labor camp near Munich where new arrivals passed through a gate bearing the ironic motto "Arbreit Macht Frei"—"Work Sets You Free."

Anti-Semitism continued to fester in Hungary as communism took hold following the war. The Aigners grew fearful. Eventually they managed to immigrate to the United States. Speaking barely a word of English, they landed at Ellis Island, traveled by train across the United States, and ended up in a strange and distant place called Portland, Oregon. There, they forged fulfilling lives. They raised two children, became US citizens, and for many years said little about their wartime experiences. Then came the Holocaust deniers, and they knew they had to speak out. The Aigners agreed to tell their story for this book because, as Eva put it, "Hate is still with us." Hate, she said, "is a little spark, and it can become a fire."

Sadly, we lost Les Aigner in 2021. He was ninety-two years old. We are so honored and so grateful that he and Eva chose to share their stories for this book. The Aigners' words—their lived experiences—give power and perspective to the grim statistics of the Holocaust. Theirs is a first-hand view of the horrors that claimed six million Jews, Roma, LGBTQ, and others in Europe in World War II. Their clear-eyed account, told in their own voices, conveys both immediacy and legitimacy. They were there; this is what they lived through.

Our choice of the narrative format for this book was quite intentional. We share the view of numerous scholars that storytelling is a vital form of gathering and analyzing data. To quote from James Phelan, Distinguished University Professor of Arts and Humanities and director of Medical Humanities at The Ohio State University, "narrative is a way of organizing, giving meaning to and creating understanding of" the human experience. We are in accord with Phelan's "narrative theory" approach to research, in which the storyteller gives shape to the raw material underlying the narrative. In describing what is widely accepted as rhetorical narrative theory, Phelan stresses both the purposeful quality of narrative and its multidimensional validity. Good stories, Phelan asserts, engage us cognitively, emotionally, politically, ethically, ideologically, and morally. Narrative, he explains, is "a way of knowing, a way of thinking." In short, narrative is recognized as a way of bringing qualitative understanding to events and experiences. By lending a human and temporal face, narrative also can enrich abstract numerical data.

Central to the notion of narrative theory, according to Professor Sarah Cobb of George Mason University, is that "stories do not just describe reality." The use in narrative of the first-person voice—i.e., that of the subject—also legitimizes the content. For instance, she explains, when people tell a story about a problem—for example, a political event such as war—the story will encompass context, characters, and values or morals. "Emotional resonance" allows readers to connect to the story, Cobb contends. "Intellectual resonance," she says, ensures credibility. In addition, psychology Professor Michael Bamberg of Clark University maintains that narratives, often in the form of small stories, can be employed as a general strategy to clarify bigger ideas. Bamberg calls this tool narrative analysis. We are in debt also to the late H. L. Goodall of Arizona State University, who coined the term "narrative ethnography" as he explored new forms of qualitative writing within the social sciences. Goodall focused on qualitative research into systems, processes, and relationships.

The use of narratives—storytelling—can be especially valuable in unraveling the complexities of immigration, according to a trio of scholars who prepared a 2021 report for the Migration Policy Institute, Metropolitan Group, the RAND Corporation, and the National Immigration Forum. "The stories about migration and migrants can paint a rich picture of how people view the opportunities and challenges associated with the movement of people, and through what lenses," wrote Natalia Banulescu-Bogdan, Haim Malka, and Shelly Culbertson. "The building blocks of narratives are stories," they continued. "The stories people hear, see and experience over time shape how they view opportunities and threats around them." (Their findings were published in a report called "How We Talk About Migration: The Line Between Migration Narratives, Policy and Power.")

Echoing this viewpoint, public health analysts Drue H. Barrett of the Centers for Disease Control (CDC), Leonard W. Ortman (CDC) and Stephanie A. Larson, a bioethics fellow in Cleveland, wrote in the *American Political Science Review* (2021): "The advantage of the use of narrative is that it prompts the reader to connect to the issue in a more personal level compared to the case-study approach."

Finally, it's important to note that we remained mindful of the sensitive nature of each narrative in this book—so much so that we engaged in active collaboration with our subjects. Our subjects reviewed their stories in order to assure accuracy. We welcomed their input and worked interactively. So from the start, our process was entirely transparent, giving our subjects agency over their own narratives. This synergistic process also diminished the power imbalance that can sometimes emerge between subject and storyteller. Our goal at all times was to honor and elevate our subjects' authentic voices, and so we sought to write less about them than with them. These stories are the products of strong back-and-forth relationships. Indeed, we allowed each subject not only the opportunity to review his or her story prior to publication, but to make editorial changes as appropriate. We wanted to make sure that each subject had an active role in telling his or her story.

And so we present this collection of profiles of survivors of the Holocaust, genocide, and unthinkable atrocities of war. These stories can be difficult to read. They are united by the troubling truth that human cruelty sometimes knows no bounds. But each chapter is also a portrait both of courage and of human resilience. In the face of unimaginable loss, these men and women bravely embraced new lives.

Or as Eva Aigner put it so succinctly, "Somehow, our spirit was not broken."

As another example, consider Myanmar, where twenty-first-century government forces methodically emptied Rakhine State of its Rohingya Muslim population. Houses were burned, villages were flattened, cemeteries were bulldozed and many, many thousands were slain. Even more—close to one million, by most estimates—were driven from their home country. Most fled to neighboring Bangladesh, where the world's largest refugee camp now houses between 800,000 and one million Rohingyas. They are stateless, because Myanmar dubbed the Rohingya "illegal immigrants" and denied them citizenship, based only on their ethnicity. Mohammed Husson Ali was among those who managed to flee to the United States, though most of his family remains in a lean-to at the Bangladesh refugee camp. Fires spread quickly in the flimsy housing the camp's residents have constructed. Disease is rampant. For children, education is at best sporadic.

"This place should be called a twenty-first century concentration camp," he said. "People cannot go outside. There is arrest. There is killing. It is no way to live."

At any moment in history, the story of Mohammed and his fellow Rohingya would merit recording. But today, this testimony to the remarkable tenacity of the human spirit seems more timely than ever.

Listen to Emmanuel Turaturanye as he sings—sings!—the songs he has composed about love and faith. Those lyrics eluded him as, clutching the small hand of his little sister, he ran from marauding Hutu troops intent on killing every Tutsi man, woman, and child in Rwanda. About one million Rwandans, most of them Tutsi, were slaughtered in one hundred days of terror in 1994. Emmanuel Turaturanye came from a large, extended family. They were Tutsi, and his father was the village pastor.

Though nearly everyone else in his family was slain, Turaturanye and his sister were spared through good luck, quick wits, and a brave family friend who dared to show kindness and compassion. Now he is married to a beautiful American woman and lives in Beaverton. He drives a bus for Tri-Met, the county public transit system in greater Portland, and cannot stop smiling when he talks about his US-born nieces and nephews. Emmanuel Turaturanye believes that the reason he survived the killings in Rwanda was so that his story—the story of what can happen when anger and hatred run amok—would not go unheard.

"Anger," he said. "It just kills, and it destroys the soul."

Starting when he was a teenager in Baghdad, war and killings were more or less a daily diet, noted Dr. Baher Butti, an Iraqi psychiatrist. "In the Middle East, you get used to violence," he said in a remarkably even voice. But the perils kept coming closer and closer. His second-grade daughter was gravely injured when her school bus was bombed. His wife, a physician, narrowly escaped a car bombing. He was reluctant to leave because he loved his country and was committed to his work there as a mental health specialist. But the final straw came when he saw his own name on a list of political enemies of the state who were targets for assassination. That was when he rounded up his family and fled his homeland.

"This is the issue," he explained. "Staying in Iraq, I am sure I would have been killed. I just didn't know who was going to kill me, the al-Qaeda or the pro-Iranians."

As unsettling as these profiles in endurance may be, many of them also exude a quiet optimism. The subjects are, after all, survivors who have made new lives in this country. Those who have become US citizens tell us they have not missed an opportunity to vote in a city, state, or national election. Some, like Dr. Butti, rejoice and also marvel that in this country, they can voice their political opinions without fear of violent retribution.

Inside each chapter of this book is a cautionary tale. Life is fragile. Neighbors can turn on you; they can also save you. Political adversaries seldom think about the human toll of their actions in terms of individual lives. Repressive regimes can arise almost anywhere. Kindness sometimes appears in surprising places. So does cruelty.

Most Americans traditionally have viewed their freedom as an assumption. The subjects of this book know better than to take any right or privilege for granted.

These stories feel especially germane as we emerge from the fog of a pandemic. As so many Americans spent several years in social isolation, many people in our country paused to reexamine not just their personal histories, but their very sense of national identity. The once-sacred myth of the American melting pot has undergone challenges as many Americans have gazed inward, wondering how each of us fits into the grand cultural tapestry of this place—this noble experiment in self-governance—called the United States of America. Who are we, anyway? Who do we want to become?

Here in Oregon, this reckoning has occasioned an often-uncomfortable awakening to the burden of the state's racist history. The same region renowned (and sometimes reviled) throughout the country for its climate of liberal tolerance was forced to look back on a state constitution that included Black exclusion laws well into the twentieth century. Suddenly, conversations among Portland neighbors were as likely to include the words "systemic racism" as they were to center around newly discovered hiking trails. If ever there were a moment when citizens were searching for the redemptive power of resilience, it was happening in the streets, in impassioned dialogue, in real time.

For the subjects of this book, these scenes can only have evoked a sense of deja vu. What they have endured at the hands of soldiers from their own governments is in equal parts unfathomable and unconscionable. Be reminded once again that these are not easy stories. Some subjects of these stories cannot return to their homelands for fear of being tortured or killed. In at least one case, we changed surnames and did not disclose village names because the subject's family could be harmed if they were named or if their location was revealed. Be aware that each narrative in this collection will invite tears. But you will also cheer as you celebrate the survival of people you may know here in Oregon. They are social workers, public transit drivers, religious leaders. They work for TriMet, and they sterilize lab equipment at the Oregon Health & Science University. They shop at Costco. They cheer for the Portland Timbers and the Portland Trail Blazers. They send their children to local schools, and they worship within the community.

They have so much to tell each of us.

Pause, if you will, to take stock of your own life experiences as you read these stories. Ruminate on what motivates human beings to inflict colossal cruelty on other human beings. Reflect on abstract terminology—words like courage, persistence, determination, and hope. What do these words mean in your own life?

These stories are offered in hopes that they will inspire, inform, and possibly instruct. Keep in mind, not one of the subjects in this book is grandstanding. No one is presenting his or her story in search of sympathy. No one is preaching. To be sure, there are flashes of righteous anger within this volume. But there is not one narrative in this collection that approaches the tone of a screed. Rather, every one of the subjects of this book will tell you that helping to end the evil and the enmity that has touched their lives is what has prompted them to speak out.

Listen as these men and women describe what they have endured.

They have so much to tell us all.

Les Aigner. Photo by Sankar Raman

Eva Aigner. Photo by Sankar Raman

CHAPTER 2

The Holocaust in Hungary

Les and Eva Aigner (Hungary)

For all my life, I have been an anti-Semite.

— Miklós Horthy

In 1940, the regent of the Kingdom of Hungary made no secret of his views toward Jewish people. In clear, unambiguous terms, Miklós Horthy wrote: "I have considered it intolerable that here in Hungary everything, every factory, bank, large fortune, business, theater, press, commerce, etc., should be in Jewish hands, and that the Jew should be the image reflected of Hungary, especially abroad."

Horthy was an admiral in the navy of a landlocked country. As regent, he presided over a kingdom that had no king. Under Horthy's leadership, Hungary became the first post–World War I government in Europe to impose a quota on the number of Jews who could attend universities. Horthy's government also enacted a 1941 law prohibiting Jews from marrying non-Jews. Another Horthy-era measure imposed a three-year prison sentence on any Jewish man in Hungary who had sex with a non-Jewish woman.

By then, Jews had been part of the Hungarian population for centuries. By some accounts, the Jewish presence in Hungary dated back to the Roman Empire. In the capital city of Budapest, Jews accounted for nearly a quarter of the population as Europe geared up for the devastation of World War II.

As early as 1933, when Adolf Hitler took power as chancellor of the German Reich, Hungary began exploring an alliance with Germany. The partnership was logical, for both governments shared certain authoritarian principles. The alliance worked to Hungary's favor as it reclaimed land it had lost in World War I. As the current war and the extermination of Jews escalated elsewhere in Europe, Hungary took anti-Jewish actions of its own.

The first massacre of Hungarian Jews took place in July 1941. Over a six-week period, Hungarian authorities identified more than 20,000 Jews as "Jewish foreign nationals" and shipped them off in freight cars to a German-occupied area of Ukraine. Almost upon arrival, most were murdered. In 1942, Hungarian Prime Minister Miklós Kállay ordered the expropriation of Jewish property. Calling for a "final solution to the Jewish question," Kállay urged "resettlement" of the country's 800,000 Jews.

By 1943, Germany was putting increased pressure on Horthy to send his country's Jewish population to Auschwitz. Horthy, however, expressed reluctance to comply. On March 18, 1944, Hitler summoned Horthy to a meeting in Germany. The German führer scolded Horthy for being soft on Jews, although Hungary had already enacted nearly three hundred anti-Jewish laws. And with Horthy away from Hungary, Hitler sent German troops into Budapest.

While Horthy was placed under house arrest in Bavaria, Hitler's second-in-command, Adolf Eichmann, set up shop in Budapest's Majestic Hotel. At first, Jews were isolated, with radio or telephone communication shut off. All were forced to wear the yellow star identifying them as Jews. Jewish property was swiftly seized. And within months, Eichmann had overseen the deportation of more than 400,000 Hungarian Jews. Most were sent to Auschwitz, where they were gassed on arrival.

Well before Eichmann arrived, a right-wing party in Hungary called the Arrow Cross had been fomenting anti-Jewish rhetoric. Calling itself the "Party of National Will" and urging a "government of national unity," Arrow Cross openly modeled itself after Germany's Nazi Party. Rather than settling for anti-Semitism, Arrow Cross advocated "a-Semitism"—that is, a society entirely devoid of Jews.

With Horthy forced into resignation, Arrow Cross stepped in to take control of Hungary's government. Whatever Jews remained in Budapest were rounded up and housed in a central, enclosed ghetto. Arrow Cross also instituted a grim ritual that became synonymous with Hungary's involvement in the Holocaust. After they were marched to the edge of the Danube River, Jews were forced to remove their shoes. Then they were shot, their bodies hurled into the swirling waters below. Records from Arrow Cross suggest that between 10,000 and 15,000 Hungarian Jews were murdered in this fashion. The Nazis, of course, wasted no time in repurposing the shoes.

Soviet troops liberated the Budapest ghetto on January 18, 1945, freeing an estimated 119,000 Jews from deplorable conditions and the threat of impending death at the hands of Arrow Cross foot soldiers. Communism, however, brought no safe haven for the surviving Jews of Hungary. From 1948 to 1988, under communist rule, Zionism was outlawed in Hungary.

Horthy died in exile in Portugal. Hitler took his own life in a German bunker. Adolf Eichmann was captured in Buenos Aires, Argentina, convicted of war crimes and executed by hanging. Hungary maintained an uncomfortable relationship with its role in the Holocaust, at times going so far as to portray itself as yet another victim of Hitler's evil.

But a 2019 study called the "Holocaust Remembrance Project" found otherwise. The report, conducted by scholars from Yale University, Grinnell College, and the European Union for Progressive Judaism, pointed to Hungary as a country that practiced Holocaust revisionism. The project concluded: "Hungary suffers from grave deficiencies in its Holocaust education, memory and commemoration."

Estimates of the number of Jews in Hungary today range from 50,000 to 130,000. The Dohány Street Synagogue, seating three thousand people, is Europe's largest synagogue. During the winter of 1944–1945, the synagogue provided shelter for many as part of the Jewish ghetto in Budapest. The synagogue's courtyard houses the graves of more than two thousand victims who died from cold, hunger, disease, or other causes during that dreadful time.

MIRACLES, MEMORIES, AND A MESSAGE

Life's hardest lessons can come at a steep cost. Tragedy, trauma, and misfortune often breed bitterness, anger, and hatred. Les and Eva Aigner, octogenarian Nazi Holocaust survivors at the time of this interview, might have had every reason to fill their days with any of those emotions. But they did not.

Les Aigner died at home in Tualatin, Oregon, on August 18, 2021. In an interview three years earlier, he and Eva—immigrants from Budapest, Hungary—focused on the good life they found in their adopted home country. In their cozy living room, Eva served homemade cake as the couple marveled at the miracles and random acts of compassion that allowed Les to survive internment, beatings and near-starvation at four Nazi concentration camps and made it possible for Eva to endure hideous conditions during World War II in the grim and grossly overcrowded Jewish ghetto of Budapest.

One such miracle occurred near the end of the war, when Eva and her sister were forced to march on a frigid winter night to the banks of the Danube River with scores of other Jews from the ghetto. Nazi leaders knew their days of domination in Europe were numbered, and they were rushing to finish their work of doing their best to eliminate the continent's Jewish population. The prisoners were ordered to form a line. As each prisoner reached the line's front, Nazi soldiers commanded them to remove their shoes. Consumer goods had grown scarce during the course of the war, and the Nazis knew their prisoners' footwear was marketable.

As Eva and her sister shivered in line, the prisoners standing ahead of them were shot, their bodies conveniently slipping into the icy river below. To the two sisters, their fate seemed inescapable. But then, moments before the two sisters were to have arrived at the front of the line to be shot, their mother appeared—literally, out of nowhere. She had been taken from them days before and was herself headed to a death camp when she leapt from a freight car to stage a daring escape. Determined to rescue her two girls, she had bravely made her way back to Budapest. Standing beside the river, she slipped off her one remaining object of any value, her wedding ring, and used it to bribe a Nazi guard into releasing her daughters.

“A miracle,” said Eva. “There is no other word for it.”

LIFE AND MEMORY IN AMERICA

For most of their lives—“Sixty-two years, married, to the same woman, and happy,” Les said, beaming—the Aigners avoided discussing their wartime experiences. The past was just that, they reasoned: past. Plus, they had lives to live in a country that celebrated freedom, not the Nazi atrocities or Communist despotism they had left behind. They got jobs, paid taxes, and bought a lovely home. They sent two children to college and rejoiced at the births of four grandchildren—and now, a great-grandson as well.

But the events of recent years made the Aigners feel they needed to speak out. For Les, it was the Holocaust deniers that tipped the scales of silence.

“How could anyone say this did not happen?” he said. “The Holocaust is one of the most documented events in modern history. Eleven million people killed, six million of them Jews. How can anyone deny that this took place?”

Just fifteen years old when he was plucked out of a line of Jewish captives headed to their deaths at Auschwitz and sent instead into slave labor, Aigner spotted the chimneys at the camp and assumed, since they puffed out smoke twenty-four hours a day, that they must be churning out the camp’s bread supply.

An older prisoner set him straight. “No, kid,” he told the newly arrived teenage prisoner. “Those are not bakeries. Those are crematoriums.”

It did not take long for Les said to find out for himself that what he had just heard was the truth. But there was no time for fear or disgust or any other emotion. Dehumanization of their prisoners was central to the Nazi strategy. For those who were not killed immediately, each day was a personal endurance test. Prisoners at Auschwitz served essentially as slave laborers for their captors. Nutrition was scant. Among the prisoners, hunger was chronic. A prisoner’s typical daily ration began at sunrise with a cereal-based beverage masquerading as coffee. A normal midday meal was a thin soup, often prepared from rotten vegetables. At bedtime, prisoners received a slender crust of bread, sometimes with a small serving of margarine.

Experts have subsequently estimated that the total daily calorie count for these prisoners seldom exceeded 1,300–about half of what is recommended for an adult male. Many prisoners developed debilitating diarrhea. Others died from weakness. For prisoners, starvation sickness all but guaranteed a nonstop trip to the gas chamber.

Les Aigner did his best not to focus on the deplorable conditions or the constant enervation that came with forced manual labor.

As Les later recollected, "There was a saying at Auschwitz: 'You cry, you die.'"

For Eva, the urgency of talking about the Holocaust centered around the importance of learning from history. Increasingly in recent years, venom had crept into the national dialogue, and she cringed at what she saw as a slow but inexorably rising tide of intolerance. She despaired as she heard national leaders in the United States denigrating immigrants and decrying the contributions of men and women born outside this country. For Les and Eva, the rhetoric had an eerie familiarity, as if they had vaulted back to the era when Jews and Roma and other objects of Nazi vilification were spat at and described with ugly phrases of enmity and contempt.

"I truly feel that the lessons of the Holocaust are more important today than ever," she said. "Because hate is still with us, and some people still like to discriminate. And we know what can happen when there is hate or discrimination. Hate is a little spark, and it can become a fire."

Sitting beside her, Les interjected: "And unfortunately, history can repeat itself."

HISTORY REPEATING

Simply because he was Jewish, Les Aigner suffered endless cruel indignities throughout World War II. At Auschwitz, he was examined—scrutinized, really—by the notorious Josef Mengele, the Nazi doctor who used concentration camp prisoners (nearly all of them Jewish) as subjects for monstrous medical experiments. Mengele, an officer in the German Schutzstaffel (SS), also was one of the doctors who administered the cyanide-based gas used to conduct mass executions in the camp's gas chambers. His brutal "experiments" on prisoners included attempts to change the eye color of his subjects. Mengele's efforts to produce a blue-eyed "master race" succeeded only in inducing blindness in his subjects—who, of course, were then sent to the camp's gas chamber since because they were blind, they were no longer useful.

Mengele, so ruthless that he was known at Auschwitz as the Angel of Death, escaped to South America after the war. Despite decades of efforts to locate and extradite him for trial, he eluded capture. Mengele drowned in Bertioga, Brazil, while swimming in 1975.

Not much about Les Aigner's experiences during World War II could be considered lucky, but fortunately, he did not meet the specifications for whatever hideous procedure Mengele was about to undertake that day. He was less fortunate the day he found himself face-to-face with an angry Nazi guard, armed with a pitchfork. Throughout the war, there were so many other unimaginable cruelties, all aimed at Les because of his religion. Far from embittering him, his background has made him insistent that such barbarity should not be repeated, ever.

"We don't want this to ever happen to another child or another human being," Les said, his tone soft with sorrow.

"Rwanda, Bosnia, Myanmar," he went on, rattling off countries where genocide has continued even into the twenty-first century. "And all because of origin, nationality, race, religion."

A few years ago, Les said, he and Eva were invited to speak to a middle school class in Ashland, Oregon, near the California border. Before their visit, the teacher had her class read *The Diary of a Young Girl* by Anne Frank and assigned them to write a report about it. One student made short work of the assignment. She turned in a "report" that read simply: "I hate Jews." Appalled, the teacher asked the student if she had ever met anyone who was Jewish. No, she replied, "but I hate them because my parents told me to hate them."

At another school presentation, Eva said, "This one kid, fifteen years old, got up and asked us, 'Don't you hate the Germans?'" Les replied: "We don't hate the German people, but we do not like the Nazi followers."

These experiences, said Les, make him all the more convinced that "the only way to break the cycle is to educate." He recalled that as they wrapped up their presentation at the Ashland school, a cafeteria worker came over to embrace the Aigners. Her uncle, she told them, had been a liberator at Dachau, the "work camp" near Munich where Les was imprisoned in the final days of the war. Upon his release, Les weighed just seventy-five pounds.

"I was a walking skeleton," he said, "after 'only' 10 months in the camp."

Ten months, on a diet by then of 700 calories a day.

Les spent two months recuperating in an Allied hospital. Returning to Budapest, he learned that most of his family had perished. Somehow, through another miracle, his father had survived.

EVA'S STORY

While Les was shipped from concentration camp to concentration camp, the comfortable life in Budapest of a young blue-eyed girl named Eva Spiegel also was upended. First came the yellow stars sewn on the front of the clothes she and every other Jewish child and adult were suddenly forced to wear. There were taunts of "dirty Jew!" as she walked to school. People threw horse manure at adults and children alike—anyone who wore the yellow star. It was as if a wall of pent-up hatred had suddenly crumbled, Eva said.

"The hidden anti-Semitism had always been there," Eva said. "But when the Nazis came, it was open season on hate and open season on hurt."

The area in Budapest where she and her family lived was renamed "Marked Housing." Without warning, three other families were moved into their three-room apartment. The families had not known one another, and suddenly they were living side-by-side. With strangers suddenly cohabitating with them, Eva and her family were distressed. But there was no way for them to know that what lay ahead for the family was far worse.

"It was terribly crowded, and we thought it was an invasion of our life," Eva said. "But it was only a beginning."

Her father was soon spirited from the family, and word swiftly came that he had been killed in a forced labor camp. Then, not long after the German occupation of Hungary in 1944, uniformed Nazi soldiers arrived at their door, ordering them to pack their bags. With Nazi guns pointed at them, they walked across the city to a cluster of dank, old apartment buildings. Tall fences encircled the area that became known as the Jewish ghetto. Guards stood by to make sure no contraband got in, and no people got out.

Eva and her mother and sister were shoved into a single room crammed with eighteen to twenty other people, all strangers. After years of comfortable living in their own home, Eva and her mother and sister had one blanket between them.

"My mom, my sister and I, we were huddling together, facing terrible starvation," Eva said. One day, she and her sister discovered a piece of bread in a cupboard. It was covered with mold, and it crumbled in their hands, "but we were hungry enough that we ate it anyway."

Bombings of Budapest were routine, but the basement that served as a bomb shelter for the ghetto was "so rat-infested that we decided to take a chance and stay where we were," Eva said.

The Jewish ghetto in Budapest measured less than one square mile in area. Many of the thousands of people who were sent to the ghetto were quickly sent off to certain deaths in concentration camps. Others were marched to the river to be shot. For those remaining in the crowded, filthy ghetto, diseases such as typhoid quickly spread.

Eventually the Nazis came for Eva's mother. Well-intentioned workers from the Red Cross and other organizations sometimes circulated in the ghetto, taking in children who had no parents. But there were rumors that those children did not always find safe haven, that instead those children were killed, or possibly used in sex trafficking. Eva's sister told her to lay low and tell no one that their mother was gone. It was a crafty move, Eva said.

"I guess a lot of those kids who had been taken by the Red Cross had been caught by the Nazis and killed," she said.

And then came the night as the war neared an end in December 1944 when Eva and her sister were awakened and ordered to march alongside the others to the banks of the Danube.

Three weeks later, following their mother's spectacular and dangerous rescue of her two daughters, Russian troops entered Budapest and told the residents, "You are free people."

It is not as if Eva Aigner shakes off the horrors of her young life, or in any way diminishes the misery that she and so many others lived through. But she keeps a level perspective: "Everybody has childhood memories," she said. "And somehow, our spirit was not broken."

Still, the dreadful memories persisted. As Les confessed: "I cried many nights." Eva agreed, remembering: "When we were (first) married, he still would have nightmares."

FAMILY

Les was not the only family member haunted by the horrors. Eventually, he and Eva were able to bring her aging mother to live with them in the home near Raleigh Hills, a suburb of Portland, that they owned for thirty-eight years. Eva kept a meticulously clean house and was baffled when the house suddenly became infested with fruit flies. She searched and searched for the source, and finally discovered a cache of fruit stuffed between the mattress and box springs in her mother's bedroom.

"Mom," she said. "We have plenty of food. Why are you hoarding fruit in your bedroom?"

Her mother explained that she needed the fruit "for my starving children." The war was long behind them, Eva said sadly, but still "she was constantly escaping from the Nazis."

On his side of the family, even among the few family members who managed to survive the Holocaust, said Les, "I am the only one left."

Eva nodded. "Me too," she said, "I am the only one." And then Les added, "I am the luckiest man alive. Not because I was better or stronger or special. But I survived."

ESCAPE

The pair married exactly fifty-nine days after they met. Eva was eighteen and Les twenty-six. Any hopes they might have harbored of a happy life in Hungary vanished as the Communists took power. The country's new leaders imposed a vise-like grip of authority that once again made life oppressive. Food shortages forced Budapest residents to stand in line for hours for nothing so much as a simple loaf of bread. And old prejudices began to resurface. One day, Eva heard someone in the bread line say, "Let's get rid of the Communists and then we'll take care of the rest of the Jews." She went home and told Les she could not remain in Budapest, and that there was no way she could think of giving birth to a Jewish child there. Les agreed.

"First it was genocide," he said. "Then it was communism." He offered a weak laugh, appreciating his own irony. "We were not good enough Communists. And I didn't want to be a Communist."

Les and Eva Aigner at their wedding, in Budapest, in 1956. Photo courtesy of Aigner family archives

The Aigners knew they had to get out. "We had to make a choice," Les said. "And we made the right choice."

The Aigners plotted their exit strategy carefully. They chose Christmas Eve to escape, figuring the guards would be busy with holiday festivities and therefore easy to distract. They had rehearsed their script in advance, presenting themselves as a cheerful young couple off for a holiday getaway. Guards boarded their train at every stop, demanding paperwork and interrogating them about their destination. Les and Eva smiled and said how much they were looking forward to Christmas Day in a small Austrian village whose name they had carefully memorized. After all their hardships, the Aigners sometimes encountered kindness at the hands of strangers. They got off the train at the end of the line, near the Austro-Hungarian border, not quite sure what to do next. A farmer appeared and offered to help guide them to safety.

They were so grateful, Eva said, that "We gave him everything we had."

They made it across the border in knee-deep snow. A snowcat from the village whose name they had committed to memory came to pick them up, and church bells rang out to welcome them. Village residents showered them with cookies and food, recognizing the difficulty of their journey.

"I got my first pair of nylons that night," Eva said. "A lady said, 'I have nothing else to give you.'"

Eventually they made their way to their actual destination, Vienna. But when they arrived at the American embassy there, it became clear that they were not the only ones trying to leave Europe. Lines of hopeful refugees snaked around and around the block. With so many people lined up ahead of them, the situation looked hopeless. How would they ever make it into the embassy to present their case? Eva decided to take things into her own hands. She summoned all her pluck, plus a little creative deception, manufacturing a convincing fiction that vaulted them to the front of the line. One thing that worked in their favor was that the Aigners did have a vital piece of paperwork in the form of an affidavit of acceptance supplied by a stepbrother Les had never met. He lived in Portland, Oregon—wherever that was.

The Aigners boarded the last refugee boat out of Bremen, Germany. The couple was among 1,700 people aboard a vessel built for half that many. Most were horribly seasick for the entire voyage. After all, Eva noted, none of them had ever seen the sea, much less ridden a ship over its waters. But finally the ship steamed into New York harbor. So many passengers rushed to the side to gaze at the Statue of Liberty that the captain feared the ship would list and sink. Immigration, inoculations, quarantine for two weeks at Camp Kilmer in New Jersey—and then the Aigners boarded a train for Oregon.

"Four days, three nights, not speaking a word of the language," said Eva.

They arrived in Portland to find that Les's stepbrother had rented them a furnished apartment at Northwest 21st Avenue and Irving Street. Eva was not quite nineteen. Les was twenty-seven.

Paradise, thought Eva.

PORTLAND

After Budapest, a city so cosmopolitan that it was often likened to Paris,

Portland was a backwater. Budapest boasted scores of theaters, opera houses, and world-class museums. Musicians played on street corners. Portland was a sleepy place, not quite Seattle and definitely not San Francisco.

Drawing on his skills as a machinist in Hungary, Les found work at the East Side Tool and Die Co. Eventually, he became a model maker, building prototypes for the Beaverton-based electronics company Tektronix. Eva cleaned houses and did whatever else she could do to bring in some cash for the family. But what she longed for was the career her mother had forbidden her to pursue in Hungary.

Estheticians, cosmetologists, beauticians, scoffed Eva's mother—they were no better than ladies of the night. But Eva thought otherwise. She was very beautiful herself, and she had always been interested in the intricacies of female pulchritude. She talked herself into an interview at Portland's Pacific Beauty School, portraying herself in her fractured English as "this girl from Hungary who wanted to learn the trade."

Fine, said the school's proprietor, but what about the tuition? And so they brokered a deal. In exchange for tuition, Eva would become the school's cleaning lady, scrubbing everything from floors to hairbrushes. She and Les also agreed to paint the school's interior.

Eva thrived in the beauty school's classes, and she kept her end of the bargain, staying late and showing up on weekends to scrub floors and polish hair-washing sinks. But going to work as a beautician in Oregon wasn't as simple as graduating from cosmetology school. To get a state license to practice her craft, Eva had to produce a high school diploma. For Eva, this was impossible. Yes, she had completed high school in Hungary, but more likely than not, her transcript was stuffed in some file in Budapest. If her diploma still existed, Eva knew that avaricious bureaucrats would eagerly accept bribes to agree to supply a document they had no intention of producing. She might as well be throwing money down the drain.

Hearing of her plight, someone at the beauty school suggested she take a GED (General Equivalency Diploma) exam instead. Eva was puzzled: "What's a GED?" she asked.

To pass the multiple-choice and true/false exam, Eva needed a score of seventy-five or above. Her command of English was still limited, and her knowledge of subjects such as American history or government was all but nonexistent. Luckily, the test also included a section on mathematics, and Eva had always been a math whiz. She earned a score of seventy-eight.

After graduation, Eva took a job with "Mr. Joseph" at the old Multnomah Hotel. She worked there for ten years, then opened the King Salon of Beauty, just off Northwest Burnside Street. Her reputation earned her a regal title.

"They called me the 'Queen of the King Salon,'" she said.

Eventually, Eva grew tired of working with all the chemicals involved in hair and beauty work, and she retired. Today, she is disarmingly young-looking, a product of her own skilled knowledge of esthetics. She has ginger-colored hair, a trim figure, and a paucity of wrinkles that most women half her age would envy.

REMEMBRANCE

In 1998, the Aigners took their son Rob and daughter Suzanne on a kind of "Holocaust tour" of Europe. It was difficult, said Les, and one odd byproduct was that he constantly found himself ravenously hungry, as if he were reliving the years of starvation in the camps.

"Going back, the insecurity, the abuse, the brutality came right back," he said. For Eva, however, "In some respects, it was healing."

They traveled with a group that included seven survivors, their children and two rabbis. Each night they said prayers and lit candles.

"I think it brought a little closure," Eva said.

The trip was an awakening for their children, they said. Now Rob and Suzanne had a greater understanding of the ordeals their parents had endured. Still, Les quipped, "Afterward my son said, 'Next time please take us on a real vacation, Dad.'"

Eva Aigner was among supporters who helped establish the Oregon Holocaust Memorial in 2004 in Portland's Washington Park. She and Les also helped set up the Oregon Jewish Museum and Center for Holocaust Education. They have built storyboards that depict their experiences, right down to the cartography of the different camps where

Les and Eva Aigner visit the Holocaust Memorial in Portland, Oregon, which they helped build. Granite slabs evoke the railway tracks that brought Jews to Auschwitz. Photo by Sankar Raman

Les was imprisoned. They continue to speak out, and they relish their roles as proud American citizens who have never missed an opportunity to vote—because, as both point out from hard experience, if any one citizen does not vote, despotism may follow.

Here is the big lesson, said Eva Aigner: "You have to treat everybody the way you would like to be treated. Because if you don't, they will differentiate you because of race, religion, gender, ethnicity, whatever."

Her gaze grew more stern, more focused as she spoke. "And if we allow this to happen, we are going to lose our freedom," she said.

Eva cast a loving smile in the direction of her husband of sixty-two years, the spouse who had also endured unthinkable sacrifices to be here, in a tranquil life of comfort—a life that has brought them joy, prosperity, a strong and loving family—and perhaps above all, freedom.

"And that is the lesson as I see it," she declared. "And we have lived it."

Sivheng Ung. Photo by Sankar Raman

CHAPTER 3

Pol Pot and His Deadly Utopia

Sivheng Ung (Cambodia)

In Nazi Germany, a yellow star sewn to an outer garment was a virtual death sentence. In Pol Pot's Cambodia—or Kampuchea, as he preferred to call the country—it was eyeglasses.

From 1975 to 1979, between one million and three million Cambodians were killed by the Khmer Rouge, Pol Pot's foot soldiers. As they conducted their massacres, the Khmer Rouge were not known for their precise record-keeping, so the most common death toll estimate is two million, about one-quarter of the country's population at the time.

Professionals, including physicians, were among the first to be targeted by the Khmer Rouge. Anyone connected with a foreign government was also an easy mark. So were intellectuals, handily identified as such because, obviously, they wore eyeglasses. Teachers also were seen as enemies of the regime of a dictator who was himself highly educated, but who dreamed of turning Cambodia into an agrarian Utopia.

In order to save ammunition, many victims were beaten to death with bamboo sticks, wooden clubs or metal spades. Some were poisoned. Others died from wounds inflicted by bayonets, knives, hoes, and scythes. Although most were executed, many Cambodians also died from starvation or disease. Again, precise numbers have never been established.

Most of the bodies of the dead were thrown into mass graves that became known as the Killing Fields. That ghoulish title was bestowed by a Cambodian journalist, Dith Pran, but not until he had escaped his homeland. A 1984 movie called *The Killing Fields* revealed the scope of the horror in Cambodia to a worldwide audience.

Some victims were required to dig their own graves. Those who were killed often were described by the government as "bad elements." In *Why Did They Kill: Cambodia in the Shadow of Genocide*, anthropologist Alexander L. Hinton writes that among those earning this label were city folks (who were considered class enemies of the new state) and anyone who clung to traditional Cambodian values—in other words, what Pol Pot viewed as the old ways.

Nearly all those who were not killed, children included, were forced into slave labor. Under a sweltering, unforgiving sun, they tilled the soil at rural worksites known euphemistically as collective farms. But collectivism in Cambodia was a failure, leading to widespread famine.

Pol Pot's strange, utopian vision was modeled loosely after Maoist China. His intent was to return his country to "Year Zero" for a new start as an agrarian paradise. Effectively, Pol Pot wanted to march his monsoon-prone country back to the Middle Ages.

As the Khmer Rouge rounded up its prisoners, cities were emptied. Because Pol Pot opposed the idea of an educated populace, schools were closed. Money was abolished. All citizens were forced to wear the same black clothing.

For centuries, Buddhism had been the primary religion in Cambodia. Under Pol Pot, Buddhism was first labeled a "reactionary religion," and then abolished entirely. Statues of the Buddha were decapitated. By the end of the Khmer Rouge regime in 1979, hundreds of temples and temple libraries had been destroyed or turned into prisons, according to Georgetown University's Berkeley Center for Religion, Peace, and World Affairs.

The architect of what became known as the Cambodian genocide was born in 1925 as Saloth Sâr. His father was a prosperous farmer in what was then known as French Cambodia. The young Sâr won a government scholarship in the late 1940s to study radio technology in Paris, where he fell in with a circle of student radicals and was willingly indoctrinated into the ideology of Marx and Lenin. Ironically, considering his later attempt to eradicate all educators, Sâr himself worked as a teacher at a private high school after he returned to Cambodia. But he also plunged into politics, serving as general secretary of the Communist party of Kampuchea beginning in 1963. It was around 1970 that he adopted the name Pol Pot. His new name had no ulterior significance but allowed him to create a fresh biography to suit his political aspirations.

The Khmer Rouge assault on the country's capital, Phnom Penh, took place in April 1975. About 2.5 million people were marched out of the city, carrying whatever they could hold in their arms. Along the evacuation route, about 20,000 people died, according to Philip Short, author of *Pol Pot: Anatomy of a Nightmare.*

It is impossible to exaggerate the effects of the Khmer Rouge years of mass killings and repression on a country about the size of Washington State. Today, about 17 million people live in the renamed Kingdom of Cambodia—double the population of Washington state, and then some. With so many of its elders murdered, the country is young. With the infrastructure, including schools, smothered by Pol Pot, large swaths of Cambodians have little education. Widespread poverty and corruption persist. Food insecurity is high, and political freedom is, at best, low.

In *Political Transition in Cambodia 1991–99: Power, Elitism and Democracy*, David Roberts calls Cambodia "a relatively authoritarian coalition via a superficial democracy." The United Nations has designated Cambodia as a "least developed country."

The country remains mostly rural, with more than half the population living away from cities. True to Pol Pot's agrarian dream, agriculture remains a strong force in Cambodia's economy, accounting for more than 20 percent of the country's gross domestic product, according to US State Department statistics. But food insecurity remains high, and in 2022, the US State Department announced a $25 million aid package for Cambodia, aimed at promoting agricultural development and reducing food insecurity.

Cambodia comes from the French word *Cambodge*, itself a transliteration of the Khmer word *kampuciə*. Maps and diaries made by early Portuguese explorers show that by the early sixteenth century the name Cambodia was already in use. Earlier still, during the twelfth century, the Khmer Empire was the largest continuous empire of Southeast Asia. The city of Angkor may have supported up to one million people at that time, making it among the largest cities in the world all the way through to the modern Industrial Revolution.

It was at this time that construction was begun on the vast series of temples at nearby Angkor Wat. As the country struggles today, the tourists from all over the world who flock to this massive historical site serve as one of Cambodia's major economic engines.

The French colonial flavor of parts of Phnom Penh also draws travelers from around the globe. In 1887, at the request of the Cambodian king, Cambodia was integrated into French Indochina, the Southeast Asian arm of the French Colonial Empire. The country's protectorate status was abolished by France in 1949, and in 1953, Cambodia achieved independence.

The country's subsequent disunity and ongoing unrest paved the way for the buildup of the Communist Party of Kampuchea (CPK), and the group's formal takeover of the government in 1975. On December 25, 1978, neighboring Vietnam invaded Cambodia, the Khmer Rouge regime was removed from power and a pro-Hanoi government, the Peoples' Republic of Kampuchea, was formed.

The Cambodian monarchy was restored in 1993, returning Norodom Sihanouk to the throne in what is described as a constitutional monarchy. But although the king is widely revered, he has little power. Government authority rests instead with Prime Minister Hun Sen. Hun, one of the world's longest-serving heads of state, is a former Khmer Rouge commander.

Thousands of Khmer Rouge guerrillas who had sought refuge in Thailand and elsewhere returned to Cambodia under a government grant of amnesty in 1994. Still under house arrest, Pol Pot died in his sleep at his home in a jungle hut near the Thai border in northern Cambodia.

"When I die, I will die peacefully," he wrote in 1987. Apparently, he did.

"BE A BLADE OF GRASS, NOT A TALL TREE"

Of thirteen siblings, it was Sivheng who most resembled their father. Kiling Ung was a businessman who traded in the teak and rosewood used in construction and furniture throughout Southeast Asia. He spoke French, Cantonese, and Vietnamese, along with his native Cambodian, or Khmer, and could also read and write in Thai. He also spoke some English. He taught all the children to fix things, even sending them up—boys and girls alike—to repair the roof.

But it was Sivheng—the family tomboy, the girl who climbed mango and tamarind trees and picked fights with neighborhood boys, the girl who refused to learn how to cook—to whom he was most close. Beginning when she was just two years old, he taught her to read. He imparted his wisdom, including this admonition: No matter how bad you've got it, someone else has it worse. In dire moments, he counseled, don't look up. Look down.

"My dad's words, they helped me through the Killing Fields," said Sivheng Ung, now a widow in her seventies, living in a trim house in Northeast Portland.

The brutality inflicted upon the Cambodian people during the five-year reign of terror by the ultra-Maoist Khmer Rouge is beyond comprehension. In addition to the mass executions and forced marches, physical and sexual abuse abounded, as did malnutrition and disease.

The Khmer Rouge operated between 150 and 196 prisons. About 20,000 people passed through just one such facility: Tuol Sleng, more commonly called Security Prison 21 (S-21). The prison, housed in a former high school, is now a tourist attraction known as the Tuol Seng Genocide Museum. The name Tuol Seng translates to "Hill of the Poisonous Tree." The prison was also a torture, execution, and interrogation center whose buildings were circled with electrified barbed wire. Prisoners were shackled to walls or to long iron bars. Prisoners slept on the floor and were forbidden to speak to one another. A prisoner's daily diet almost ensured starvation or malnutrition: four spoonfuls of rice pudding and a watery soup made from leaves, twice a day.

Embracing practices reminiscent of the notorious Dr. Josef Mengele in Nazi Germany, the Khmer Rouge used live prisoners for medical experiments and surgical studies at Tuol Sleng. No anesthetic was used for these procedures. Prisoners were forced to write lengthy confessions listing not only their own purported transgressions but also naming friends, neighbors, and colleagues who, according to Khmer Rouge standards, had been equally treasonous. Only seven adults and five children survived to recount the horrors of Tuol Sleng.

Pol Pot took the most venal lessons of both Nazism and Stalinism and applied them to his own people. From the former, the Nazis who exterminated six million people because they were Jewish, LGBTQ, Romany or otherwise non-Aryan, Pol Pot embraced racial determinism. From Stalin, Pol Pot took contempt for a class system that rewarded educational achievement or accumulated wealth. He endorsed a harsh new social system that meant breaking the spirits of all but those who were most blindly loyal to him.

Anyone associated with the former Cambodian government was especially targeted. Professionals, intellectuals, and followers of any religion were murdered by rebels who espoused state atheism. Around 50,000 Buddhist monks alone were killed. The elderly, the infirm, and the disabled typically were shot on the spot. A person could be killed for speaking a foreign language, wearing eyeglasses, smiling or crying. "To spare you is no profit," went a familiar regime slogan. "To destroy you is no loss."

"MONKEY-GIRL"

In Sivheng Ung's household in the northwestern city of Battambang, the first clear indication of what the Khmer Rouge invasion of 1975 would bring came in the form of an immediate, dramatic decline in the family's lumber-hauling business. Sivheng had just finished high school, a rigorous program that awarded three diplomas to those who passed the tough state exams.

"Many people did not pass, but I did," she said.

But the schoolgirl who scored an equivalent of a straight-A average in the United States was also famously mischievous. Her tree-climbing prowess prompted one friend to nickname her "monkey." The monkey girl, just four-feet-eleven-inches tall, knew she could stir up trouble with little consequence because of her family's prominence.

"They considered my father 'the Man' in the village," she said. "I knew they couldn't touch me. That gave me confidence. I could do anything."

Within reason, she stressed: "I didn't do bad things. Even today, I don't curse."

The unrest that pushed Pol Pot into power actually began well before the French-educated tyrant seized control. As noted, a century of rule from Paris ended in Cambodia in 1953 during a time when France decolonized its numerous holdings in Southeast Asia.

In 1970, Cambodia's Prince Sihanouk was deposed in a coup led by his own prime minister, Lon Nol. Lon Nol promptly declared himself president, embarking on an erratic five-year tenure that allowed Khmer Rouge rebels to establish deep inroads. When Lon Nol fled to exile in the United States in 1975, his name was first on the list of officials the Khmer Rouge intended to assassinate.

As the Khmer Rouge proliferated, gaining steadily in power through their ruthless tactics, Sivheng Ung's father watched his business dry up. His very acumen as an entrepreneur all but painted a bull's eye on his back for the Khmer Rouge. As his daughter said, "He could not go to the forest for wood, or he would be killed."

With so many children, it was Sivheng in whom her father was most likely to confide. He took her to movies and taught her about historical events, notably the Nazi Holocaust in Germany. "We talked about the Gestapo, about how they would kill you," she said. "And then we talked about the Chinese communists. He told me, 'When the communists come, they're going to kill a lot of people. They're going to take away everything you own. They will give you only one plate and one spoon.'" At night, he warned, "There will be spies under your bed."

From her father she knew that the Khmer Rouge invasion was taking place. And she came later to remember his political prescience. "During the communists, Pol Pot, it was just like everything my dad told me," Sivheng said.

Still, even her own father could not have foreseen the full extent of the Khmer Rouge horror.

MARRIAGE AND THE FORCED MARCH

Just months before the communists took control in Phnom Penh, Sivheng married a young accountant named Savat. She was twenty-three; he was just twenty-one. As was not uncommon in their culture, they were "kind of related" through her mother's side of the family. She met him once at age seven, and "he stuck in my heart." Years later, they reconnected when Sivheng traveled to the capital, hoping to become a teacher, or possibly a banker. When she spotted him at the bank where he worked, she waved.

"And then we connected," she said. "I think it was fate. From seven years to twenty-three years, I remembered him."

The two families gathered for a traditional wedding, "no bombs or anything" in spite of the rebel activity. But when the newlyweds drove her mother to the airport to fly back to Battambang, "there were bombs, bombs, bombs."

Soon enough, the bliss of their new marriage was interrupted. Moving from door to door in April 1979, the Khmer Rouge fighters ordered residents out of their homes on the pretext that Americans were about to drop bombs on the city. The dissidents came during the day, when men were traditionally in the workplace. Sivheng's mother-in-law and her husband's siblings had gathered at her house, when they were told to leave.

"We had no choice," she said.

Trauma is a well-known breeding ground for black humor. Sivheng still laughs when she talks about what her mother-in-law insisted on carrying with her: "For my mother-in-law, a television was a big luxury. It meant you had class. It meant you had money."

So her tiny Cambodian mother-in-law lugged the television set out with them. She also brought Sivheng's fancy wedding shoes along with her daughter-in-law's best clothes and jewelry. She had seven children with her, but neither her husband nor Sivheng's was with them, as both had gone to work that day at the bank. The women had no idea what had happened to their husbands. Had they, too, been marched away by the Khmer Rouge? Had they been taken prisoner? Or worse, had Pot's troops singled them out as representatives of the merchant class, and then murdered them?

"We didn't know where they were," said Sivheng, "if they were dead or alive."

At around 10 a.m. on April 17, 1975, loudspeakers began blaring throughout the city, ordering residents to leave within twenty-four hours. By some reports, the announcements were interspersed with the sounds of gunshots.

Because the forced depopulation of Phnom Penh was so rushed, and so massive, precise figures are difficult to ascertain. But in the aftermath of the fall of the Khmer Rouge, the Extraordinary Chambers in the Courts in Cambodia—a special court created jointly by the United Nations and the government of Cambodia, but independent of both—estimated that between 1.5 and 2.6 million people were driven from their homes and businesses. What a sight the evacuation must have been: Men, women and children of all ages walking in the streets, a throng headed in a common direction toward a destination they could not guess. Soldiers with guns drawn, some as young as seven or eight years old, lined the streets. Anyone who hesitated was shot. Sivheng and her family held hands, knowing that if they were separated they might not find one another again. The crowd was so deep they could not see the ground. It was April, the hottest month of the year in Cambodia. Steam rose up from the street and dirt flew.

"I felt so numb, scared. I didn't know what to think," Sivheng remembered. She let out a bittersweet laugh. "Even then, my mother-in-law would not let go of the TV and my wedding shoes."

At nightfall, as they marched, they were ordered to stop and sleep along the road. No food was offered. But Sivheng had a small advantage: "The tomboy thing helped me. I snuck out to forage for us. I saw an empty house and grabbed some pots and pans and whatever I could find. We lived like animals. Like animals."

Two weeks into the evacuation, Sivheng saw a friend from high school and begged him to take her fishing. Enormous craters from bombs dropped from B-52 planes had produced basins that were now filled with water and fish. At last there would be some protein for her family. Along the road, people regularly collapsed from exhaustion. Decomposed bodies littered the landscape. One night, Sivheng fell asleep next to someone who by daylight turned out to be dead. That chilling memory has never left her. "When I tell you this, I can still smell him," she said.

As the trek to a remote, still-unknown area continued, they dodged land mines on the dirt roads and passed through dark clouds of mosquitoes. "In the morning, we looked like we had the measles," she said, not laughing this time. They were barefoot and had no food.

When they arrived in the village that the Khmer Rouge had transformed into a forced labor camp, there was her husband. With or without mosquito bites, he was overjoyed to see her.

"He hugged me so tight I couldn't breathe," Sivheng said.

ESCAPE

And then they were herded into the fields to begin their assigned work, picking potatoes under the blazing Southeast Asian sun. Families crowded together in small, primitive huts. The soldiers gave them no rice, only dried corn—inedible unless it was cooked for hours. But they had no firewood, and venturing into forests filled with tigers and other wild animals was too dangerous. In any case, child spies followed them everywhere. Even to cross the street, they had to ask permission.

"We had no rights," she said.

But they did have a new collective name. "They called us New People, the Enemy," she said. "They hated people like us from the city. They called us American slaves. All the women, they considered us like sluts, no morals. They looked at us with disgust."

Money had also been abolished. So the cash her mother-in-law had spirited out now meant nothing. Secretly, and at great personal risk, the New People sometimes traded clothes in exchange for favors from the communist soldiers—who, it turned out, were not all ideologically above nice things. One day, Sivheng asked her mother-in-law what had happened to the TV set. She explained that the soldiers had pointed a gun at her and ordered her to leave it. The absurdity was inescapable. Even in their dehumanized state, Sivheng said, "We all laughed."

And then, at gunpoint, soldiers came and dragged her fourteen-year-old sister-in-law away. "They killed her, but before they killed her, they raped her," Sivheng said.

One day, the soldiers took her husband and father-in-law aside for questioning. The family knew this was nothing resembling a friendly conversation. In fact, said Sivheng, "questioning" by the Khmer soldiers could only bode the worst: "You know, when they question you, they will come back and kill you."

Sivheng told her husband they had to escape, right away. "If we stay," she told him, "they are going to kill all of us." Her in-laws agreed, telling her: you need to go.

Somehow, they managed to elude the Khmer guards as they slipped out of the camp. They could not take anything more than the clothes they were wearing. They walked slowly, almost casually, so as not to attract attention. Along the way, when soldiers demanded, "Comrades, where are you going?" they said they were headed to the next village to get some fish. They continued this ruse for a week, walking at a leisurely pace. By night they slept wherever they could, no longer fearful of tigers or other forest predators. Whatever animal foes they might encounter could be no worse than the soldiers of Pol Pot.

Survivor skills kicked in. As they gained distance, they changed their story. They asked children in each village they passed what the name of the next village was. Then, adopting anguished expressions and using the name of the village, they told guards at the checkpoints: "My mother in the next village, she is very, very sick."

Sivheng feigned illiteracy. But she would also learn the name of each village chief. Then she forged a permission slip, "signed" with the chief's name. The guards could not read, so when she showed them the so-called document, they would pretend to examine it and then wave them on.

At one point, a security guard tried to stop them. Instead, they persuaded the village chief that the document was real and were allowed to sleep there. Sivheng addressed the chief and his wife as "Father," or "Daddy" and "Mother," showing them the respect their titles afforded. She complimented them constantly, making them feel important.

When a friendly village woman whispered to Sivheng that she would blend in better if she cut her long, silky hair, Sivheng found scissors and hacked her hair to just below her ears. Again, she found herself summoning a lesson from her father.

"Don't be a tall tree, be a blade of grass," he advised. "The grass blows in every direction," he counseled. "The tree falls down."

Eventually, the couple told the man they were calling "Father" or "Daddy" that they were going out to find fish. Again they escaped. They walked and walked until a young soldier surprised them. Instead of killing them or taking them prisoner, he offered to share his food with them. Even among the Khmer Rouge, Sivheng decided, there had to be a few people who still had hearts. The soldier told Sivheng and her husband that their best bet was to play dumb.

"Be blind, be deaf, be mute," he advised. "That way you survive."

Just about then a truck stopped near them. The back of the truck was open, filled with men packed as tight as livestock on their way to market. Among the captives, Sivheng spotted one of her old teachers. His hands were bound, and his face bore the saddest expression she had ever seen. She knew the soldiers were going to kill her teacher, and so did he. Without betraying anything to the soldiers, Sivheng tried to use her gaze to tell her teacher that she was so, so sorry.

THE KILLING FIELDS

Their grim odyssey continued, on and on for more than a year. Sivheng became pregnant but lost the baby—most likely, she believes, to maternal malnutrition. At one point they found themselves running from villagers armed with guns. They ran through thorns and brambles, bleeding, "just like in *The Killing Fields* movie," she said.

Rounded up by soldiers once again, they were taken to another village. "No New People, purely communists," Sivheng said. This time, they did not dare to run again. Questioned about what they were doing out there on their own, Sivheng once again summoned her ingenuity. She thought fast and said they had fled because soldiers in the last village were about to rape her. Apparently this ruse worked, for again the couple was put to work. A year passed before they were sent to yet another village, this one populated by other New People.

Conditions were terrible. "One meal a day," Sivheng says. "A common kitchen, one plate, one spoon, just like my father said. One scoop of porridge, and if you were late, you got nothing. As time passed, the porridge got thinner and thinner, just water."

When soldiers came to take her husband to be "reeducated," Sivheng knew the worst was about to happen: "Ninety-nine percent certain, he would be killed."

Fear and hardship had turned her both numb and mute. "I lost my husband, my baby—and still I could not cry," she said. "I was too afraid."

Sivheng was sent to what was known as the widows' hut. Plunged into despair, mourning a death she could not dare to imagine, she grew sick and malnourished. She could not swallow. She cried so hard at night that when she stopped, people thought she was dead. She grew bloated, swollen like a dead body that has floated too long in a river. She thought about killing herself, but remembered that "Buddha said, 'If you kill yourself, I cannot help you.'"

Hoping tainted seafood would do the trick, she ate two crabs and fell unconscious. But even in wartime, life can play ironic tricks. Instead of killing her, the crabs saved her, fueling her with needed nutrients. She grew strong enough to work her way to a Southeast Cambodian village called Leuk Dek, close to the border with Vietnam.

By then a new kind of chaos had overtaken Cambodia. Vietnamese troops had begun to invade the country. Pandemonium broke out as Pol Pot's soldiers fought against one another. Sivheng found herself surrounded by communists, the Old People. Again they were ordered to march, finally ending up in a Cambodian village she describes as "almost medieval." Rumors abounded. The Vietnamese would descend, they were told, and eat human flesh. Yet again they were moved, this time to a village near Siem Reap. Dig a trench, they were ordered. They knew the ditch was intended to house their own dead bodies.

But among the soldiers, there was a sense of mass confusion. They issued conflicting orders. They yelled at one another. It was hard to tell who was in charge, if anyone. Sivheng saw a Vietnamese tank rolling in and didn't know quite what to think. She was excited, worried, and confused. Right in front of her, she saw Khmer Rouge soldiers being beaten to death. What did any of this mean? At this point, she knew she had nothing to lose. Either things were going to get a whole lot worse, or she might have a window of hope. She sidled up to a Vietnamese captain and told him she wanted to see her family. Demanding nothing in return, he said he would give her a ride back to her hometown.

"I expected to see my mom, my dad, my family," she said. "But I got there and there was nobody. My mom, my dad, my grandma—all gone. My younger sister, gone. All the in-laws, gone. My older sister, first and second sister and then the fourth sister and the sixth, and all the men—all killed." Sivheng was twenty-eight years old.

In fact, among such a large family, four sisters had managed to survive. Terror persisted. No one knew if the mass killings would continue. When a man from Phnom Penh named Van Touch, who had been married to her cousin, came to say he was leaving for Thailand, Sivheng begged him to let her come along. He hesitated, then assented. He was not happy when Sivheng insisted on bringing her youngest brother, just twelve years old, with them.

Van Touch was only a year older than Sivheng. He was handsome, with curly black hair. Their birth years made them compatible.

"He's a Tiger, I'm a Rabbit," she explained. "In our mythical way, a Tiger is very strong and a Rabbit is very smart. You can get out of any situation."

Already, that had proved true. After all, the communists had forced her to dig her own grave, and still she had escaped.

WINDOWS OF HUMANITY

Their final attempt at freedom was unencumbered by suitcases or other possessions because, as Sivheng pointed out with a justifiable note of bitterness, by that time they had nothing. In one village on the way to the Thai border, Van Touch found his sister. She joined them in a trek still fraught with peril.

"The Khmer Rouge, they were always around, especially at night," Sivheng said. "They were so inhumane, so evil."

For instance, she said, Khmer Rouge soldiers who came upon escape parties such as theirs would rob them of whatever they could take. For further humiliation, they forced their Cambodian countrymen—and women—to disrobe. They then conducted invasive body examinations, searching for jewels or money that might be hidden in private areas, but also seeking to demean and dehumanize their captives. Whenever this happened, Sivheng said, "I was sure I would be killed, and certain that I would be raped."

Van Touch had the advantage of understanding English, so in villages he could listen to American radio broadcasts that gave accounts of regional fighting. Land mines were everywhere. The only way to be sure to avoid these explosives was to walk in footprints already on the ground. With no money to bribe a guide to help them, they were on their own.

"Even going to the bathroom, people were blown up," she said. "We didn't see it, but we heard the blasts and the screaming."

They met up with a wealthy man who claimed he could get them all across the border because he had a rich relative in Bangkok. Halfway to the border, he abandoned them, too. But there were tiny shreds of humanity as well. Sivheng was fearful when they came across a cluster of people with guns who spoke only Thai. When they ordered Sivheng and the others to sit, she assumed they were about to be killed. Instead, they passed around some of the food they had brought with them. To this day, Sivheng marvels at the miraculous culinary fortune that had befallen them: "Canned tuna!" It might as well have been a five-star meal: "I hadn't eaten anything like that in five years. Each bite was heaven."

Their benefactors led them through the thorny jungle to the river that divided Cambodia from Thailand. They plunged in and swam across. Instantly they spied the reward for their arduous journey and their years of suffering. "We saw the camp, and we thought, 'That's freedom!'" she said.

For five years, under the tyranny of Pol Pot and then the Vietnamese, all they had been permitted to wear was black and white. Any expression of happiness carried the risk of torture or death. Now, said Sivheng, the people they saw wore beautiful colors. And there was another sign of jubilation. Under Pol Pot, Cambodians had worn expressions that reflected their unhappiness and suppression. At the Thai camp, Sivheng said, "They smile!"

Until then, Sivheng thought of Van Touch as a friend, little more. They had traveled together under perilous conditions. He had protected her and her brother, and in the Thai camp, he found fish and vegetables for them. "I thought, 'Good man,'" she remembered.

But others suspected that more than friendship might be involved. They called Van Touch and Sivheng "kissing cousins," even though neither of them had a mind at that time for love. As was required of them, they called each other "Comrade," never using a formal name.

More than once in the Thai camp, Sivheng was approached by men offering her promises of a glamorous life filled with luxury and excitement. Sivheng was savvy enough to know that what they really had in mind for her was sexual slavery. "They made it sound like heaven—a house, gold," she said. "But I am not stupid. I am starving (at that time), but I am not stupid."

A FINAL CHOICE FOR FREEDOM

From their first refugee camp, Kok Suong, they were transferred to a camp called Mai Rut. Van Touch's proficiency in English made him a vital assistant to United Nations officials who wanted to develop medical records and other documentation for the refugees. He met up with an American named Stanley Moneyham who had been a missionary during the war and now headed a global Christian organization called World Vision. Moneyham promised to help Van Touch and his companions, by now a sort of ragtag de facto family, find speedy passage to safety.

"They asked us, do you want to go to France, Russia, China or the United States," Sivheng said. Though Van Touch had friends in France, he had set his mind on America as the ultimate symbol of freedom. For her part, Sivheng was indifferent. "I didn't know one from the other," she said. "I just wanted to survive."

And seemingly just like that—just that simple after so much suffering—they were on a plane to San Diego. It was 1979. Sponsors found them housing. Van Touch found work as a teacher's assistant and Sivheng enrolled in school, hoping to learn English. After seven months, Van Touch discovered that his brother had made his way to Portland. And so, said Sivheng, "we moved to Portland."

Though they shared an apartment for nearly four years, Sivheng insists that romance was not part of their relationship. Still, she knew Van Touch was interested in more than friendship. They married in 1984.

"I go with my heart," she explained. "This man, he had been taking care of me. He asked nothing in return."

Blessings and sadness alike have marked the years in the United States.

"Plucked out of the jungle and into the city," as Sivheng describes it, their cultural learning curve was steep. The cruelties they had witnessed and lived through took their toll. Sivheng experienced what can only be called post-traumatic stress disorder, or PTSD, falling into deep depression. Van Touch, too, battled demons in his soul.

Van Touch held many jobs, eventually attending culinary school and opening a restaurant in Beaverton called "The Grape Leaf." He channeled his personal anguish into hard work, to the point, Sivheng said, where he couldn't make time for his own family. In 2018, Van Touch died. The official cause was a heart attack, but Sivheng believes he worked himself to death, a kind of fatal compensation for all their years of deprivation.

By 1990, Sivheng and Van, with David and Tony Touch, had become an all-American family. Tony Touch died in 2009, and Van passed away in 2018. Photo courtesy of Ung family archives

Thirty-eight years had passed since their ordeal in Cambodia, she noted, "and still he felt it."

Their son, Anthony, known as Tony, died in a motorcycle accident at age twenty-three. Sivheng had little use for those who praised her strength in the wake of her son's death. She knew too much about death, she wanted to tell them, too much. And again, she seized on her father's admonition to remember that someone always had it worse. Unlike so many mothers in her own country, she said, she at least got to say goodbye to her son.

Kilong Ung, the younger brother Sivheng rescued, won a scholarship to Reed College, earned a graduate degree, and married his high school sweetheart. An American family, the parents of his best friend, formally adopted him. He wrote a book, *Golden Leaf: A Khmer Rouge Genocide Survivor,* recounting not only his own difficult journey to freedom, but the struggles of his country as a whole. The title, *Golden Leaf,* refers to "one who survives against extreme odds."

One irony of her time in the labor camps was that Sivheng lost—or gained, depending on how you look at it—five years. Her actual birth year was 1951, but somewhere along the line it was recorded as 1956. Many women would kill for such an error, but Sivheng notes "I had to work longer for retirement."

In actual fact, she is not one to sit around and do nothing. "It's boring," she said. Working helps her to concentrate and not think about what she has been through. "It beats depression," she said.

FRIENDSHIP AND ADJUSTMENTS

It was one of her brother's Portland schoolteachers, Clara Buck, who launched Sivheng on a path that became both a passion and a profession. Arriving at their apartment to pay a visit, Buck brought flowers to Sivheng. Sivheng was intrigued by the artful display, and soon Mrs. Buck had taught Sivheng the art of flower arranging. Sivheng's home today is filled with colorful and complicated arrangements of artificial flowers. Their friendship has lasted for forty years.

"Clara," said Sivheng, "she became my mentor. Everything you see here," she said, gesturing around her living room, "everything is inspired by her."

Sivheng may have endured unimaginable horrors under Pol Pot and the communists, but in a new country, with a new language and a new culture, she had new obstacles to overcome.

"Clara, she taught me how to survive," said Sivheng.

Along with her flower business, Sivheng did housecleaning for "rich ladies," women who paid her handsomely and often made gifts of furniture, clothing or other essentials. These random acts of generosity helped cement a sense of connection to the United States, even before they attained full citizenship.

"My husband always said 'America is full of angels,'" she said. "And my husband did not give many compliments. He was very critical." Sivheng is quick to agree with the assessment of Van Touch.

"I appreciate America. I appreciate people here," she said. "Look where I come from. I come from Cambodia, where they killed two million of our own people."

Twenty years ago, Sivheng began working as a parent-educator at IRCO, the Immigrant and Refugee Community Organization in Portland. From her own experiences, she has learned a great deal about plodding through difficulties and adjusting to confusing new circumstances.

She tells her story today in hopes that knowledge and information will help break the chain of human cruelty that continues with mass killings and repression, even in the twenty-first century. She cautions: "I am not looking for sympathy. I just want to make people aware."

And still she has dark days. She has lost two husbands and a son, along with too many other family members to count on two hands. Instead of dwelling on these tragic events, she heeds her father's lesson. Someone, somewhere, is suffering even more. These same words that got her through the Killing Fields continue still to inform her life.

Mohammed Husson Ali. Photo by Sankar Raman

CHAPTER 4

Myanmar and the Plight of the Rohingya People

Mohammed Husson Ali (Myanmar)

In cold, clear tones, two soldiers from the Tatmadaw, the army of Myanmar (formerly Burma), testified to the orders they received in August 2017 as part of their government's campaign against the Rohingya people in Rakhine State. "Shoot all you see and all you hear," Pvt. Myo Win Tun said his commanding officer told him, according to *The New York Times*.

Pvt. Zaw Naing Tun, once a Buddhist monk, said he was given similar instructions as his division prepared to attack a neighboring village: "Kill all you see, whether children or adults."

The soldiers and their troops followed orders. In a chilling videotape submitted to the International Criminal Court in The Hague, Zaw Naing Tun said the Tatmadaw troops "wiped out about twenty villages" in Rakhine State, an area of about 14,000 square miles on Myanmar's west coast. They then dumped their victims' bodies into mass graves.

At least 24,000 people were killed in what the Myanmar government called "clearance operations" aimed at the Rohingya, an ethnically distinct population that for centuries had inhabited the area of Rakhine. In a country that is 80 percent to 90 percent Buddhist, the Rohingya were followers of Islam.

Many human rights groups have called the massacres genocide. Officials from the United Nations described the actions as "a textbook example of ethnic cleansing." That term first surfaced in the context of the 1990s conflicts in the former Yugoslavia. A United Nations Commission of Experts went on to define ethnic cleansing as "rendering an area ethnically homogeneous by using force or intimidation to remove persons of given groups from the area." The same commission elaborated by stating that ethnic cleansing involves "a purposeful policy designed by one ethnic or religious group to remove by violent and terror-inspiring means the civilian population of another ethnic or religious group from certain geographic areas." The United Nations (UN) commission also concluded that the "coercive practices" used to remove the civilian population can include: murder, torture, arbitrary arrest and detention, extrajudicial executions, rape and sexual assaults, severe physical injury to civilians, confinement of civilian populations in ghetto areas, forcible removal, displacement and deportation of civilian populations" and more.

The Commission of Experts determined that these practices can "constitute crimes against humanity and can be assimilated to specific war crimes." Furthermore, the Commission continued: "Such acts could also fall within the meaning of the Genocide Convention." Adopted on December 9, 1948, the Genocide Convention was the first human rights treaty adopted by the United Nations General Assembly. The Genocide Convention marked the first time that the crime of genocide was codified as international law.

One UN report said that close to four hundred Rohingya villages were destroyed in the violence that began in August 2017 and continued into the following years. The settlements were torched, sometimes with people still in the buildings as they were set afire. Later, the Myanmar military bulldozed the area so that nothing remained. Fields that once yielded rice and other crops now lay barren. Coconut, mango, and jackfruit trees were turned to matchsticks.

The Tatmadaw's weapons included guns, flamethrowers, swords, and machetes. Old men were beheaded. Sexual violence was rampant. An estimated 18,000 young girls and grown women were raped, often by gangs of uniformed soldiers. Sometimes the attackers ripped the headscarves off their victims—all of them Muslims—and used them as blindfolds to ensure they could not be identified, just in case the rape victims managed to survive.

The Myanmar government's effort to eliminate the Rohingya

produced one of the largest mass evacuations in modern history. As the brutality escalated, around one million people were forced to flee to other countries from Rakhine State. Most made their way to neighboring Bangladesh.

Already, thousands of Rohingya had escaped to Bangladesh after the former Burmese military initiated a program called Operation Clean and Beautiful Nation in the early 1990s. They settled in a camp in the Cox's Bazar district of Bangladesh called Kutupalong. The United Nations High Commissioner for Refugees (UNHCR) started the camp with support from the European Union, the United States, Japan, Finland, Sweden, Canada, and the IKEA Foundation. By July 2017, Kutupalong and another nearby refugee camp, Nayapara, had a combined population of 34,000.

Bangladesh is a predominantly Muslim country, and as the camps' populations surged, authorities there vowed that no restrictions would be placed on Rohingya refugees entering the camps. Refugees would be sheltered for as long as necessary, the authorities said. But as the Rohingya refugee population in Bangladesh soared to almost one million, human rights observers began describing Kutupalong as an example of what is known as refugee "warehousing."

Camp residents live in flimsy shelters built close together on the steep hillsides of what was once a forest. The camps are prone to flooding, especially during the monsoon season. Fires that spread quickly are commonplace, including a large fire in January 2021, that leveled more than five hundred flimsy shelters as well as shops and other facilities. Several months earlier, another fire killed at least fifteen people and destroyed four hundred homes in an adjacent camp populated by Rohingya. Crime and disease are rampant, and camp residents also are prey for human traffickers. Rohingya women and children are easy targets for exploitation in Asia's sex trade.

By late fall 2019 Bangladeshi authorities encircled the refugee camps with barbed wire, justifying this move as a means to combat human trafficking. Next, the Bangladeshi government restricted telecommunications within the camp. Sales of cell phone SIM cards to Rohingya were restricted, and cell phone reception was reduced. Months later, fires swept through the camps, destroying hundreds of shelters. In the spring of 2020, COVID-19 arrived at the camps, as it had throughout the world.

Months later, in violence that broke out between two rival factions in the camp seeking to control the illicit trade of contraband drugs, about a dozen Kutupalong shelters were burned to the ground. Conditions deteriorated to the point that Human Rights Watch dubbed Kutupalong "an open-air prison" where conditions are "beyond the dignity of any people."

As the overcrowding reached dangerous proportions, Bangladesh in 2018 offered to repatriate some of the Rohingya to Myanmar. But the Rohingya refused to return, citing fears of ongoing persecution and violence. There was also the fact that the Burma Citizenship Law of 1982 had stripped Muslims in the country of their citizenship. In addition, the government of Myanmar had seized most of the agricultural land abandoned by the Rohingya as they fled. Most refugees had no documentation to prove that they had lived in Rakhine or had once owned land. The Rohingya were stateless; indeed, today the Rohingya comprise the world's largest stateless population. Even the name "Rohingya" was no longer acknowledged in Myanmar. Officials there called the Rohingya "illegal immigrants," "terrorists," "foreigners" or "Bengalis." (The latter is not considered a compliment.)

Next, the Bangladeshi government came up with a plan to move up to 100,000 of the Rohingya refugees to a remote island in the Bay of Bengal known as Bhasan Char. The name translates to "floating island," an appropriate image since the tiny, low-lying land mass is prone to floods that can cause parts of the island to disappear. Cyclones, typhoons, and tidal waves are a constant threat. The island is made of silt and encompasses just fifteen square miles, smaller than Santa Catalina Island in California. Travel to Bhasan Char from the mainland requires three to five hours by boat. In what can only be described as diplomatic understatement, a report by the United Nations dubbed the Bhasan Char plan "logistically challenging." Human Rights Watch officials were more blunt, calling the idea of turning Bhasan Char into a sort of satellite settlement area for the Rohingya refugees, "a human rights and humanitarian disaster in the making." Or as one Rohingya in the camp was quoted as saying in a 2019 Amnesty International report, "Sometimes it feels like a small corner of hell."

But Bangladeshi officials insisted that establishing the new island refugee settlement was essential to reduce the crowding at Cox's Bazar. By March 2021, about 13,000 Rohingya were living on Bhasan Char. A year later, the number had grown to close to 30,000. Bhasan Char is patrolled by armed security forces, making it all but impossible to leave. A Rohingya child interviewed by Human Rights Watch in 2021 described Bhasan Char as "an island jail in the middle of the sea."

In their home country, many of the Rohingya lived an agrarian life, raising their own crops and trading produce with their neighbors. On Bhasan Char, they argue, they have no means of subsistence. What work opportunities can they possibly find? At Bhasan Char and at Cox's Bazar alike, Rohingya parents also worry that their children are receiving inadequate education. Health care at the camps is limited. Rohingya also are not allowed to work in Bangladesh, leaving camp residents almost entirely dependent for survival on humanitarian assistance.

Indignities aimed at the Rohingya stretched back for decades. For its part, the United Nations has called the Rohingya "the most persecuted minority in the world." Prominent scholars and theologians, as well as two Nobel Peace Prize winners—the late Archbishop Desmond Tutu and Malala Yousafzai—have condemned the treatment of the Rohingya.

"I am now elderly and decrepit and formally retired, but break my vow to remain silent on public affairs out of profound sadness about the plight of the Muslim minority in your country, the Rohingya," Tutu wrote in 2017 in an open letter to fellow Nobel Peace Prize winner Aung San Suu Kyi, who at the time was the titular leader of Myanmar, and had remained silent about the plight of the Rohingya.

"My dear sister," the then-eighty-five-year-old cleric continued, "if the political price of your ascension to the highest office in Myanmar is your silence, the price is surely too steep."

Politician, author, diplomat, and outspoken advocate of democracy in the country formerly known as Burma, Aung San Suu Kyi was confined to house arrest when she won the 1991 Nobel Peace Prize. Her detention meant that she was unable to travel to Stockholm to hear Swedish officials laud her as "an outstanding example of the power of the powerless." Educated at Oxford University, she was the daughter of Burmese independence leader Aung San, known as the father of Myanmar. He was assassinated in 1947. In 1988, she returned to her home country to take part in Burma's 1988 democracy uprising and general strike, known as the 8888 Uprising. The Burmese government retaliated with a brutal crackdown. At least three thousand demonstrators were killed. Thousands were sent to prison. Around ten thousand activists fled the country. Aung San Suu Kyi's government-ordered house arrest began in 1989.

Released from house arrest in 2010, Aung San Suu Kyi was elected to the Assembly of the Union (Myanmar's legislative body or Parliament) in 2012. In 2015, she was appointed State Counsellor, the country's equivalent of a prime minister. (Under the country's constitution, Aung San Suu Kyi was not eligible for the presidency because she was the widow of a foreigner and the mother of two foreign-born children.) But despite her diplomatic star power as a Nobel Peace Prize winner, Aung San Suu Kyi steadily refused to speak out in support of the Rohingya. Numerous organizations responded by rescinding honors previously bestowed on her for her pro-democracy work.

Tutu was among nearly two dozen human rights activists who called on the United Nations Security Council to intervene in Myanmar. Aung San Suu Kyi herself declined to attend a United Nations meeting set to address the Myanmar crisis. A Myanmar government spokesman said she had "more pressing" matters to attend to.

In February 2021, Aung San Suu Kyi was deposed and placed in detainment following a coup staged by Myanmar's military, the Tatmadaw. By late summer 2021, she was facing a series of corruption charges, as well as accusations of breaching the constitution. Coup leaders detained her in a secret location and convicted her of illegally importing and possessing walkie-talkies. By 2022, she was being held in solitary confinement, with a variety of charges pending against her, including bribery. If convicted, she will likely spend the rest of her life in detention.

Meanwhile, much of the Rakhine state has been bulldozed by Myanmar leaders. Entire villages have been eliminated. Staunchly denying any allegations of genocide, ethnic cleansing or "clearance operations" aimed at the Rohingya, Myanmar officials have gone so far as to suggest that the Rohingya burned down their own villages in the Rakhine State in order to attract international sympathy. All the while, refugees such as Mohammed Husson Ali are separated from their families and their country by tens of thousands of miles—and many rivers of tears.

Rakhine State is on Myanmar's western coast. The name "Rakhine" means "one who maintains his own race." Sanskrit inscriptions found in the region formerly known as Arakan have led archeologists to believe that the earliest settlers were of Indian origin. After centuries of rule by monarchs and princes, the kingdom fell to the invading forces of Burma's Konbaung dynasty in 1784. In 1826, the British assumed control of the entire kingdom of Burma. With its broad coast, the region was an active center for trade. Islam is said to have arrived with Arab traders in the eighth century. The Rohingya language is part of the Indo-Aryan family of languages.

In 1962, all Burmese citizens were required to carry national registration cards. The Rohingya were issued foreign identity cards. Two years later, a group called the Rohingya Independence Front (RIF) announced its intention to create a designated Muslim zone for the Rohingya. Ironically, the group was headquartered at Cox's Bazar, Bangladesh, near the current refugee camp of Kutupalong. The organization was also known as the Rohingya Independence Army. In 1972, its name was changed to the Rohingya Patriotic Front. The Rohingya Liberation Party, founded in 1972, was based in jungles and armed with weapons from Bangladesh. Ten years later, the Rohingya Solidarity Organization (RSO) formed.

Operation Clean and Beautiful Nation sought to apprehend RSO rebels and expel "foreigners"—mostly Muslims. By 1992, the effort had pushed more than 250,000 Rohingya civilians out of Rakhine State.

Along with a steady flow of Muslim refugees headed to Bangladesh from Myanmar, the 1990s brought frequent bouts of violence between Rohingya forces and the Burmese military. It was a back-and-forth decade.

FLEEING A TWENTY-FIRST-CENTURY GENOCIDE

It would be difficult to imagine a more idyllic childhood. Nearly all the 1,300 families in the Burmese village of Myo Thu Gyi were farmers. There in the northwest state of Rakhine, an area of about 14,000 square miles, they owned their land and cultivated rice and other crops. Goats, cows, sheep, and water buffaloes roamed freely. Palm trees provided shade, and sometimes, a soft breeze. Plump mangoes and sweet coconuts hung heavily from their trees. Jackfruit, with their pimply skin and greenish-yellow tinge, abounded. Guava, green on the outside and deep-deep pink inside, flourished. Bananas were everywhere.

At harvest time, neighbors pitched in to help one another gather the rice. Little boys worked alongside their fathers, grandfathers, and uncles. At the end of each day, women and girls delivered big baskets of vegetables for the hungry harvesters. Curry made of goat or chicken was served to anyone who happened to come by. Sticky rice was all but inhaled, a delectable specialty that no one could resist.

Farmers saw no need to compete over crops. No one went hungry, so no one had reason to steal. At the end of each day, after the harvesters had moved from field to field, they broke into song, "*Alleyeela Shari*," or "Farmer's Song." The tune's jaunty chorus echoed across the fields.

All in all, said Mohammed Husson Ali, "In my childhood, it was a very easy life, a very happy time."

But the idyll ended with the political transformation of the country now known as Myanmar. The people of Rakhine were an ethnic minority, Muslims known as Rohingya who had settled in the province known centuries earlier as Arakan. Based on temple inscriptions, the area is thought to have been inhabited for five thousand years. A lineal succession of 227 monarchs ruled the country; the last ruler presided over his realm until 1784. Arakan, with its broad coast, was for centuries an active center for trade. Islam is said to have arrived with Arab traders in the eighth century. The Rohingya language is part of the Indo-Aryan family of languages.

The Rohingya practiced a variation of the Sunni Muslim faith, with their own distinct language and culture. Legend holds that they descend from Arab traders who settled in the region many generations ago. In the state of Rakhine, said Ali (who prefers to be known by his first name, Mohammed), Buddhists and Muslims lived together in harmony. Until quite late in the twentieth century, each group had full citizenship and full voting rights.

"My father sold jute to the Buddhists," he remembered. "At my wedding, a lot of my Buddhist friends came to the celebration. There was no judgment, just living together. We coexisted."

He tells his story quietly, his soft voice betraying no trace of anger or bitterness. His wife, most of his children and grandchildren—those who have survived—reside in the crowded Rohingya refugee camp of Kutupalong, in Bangladesh. The township of Maungdaw, where Myo Thu Gyi was among the villages, no longer exists. As part of its "clearance operation" to eliminate the Rohingya, the Myanmar army burned all the houses, mosques, and other structures in the township and its villages. Then the army bulldozed the entire region to make sure nothing—and no one—remained.

Mohammed is a small man with a wispy white beard. Sixty-eight years old at the time of our interview, he appeared older, aged no doubt by hardship. He wore a knitted skull cap and many layers of warm clothing over his traditional sarong. Coming from a tropical country, he has struggled during his years in the United States to adapt to the chilly winters of the Pacific Northwest. He keeps a sense of perspective, though, perhaps because bureaucratic error sent him initially not to Portland, Oregon, but to Portland, Maine. It was February 28, 2011, when he arrived. In the eighteen days before he was redirected to the other Portland—the one in Oregon—he said he could not imagine how any place on Earth could be so cold.

Only when he speaks of the conditions his family and other Rohingya refugees must endure in a camp bulging with nearly one million people does his voice turn hard. "This place should be called a twenty-first-century concentration camp," he said. "People cannot go outside. There is arrest. There is killing. It is no way to live."

Young men are especially vulnerable. "All the young men, under fifty, they need to hide," he said. "In 2013, one of my sons was targeted." Like his own father, Mohammed Arfat Mohammed Husson, managed to escape with the help of a broker. The younger Ali, twenty-five at the time of our interview, remains in Malaysia.

Kutupalong, the world's largest refugee camp, sprang up in a part of Bangladesh called Ukhia, Cox's Bazar, in 1991, when thousands of Rohingya fled to escape a campaign launched by the Myanmar military called Operation Clean and Beautiful Nation. The effort by Myanmar's military regime sought to apprehend rebels from the Rohingya Solidarity Organization (RSO), an armed militia and political organization whose goal was autonomy for Rakhine state. Operation Clean and Beautiful Nation also was designed to expel "foreigners"—mostly Muslims. By 1992, Operation Clean and Beautiful Nation had pushed more than 250,000 Rohingya civilians out of Rakhine State.

By 2020, the camp at Kutupalong—like so many places in the world—was under siege by COVID. Experts at the World Health Organization warned that the camps' crowded conditions and inadequate hygiene put residents of the camps at heightened risk for contracting the virus. The continued internet and cell phone blackout ensured misinformation, leading to panic and paranoia. Tens of thousands of Rohingya also were moved to a second refugee settlement on the remote island of Bhasan Char, in the Bay of Bengal. A travel ban imposed by the Bangladeshi government in April 2020 extended to the camps and the surrounding area. This meant most aid workers could no longer enter, halting most education and mental health services. Only emergency food assistance remained.

A HISTORY OF FRICTION

Village to village, family to family, residents of the Rakhine State may have enjoyed the kind of harmony that marked Mohammed Ali Husson's childhood. But tension stemming from the religious and social differentiation between the Rakhine Buddhists and the Rohingya Muslim population can be traced at least to World War II, when the Rohingya Muslims sided with the British and the Rakhine Buddhists aligned with the Japanese.

Historians say the modern trouble dates to 1962, when Gen. Ne Win and his Burma Socialist Programme Party seized power in the capital city of Rangoon (now known as Yangon) through a coup. Rohingya were deemed "foreign invaders." This was the year the new government required all citizens to carry national identity cards. Rohingya, however, were issued foreign identity cards. The distinction was deliberate, and the discrimination persisted, preventing Rohingya—who had once held seats in the Burmese Parliament—from voting. For those Rohingya who could work their way through a rigorous citizenship test, limits were placed on how many Rohingya could enter certain professions, such as law or medicine. With the passage of the Burma Citizenship Law in 1982, Muslims in the country—meaning all Rohingya—were largely denied citizenship.

In the more than four decades since crackdowns on the Rohingya in the Rakhine State forced hundreds of thousands to flee to neighboring Bangladesh, Malaysia or elsewhere, many Rohingya say they or their family members have continued to be the victims of rape, torture, arson or murder at the hands of Myanmar security forces. The government in Yangon has steadily denied these charges, including in 2013, when Human Rights Watch said the government was conducting a campaign of ethnic cleansing against the Rohingya, or in 2016, when a United Nations official made a similar accusation. Indeed, Human Rights Watch contends that the Myanmar government has partially or completely destroyed more than 350 Rohingya villages. In turn, the government in Yangon claims that Rohingya rebels killed nine members of the Myanmar border police in 2016, and that the Arakan Rohingya Salvation Army (ARSA), a Rohingya insurgent group, launched a raid on police outposts in Rakhine in the same year.

When Pope Francis visited Myanmar in 2017, the leader of the country's army told the pontiff there was no discrimination in the country and praised the military for maintaining peace and stability. Up until she was deposed in a February 2021 coup by Myanmar's military and placed under house arrest, the country's State Counsellor, Aung San Suu Kyi, would not discuss the plight of the Rohingya.

None of which sits well with Mohammed Husson Ali, a man who taught high school physics, chemistry and math in the Rakhine State, and who worked as a senior food monitor for the UN World Food Programme in his country. After a peaceful childhood that saw him huddle under palm trees when heavy rains struck during the two-mile walk to and from high school, he has lived through stiff restrictions in his township: no access to hospitals, for instance; no facilities for Rohingya students to pursue higher education. Rohingya could not marry without government permission, a process that could take as long as a year. Rohingya couples were not allowed to have more than two children. They saw their land confiscated. They needed permits to travel from place to place. Even members of the United Nations staff, like Mohammed himself, could not move about without an authorization letter.

"Our lives were restricted entirely," he said. "If one became separated from one's family, one could not build a new house."

After Aung San Suu Kyi's appointment as state counsellor in 2016, Mohammed said, even the temporary government registration cards that had been issued to Rohingya were canceled. Rohingya, he said, became known as "illegal immigrants from Bangladesh." To be clear, he said: "No voting rights, no ownership rights, no cars, nothing. Every right, canceled."

A NEW START

Born in 1951, Mohammed had avoided certain curtailments by dint of hard work and some measure of good luck. As a youth he attended the local Madrassa, or Muslim education center, for three hours each morning before heading to the township school. In high school, he excelled at chemistry and math, but his family lacked the funds to send him to college. Instead he began working as an administrator in the education department. He also taught high school and made it a point to study for the country's rigorous university exam while commuting to and from work on city buses. In 1978, he traveled to Rangoon and handily passed the exam, giving him the equivalent of a bachelor's degree in history.

That same year, Mohammed decided for the first time that he and his family would have to leave their country. "The situation was growing worse and worse," he said. The government's new constitution excluded Muslims from any form of citizenship, and the socialist government, rife with graft and corruption, continued to clamp down on the Rohingya through a military effort known as Operation Dragon King.

Officially, the purpose of Operation Dragon King was to register citizens in the northern part of the Arakan state, Rakhine, and oust "foreigners"—i.e., Rohingya—from the region. Rohingya refugees charged that immigration officials and military personnel used intimidation, rape, and murder to expel residents from their communities. When a quarter of a million Rohingya fled the region, government officials declared that the mass exodus had proved that the refugees were in fact illegal immigrants.

Mohammed and his family were among those who headed to Bangladesh. For six months they lived in a refugee camp, before the governments of Bangladesh and Myanmar reached a repatriation agreement that made it possible for them to return to their village. Their goal was to start again, rebuilding the life they had left behind. Mohammed found work first with the World Food Organization, then the UNHCR, the United Nations agency that works with refugees, forcibly displaced communities, and stateless people. Later he returned to teaching.

"We thought everything was settled," he said. "But slowly the problems came back."

By 1992, the Rohingya population once again found itself with all rights gone. "We were told to go," Mohammed said. "But where?"

Again, hundreds of thousands of Rohingya crossed into Bangladesh. Again, the two governments formed an agreement and in 1994, the repatriation process began. Again, Mohammed found work with the World Food Program and the UNHCR. But tensions arose between Mohammed and some of his Buddhist colleagues. Mohammed suspected them of taking information from him and using it against him. His fears were confirmed when he left to attend an external workshop on school food programs in Addis Ababa, Ethiopia. When he arrived at the airport in Yangon, he learned that his passport had been confiscated. A month later, UN officials told him it was too dangerous for him to continue working there. His future looked grim: "I had no passport, no job and at the time, no money," he said.

By 2008, it became clear that he could not remain in Myanmar. He told his family he would try to find a safe place and then send for them. He had little choice but to trust the brokers who made a lucrative business of helping Rohingya and others escape from their country. Under the cover of darkness he began an arduous journey by rowboat, bus, foot and whatever means of transport he could summon. In his hand luggage he carried two shirts, some documents, and recommendation letters from assorted officials.

He landed in Bangladesh, aided by his ability to speak some of that country's language. His familiarity with the customs of Bangladesh also helped him to blend in. Soon enough, his broker delivered, and Mohammed had a Bangladeshi passport. He waited for nearly three months before the broker told him his Thai visa had been approved. At the Bangkok airport, a contact arranged by the broker took him by train to a town on the Malaysian border.

"Then the Thai person gave me some food and took me by motorbike to a small river crossing," Mohammed said. He boarded a tiny boat, just the rower and Mohammed, and entered Malaysia late at night, when river guards were off duty. The stress of the journey was taking its toll. Mohammed felt weak and feared that the pains in his chest signaled something serious. He was right.

From the border, a family took him to a bus station and bought him a ticket to Penang. At two in the morning, he arrived in Malaysia's second largest city, hugging the country's northwest coast. A local Madrassa gave him shelter until he could make contact with someone from UNHCR in Kuala Lumpur. Then, "Fifteen days later, alone, I went to Kuala Lumpur." His youngest son was living in the Malaysian capital, and Mohammed found his way to his home. He also made contact with some of his former students, also Rohingya refugees, who were living there as well, as was one of Mohammed's brothers.

Mohammed told his brother he believed he was seriously ill. After nearly a year-long odyssey, fraught with danger and uncertainty, he was weak and suffering from high fevers. The debilitating condition persisted, and several months later, he realized he was having a full-scale heart attack. The nearest hospital was two hours away, and the only means of transport available was a motorbike. Mohammed clung to the driver while his heart screamed out in pain. His convalescence, "back and forth to the hospital," took two years. During that time he had applied to UNHCR to go to Australia. It was a safe enough destination. When the UNHCR came back with an offer to send him to America, "My brother told me, 'Go.'"

In Portland—the one in Oregon, not Maine—he shares a house owned by a fellow Rohingya with other refugees. He worships at a nearby mosque. He misses his family terribly and prays that they will join him in America one day. He mourns the devastation of his home community and the ongoing violence that continues to claim lives there. His own nephew, for example, was gunned down and killed on his way to the rice paddies in 2016 when Myanmar authorities retaliated against an insurgent attack on a military encampment at the border.

"He was shot down in front of my house," Mohammed said—a house that no longer stands now that the government has erased the existence of the village. "They killed three people in my village that evening." Minutes later, he said, the Army struck another nearby village, killing seven young children on their way to sell produce in the village market. "No one could escape," Mohammed said.

Just to make sure the remaining Rohingya were kept in line, "the government removed all fences, even the walls around toilets. There was no privacy, none at all. House by house, village by village, they cut down all the trees so no one could hide." The following year, "the military entered my village and burned all the houses, one by one. The whole village—nothing was left." Even the cemetery was later bulldozed, along with fourteen mosques, flattened.

In the aftermath, his wife, two sons, and three daughters managed to cross to Bangladesh, where they remain in the vast Rohingya refugee camp. When cell phone coverage permits, Mohammed tries to speak to his family twice a day. All are healthy, he reports, despite the difficult conditions. But they are trapped in their stateless and refugee status, with no passports, no national identity, and no funds for travel.

Even in the arduous conditions of the Leda refugee camp, Mohammed's wife Asha Katun maintains the Muslim tradition of female modesty, covering her head as she peers out from behind a curtain to hear the men's conversations in the shelter's main room. Katun, age sixty-six, has been in the Leda refugee camp since 2017. Mohammed has not seen her or the sons who accompanied her to the camp in ten years and has never seen his grandchildren. Photo by John Rudoff

"Immediate intervention" is needed to solve this conundrum, Mohammed maintains. He sets his hopes on action by the US government but concedes that the predicament of the Rohingya is not a high priority.

"Nobody even knows who the Rohingya are, or where the Rohingya are from," he laments. "The Rohingya genocide movement needs to be organized."

For his part, Mohammed appreciates the good fortune that allowed him to escape the twenty-first-century genocide that has claimed the lives of so many of his people.

"I found this to be a nice place, America," he said. "Since I am aged, old, I get all sorts of facilities—medical care, food, everything." In the United States, he said, he has found "no discrimination against religion, skin color, race. Here, the rule of law means everything." Among the standout benefits, Mohammed said in a voice filled with appreciation as well as admiration, "There is free education here!"

He paused, then added: "I want my family and my community to have this kind of society."

Emmanuel Turaturanye. Photo by Sankar Raman

CHAPTER 5

Broken Bodies, Damaged Psyches, and an Elusive Search for Justice in Rwanda

Emmanuel Turaturanye (Rwanda)

Not so many years ago, Rwanda held a firm grip on the popular imagination—not for its bloody civil war, but for the legend of the landlocked country as a haven for peace-loving gorillas made famous by an American primatologist named Dian Fossey.

Fossey—a thirty-one-year-old San Francisco native whose love for animals dated from childhood—used her life's savings to travel to Africa in 1963. Captivated by the habits of some of the world's largest, most powerful primates, she set up camp in Rwanda's Virunga Mountains and launched what became a lifelong study of the mountain gorilla.

At her Karisoke Research Center, Fossey lived among quadrupeds who grow from four to six feet tall, and whose weight can range from three hundred to nearly five hundred pounds. Mountain gorillas, she discovered, vocalize with sixteen distinct calls. When a male mountain gorilla wants to fend off a rival, he stiffens his legs and struts aggressively. When a female gorilla is feeling amorous, she makes sustained eye contact as she slowly approaches her chosen male, then purses her lips. If that doesn't work, she slaps the ground as she heads toward him.

Mountain gorillas form family groups, Fossey found. Individuals can live to be forty years old. Fossey's enthusiasm was contagious. Her 1983 book, *Gorillas in the Mist,* topped best-seller lists for several years and became a successful film starring Sigourney Weaver as Fossey.

But violence has a way of foreshadowing itself. Fossey was hacked to death with a machete in her tent at Karisoke in 1985. Her murder remains unsolved.

Along with animal researchers around the world, the crime shocked one of Africa's smallest countries. Rwanda—officially, the Republic of Rwanda—is located just south of the equator. The area was settled by hunter-gatherers during the Stone and Iron ages. Its three primary ethnic groups are the Hutu (85 percent), the Tutsi (14 percent) and the Twa (1 percent).

The mountainous topography of Rwanda gave rise to its nickname, "land of a thousand hills." In fact, the entire country is at such a high altitude that its lowest point is the Rusizi River, at 3,117 feet above sea level. Along Rwanda's northern border, the Virungas—a chain of extinct volcanoes—soar to more than 14,000 feet. Rwanda's breathtaking scenery and temperate climate have prompted some to liken the country to a tropical Switzerland.

Bordering Rwanda are Democratic Republic of the Congo, Burundi, Uganda, and Tanzania. Its population of 12.6 million makes tiny Rwanda the most densely populated mainland African country.

Rwanda's primary language is called Kinyarwanda. English, French, and Swahili also are widely spoken. With their own long oral traditions, the Hutu, Tutsi, and Twa tribal people laid the groundwork for a rich heritage in Rwanda of poetry and folk tales. Before European colonization began in the late nineteenth century, a form of epic poetry was performed in Rwanda's royal courts. Ibitekerezo told the history of the country's dynasties through poetry that was performed as song, accompanied by a musical instrument.

The early Hutus were largely agrarian, while the Tutsis traded in cattle. For centuries, Rwandans lived in a series of small kingdoms. Then, in the nineteenth century, Rwanda—like so much of Africa—became a target for European colonization. The territory went first to Germany, and then to Belgium.

Playing on underlying tensions between the tribes brought on by longstanding economic imbalance, the Germans and the Belgians promoted the idea of Tutsi supremacy. In 1926, Belgium further emphasized ethnic differences by imposing identity cards designating people as either Hutu, Tutsi, Twa or "Naturalized."

The strife turned violent in 1959. After Tutsi extremists fatally assaulted a Hutu sub-chief, Hutu activists retaliated with a series of arson attacks on Tutsi homes. The same year, Hutu rebels launched what became known as the Rwandan Revolution, a full-on rebellion against Belgian rule. This period also is sometimes called the Social Revolution or Wind of Destruction. The Kinyarwanda word for this conflict is *muyaga*.

Not until 1962 did Rwanda achieve full independence from Belgium. That year, a Rwandan revolutionary named Gregoire Kayibanda—a Hutu—became the country's first elected president. Thousands of Tutsis fled to neighboring Burundi as the 1960s and 1970s brought the purging of Tutsis from universities and ethnic quotas that restricted Tutsis to 9 percent of government jobs.

In a 1973 coup aimed at overthrowing Kayibanda, one of Rwanda's senior military officers, Juvenal Habyarimana, took power. Habyarimana—whose nickname was Kinani, the Kinyarwanda word for "invincible"—promised to restore order and national unity. Instead, exclusion of Tutsis and preference for Hutus in military and public service jobs persisted.

Decades of continuous ethnic strife continued up to 1990. Habyarimana was attending diplomatic meetings in New York City when a rebel group called the Rwandan Patriotic Front (RPF) invaded northern Rwanda from outposts in Uganda. The attacking forces were made up largely of Tutsi refugees who had fled persecution in their own country. The three-year confrontation that followed became known as the Rwandan Civil War, an explosion of the long-running enmity between Hutus and Tutsis.

While the Rwandan army sought and received assistance from French troops, the RPF staged what amounted to a guerrilla war. Among the RPF leaders was Paul Kagame, the country's future president.

An uneasy truce settled into place in late 1993. Then, on April 6, 1994, a plane carrying Rwandan President Habyarimana, Burundian President Cyprien Ntaryamira, and other dignitaries was shot down above Kigali International Airport, killing everyone aboard.

Habyarimana's death became the catalyst for the Rwandan genocide. Just hours after his death was announced, Hutus began a deadly campaign against the Tutsis. To prevent anyone from escaping, the Hutus set up roadblocks, then systematically moved from house to house, slaughtering Tutsis and moderate Hutu political figures.

Exact figures remain in dispute. But over the course of one hundred days, between 500,000 and one million Tutsis are believed to have been killed in well-planned attacks. Thousands of Hutus also died in the violence, often while attempting to oppose the slaughter. Seventy percent of the Tutsi population was decimated in attacks perpetrated largely by nail-studded clubs, machetes and sometimes, firearms.

Rape, often a weapon of war, was widespread, promulgated in many cases by groups of insurgents known as rape squads. No official tally exists, but it is believed that between 250,000 and 500,000 women were raped. Thousands of widows, subjected to rape, became HIV-positive as a result.

The killings in Rwanda gave rise to a chilling new phrase in the lexicon of warfare. "Intimate genocide" referred to the fact that, among other atrocities, Hutus married to Tutsis were expected to kill their spouses and children. Hutu neighbors who had lived as friends with the Tutsis next door also were on orders to slay their acquaintances.

The Rwandan genocide received limited international response and essentially no attempts at intervention.

Philip Gourevitch, an American journalist, is the author of a book called *We Wish To Inform You That Tomorrow We Will Be Killed Along With Our Families*, one of the definitive accounts of the Rwandan genocide. According to Gourevitch, the mass murders in Rwanda cannot be explained simply as the product of hostility between competing ethnic groups.

"The genocide was the product of order, authoritarianism, decades of modern political theorizing and indoctrination, and one of the most meticulously administered states in history," he writes.

In an interview with the PBS program *Frontline*, Gourevitch said of the Rwandan genocide, "The logic was to kill everybody. Not to allow anybody to continue."

Gourevitch makes a clear distinction between civil war in Rwanda and the country's genocide.

"In a civil war, you have essentially two combatant forces," he explains. "Sometimes they are fighting against one another. Sometimes civilians get involved as militia men or so. In a genocide, there is no political objective. The idea is to eliminate what is perceived as a bloodline. It means anybody who carries that blood must be eliminated. So it doesn't matter if you're a baby. In a civil war, a baby is not a serious enemy element. Here, it is, because sixty years from now, that baby could be an adult."

A 1999 report from Human Rights Watch called *Leave None to Tell the Story* draws much the same conclusion.

"The Rwandan genocide of 1994 was one of the defining events of the twentieth century," the report asserts. "It ended the illusion that the evil of genocide had been eradicated and spurred renewed commitment to halting genocides in the future."

The book-length report assesses the implications of the genocide, both within Rwanda and for the international community. It's worth quoting at length.

"For Rwandans, whether inside the country or abroad, the consequences of the genocide are direct and tangible," the report states. "They struggle daily to heal broken bodies and traumatized psyches, to seek justice, and to recreate trust among themselves. Yet the consequences of this genocide, enormous as they are for Rwandans, do not stop at the border of that one small country but spill onto the people of neighboring countries and far beyond. Those living in the region have suffered from subsequent wars of unimaginable cruelty and from the consequences of millions of people in flight, both refugees and killers. Those further from Rwanda pay the price of their failure to protect others, both in guilty consciences and in the material costs of humanitarian aid and assistance in rebuilding shattered societies."

Timothy Longman, a professor of political science and international relations at Boston University, was among the authors of *Leave None to Tell the Story*. Longman directs the university's Institute on Culture, Religion and World Affairs and has served as acting director of BU's African Studies Center. Longman worked with Human Rights Watch in

Rwanda following the genocide and has been called as an expert witness in several Rwandan war crimes trials.

Longman stresses that entrenched views about Africa on the part of many Westerners may help to explain the failure to intervene in the Rwandan genocide. In an interview with BU Today, an internal publication at Boston University, Longman said, "Our approach to Africa is still shaped by racist ideas. There's a tendency for Americans—but I think it's true for Europeans as well—to view Africans as inherently savage, to still believe that Africans are just prone to violence, and that's why violence happens.

"In dealing with Africa," Longman continued, "when violence happens, we assume that it is primal and a reflection of backward cultures rather than something that is, in fact, modern and well-organized. The genocide in Rwanda was only possible because of a modern bureaucracy, because of the type of organization that a modern state made possible. It was well-organized and well-planned."

The Rwandan genocide ended in July 1994 when Rwandan Patriotic Front forces took Kigali, the nation's capital. Hundreds of thousands of Hutus fled as Kigali fell to forces led by Paul Kagame.

A sense of global horror and shame took hold as the extent and calculus of the mass killings became evident. In 1994, the United Nations Security Council established the International Criminal Tribunal for Rwanda (ICTR) with the goal of bringing to justice those who had perpetrated the massacres. Within Rwanda, a traditional village court system known as Gacaca was reintroduced as an additional step to ensure justice.

According to Human Rights Watch, at least ten thousand Rwandans have been tried for crimes associated with the massacres. The country's civilian-run Gacaca courts have handled more than a million such cases. After ten years, the Gacaca ended formally in 2012. In 1998, twenty-two people were publicly executed for their roles in the killings. Other death sentences were commuted when Rwanda abolished the death penalty in 2007.

In the aftermath of the genocide, several countries offered formal apologies to Rwanda for failing to take steps to halt the killings, according to *Rwanda: Justice After Genocide—20 Years On*, a 2014 report from Human

Rights Watch. Without actually apologizing for his country's failure to intervene in Rwanda, former US president Bill Clinton, who was in office during the atrocities, said in 2012, "I don't think we could have ended the violence, but we could have cut it down. And I regret that."

A report from Human Rights Watch cast a wide shadow of shame, concluding that "Despite repeated warnings by Rwandans and international human rights organizations, diplomats, U.N. staff and others that a genocide was being prepared, governments and intergovernmental bodies . . . dramatically failed to act to prevent the genocide as it unfolded in 1994." Within Rwanda, a new constitution adopted in 2003 bans political organizations that base themselves on "race, ethnic group, tribe, clan, religion, sex, religion or any other division which may give rise to discrimination."

Rwanda's 2008 Genocide Revisionism Law prohibits the advancement of what it calls genocide ideology. Included under this legal umbrella are intimidation, defamatory speeches, genocidal denial, mocking of victims and acts lumped under the term "divisionism." The new government also took steps to address gender inequity. According to the new government, a mandatory minimum of 30 percent of the country's senators are women. Not all the changes were seen as progressive. As president, Kagame had been limited to two terms in office. But he wanted more. A 2015 constitutional amendment would permit Kagame to stay in office until 2034.

The specter of the genocide weighs heavily on the soul of Rwanda. Little chance remains of burying the horrific memories—not when, twenty-five years after the slaughters ended, mass graves of genocide casualties continue to be uncovered.

The civil war and ensuing genocide also took a toll on a Rwandan economy based largely on subsistence agriculture. Ironically, before the global pandemic caused by the coronavirus virus closed most international borders, tourism was strengthening the Rwandan economy. In spite of the tragic legacy of war and genocide, people still wanted to observe the mountain gorillas. As pandemic travel restrictions have gradually lifted, the mountain gorilla tourist traffic has begun to return to Rwanda.

"I LIVED TO TELL THE WORLD"

Dressed in the plaid shirt and down jacket that is the unofficial uniform of the Pacific Northwest, Emmanuel Turaturanye was riding the MAX train in Portland, Oregon, one day when a guy sitting nearby shot him an angry glare. Turaturanye has an easy smile, and his tortoise shell glasses afford him a scholarly air. He is from Africa, and his skin is very dark.

"Go back to where you came from!" the man shouted at Turaturanye.

Very soon, the man on the MAX train realized he had chosen the wrong adversary. Turaturanye stayed calm and poised. What the man had roused in him was not anger, but righteous indignation. Turaturanye knew far too much about the toll of hatred, and he knew that the best way to combat it was not to fight back, but to stand up to it.

"Freedom of speech does not give you the right to engage in hate speech," he rejoined, keeping his voice strong and even. "What you just said is a violation of my human rights."

All eyes on the train turned on the man who had spoken to Turaturanye. Still keeping his voice calm, Turaturanye challenged, "What do you think all these other passengers think of what you just said to me? What do they think of you?"

At the next stop, Turaturanye's verbal assailant couldn't get off the train fast enough. Around him, Turaturanye said, other passengers began marveling at how skillfully he had defused a potentially explosive encounter. Several people wept in admiration.

"I do not respond to anger with anger," the lanky Multnomah County transit driver—forty-one at the time of our interview—explained later. "It is like trying to stop fire with fire." More forcefully, he added, "I am a product of hate. I survived it. I respect human rights. But I will never tolerate hate."

Turaturanye was sixteen years old, "just a young boy," when his native Rwanda was ravaged by civil war. The assassination of President Juvenal Habyarimana spurred a bloody Hutu campaign that sought to kill every member of the rival Tutsi clan living in Rwanda. The worst of the killings occurred in the first six days after Habyarimana's death on April 6, 1994. But the genocide stretched on until 70 percent of Rwanda's Tutsi residents had been slain—including nearly all of Emmanuel Turaturanye's family members. Among Tutsis who survived, many sought permanent exile outside Rwanda.

In the process, the Hutu forces also murdered thousands from the Twa tribe, the country's earliest inhabitants. The Twa were aboriginal pygmy hunter-gatherers who had begun settling in the region that became Rwanda between 800 BC and 3000 BC. About one-third of the Twa population were slain in the rampage.

Experts say the rate of killing in such a short time was five times that of the Nazi Holocaust. The scale and brutality shocked the world. But Western nations, including the United States, all but ignored the careful and calculated attempt to eliminate an entire population based solely on ethnic identity.

A VILLAGE CHILDHOOD

Turaturanye, whose surname means "neighbor," was born and raised in the Ngoma district of Rwanda's Eastern Province. His father was a pastor and his mother, a farmer. Beans, cassava, bananas, and avocados provided the bulk of their income. Theirs was a self-sustaining lifestyle: "I never had to go buy food at the market," Turaturanye said. "It was just there."

Turaturanye was one of six siblings whose native language was called Kinya. Three cousins, the children of his father's brother, lived with them. "So we were eleven in the house," he said. "It was fun."

The boys and their neighbors played soccer in the village streets, barefoot. Turaturanye said no one thought about who came from which tribe. The family was active in the large church community led by Turaturanye's father, where Hutu prayed alongside Tutsi. They lived a village life, far in so many ways from the political strife of the country's capital, Kigali. If there was tension, he said, it was more about economic disparity than tribal identity.

"I was a Tutsi, but it was a social class, not a tribe," he said. "Sometimes when I talk about this, it is hard even for me to understand: How to call people who speak the same language 'different tribes?'"

But hostility toward the Tutsis had been brewing for several decades. The attacks on April 7, 1994, that began in the northern part of Rwanda, when Hutu insurgents poured in from Uganda, had been carefully orchestrated. The violence came with a mandate to leave no Tutsi man, woman or child alive.

As Turaturanye observed, "Genocide does not happen instantly. It has to be planned." The killings may have taken place in 1994, but "the seed of genocide ideology—the propaganda and the discrimination," as he put it, was planted in 1959, long before Turaturanye was born.

As a Tutsi, his father was not allowed to go to high school, nor to serve in the military. As time went on, intending to deny Tutsi children the chance for higher education, the government maintained a steady count of Tutsis attending school. In first grade, Turaturanye remembered, an official called out, "Hutus, stand."

"So I stood," he said. "I didn't know the difference."

When the same thing happened the next year, in second grade, his teacher slapped him for what she presumed was his impudence. Confused, young Emmanuel went home and asked, "Dad, what is a Hutu, and what is Tutsi?"

By the following year, when he was eight, Turaturanye began to feel the discrimination himself. "What I experienced in school was dehumanization," he said. "I was called a cockroach and a snake. I was bullied, physically, every day." When this would happen, when schoolmates would taunt him," Emmanuel would turn to his father for comfort. "He was the one I would go to, and cry," he said. "He was a really good, loving, caring father."

He has since studied the philosophy, such as it is, of tyranny. "This is how they did it, with propaganda. It was the same as the Nazis against the Jews."

Because even many Rwandans could not distinguish one group from another, the government began issuing those national identification cards. Children, however, were not required to carry ID cards. That oversight by a government bent on destruction helped many young people to survive.

The genocide came as no surprise to Turaturanye. "Growing up, Tutsi, I was told we were going to be killed," he said. "They were always telling us we were foreigners—Ethiopians."

The relentless erosion of his humanity took its toll. "I don't know if

I can explain it," he began. "It was as if I was already dead. I was not a human being." The unremitting cruelty was itself unfathomable. "You would see people wearing priests' robes," Turaturanye said—men whose very clothing was intended to inspire trust. "They would tell you they were going to kill you."

THE KILLINGS BEGIN

The mass killings of 1994 began in early April. On the eighth day of the month, machete-armed guerrillas arrived in Turaturanye's region. The Tutsi population was in shock, wondering what to do. No one could have expected such brutality, so quickly. "There was not enough time to flee," he said. If you did manage to escape, "wherever you would go, someone would find you."

Many of the people in his father's congregation were Hutus. "The people he had preached to, they turned against him," his son said. A crowd of maybe ten people surrounded the family's home. They carried guns and machetes. "Machetes were for the poor. You had to pay to be shot," Turaturanye said. "Can you imagine? Paying someone to shoot you?"

By sheer happenstance, Emmanuel Turaturanye was outside when the attack began. Cooking duties rotated among the children, and it was his day to prepare meals for the family. His five-year-old sister, Amena, was with him. Amena adored her big brother, and she loved to sit next to him while he cooked.

A group, he said, "maybe 10 people" began surrounding the family home. "They had gun and machetes." Turaturanye saw them, "and my heart started to race, the way you feel when something bad is about to happen." His body began to spasm with chills of fear. "And then my gut told me: Run!"

He scooped up his sister and took off as fast as his long, lean legs could carry him. The guerrillas chased them, but Emmanuel and Amena outran them. All these years later, a sense of amazement remains in his voice as he remembers, "My little sister, my God, she was so fast."

Inside the family home, the Hutu warriors killed his ninety-five-year-old grandmother, his mother, and his brother Steven. His cousins—Asman, Amina, and Ayat—all were killed the same day. His father, who had been at a neighbor's house when the attack occurred, also perished in the carnage. An older brother, Samuel, somehow had managed to run to another village.

As the massacre continued, Turaturanye said he lost too many members of his family to count—certainly too many to make any sense. "Oh my God," he said. "More than one hundred."

An official death toll from the massacres is hard to establish in part, he said, "because so many people disappeared."

The loss of his family and the callous nature of the violence seemed impossible to absorb. There was no time to grieve. Turaturanye knew only that he had to flee, to find a place of safety for him and his sister. "All I felt was numbness," he said. "I was in desperation mode. You don't think of anything else, just how to survive."

Emmanuel and Amena first sought refuge in the district's administrative offices. It seemed reasonable to believe that in a government office, they would be out of harm's way. The brother and sister were not alone in making this assumption. When they arrived, the offices were teeming with Tutsis in search of refuge. But far from being safe, he soon realized, "it was like walking into fire. We were six thousand Tutsis in the district office that day, a kind of ad hoc refugee camp. We thought we were safe, but they were planning to kill us all."

Three days later, the Hutu soldiers tried to lull their captives into a further sense of safety by bringing them food: rice and beans. They also brought one thousand grenades with the intention of finishing off the entire lot in one massive hit. Turaturanye is still unsure just how he managed to escape. But in his heart, "I thought, 'I do not want to die.'"

One small advantage was that he did not have a national ID card naming him as a Tutsi. But Hutus from his own village knew him and would happily have identified him as their enemy. Roadblocks were everywhere.

THE KINDNESS OF KAMONDO

With nowhere to turn, and at that point, little to lose, he knocked on the door of a Hutu woman who had been a close friend of his family. She told him she knew what was happening. Then, rather than turning him out to face certain death, she said, "Son, just come in."

Her name was Kamondo, the same as a kind of exotic bird. Inside her home, she hid Emmanuel and Amena. The gesture carried great personal risk. Her own son, Turaturanye said, "was among the criminals. He knew we were there."

But the woman warned her son: "If one of these kids is ever killed, I will kill myself." For emphasis, she told him: "If you ever, ever even think about it, I will die first. They will not be harmed. Not in my life."

When Hutus from his own village came looking for him, she hid Emmanuel and Amena under a bed. Even her son went along with the scheme. "There's no one here," he told the rebels. "And since he was one of them," Turaturanye said, "they believed him."

Who can comprehend the incomprehensible? When the killings stopped, Turaturanye could scarcely understand that he was alive, never mind why or how. Many people his own age, after all, had been bludgeoned, butchered, burned alive. He believes his survival may have been preordained for a purpose. "Being alive . . . it is not that I deserved it," he said. "I think I lived in order to tell the world."

FIGHTING BACK

For years, even the United Nations balked at applying the label "genocide" to the terrible events in Rwanda. Instead the bloodshed was called the Rwandan Civil War. "They were ashamed," Turaturanye theorizes. "'Never again,' they had said when this had happened before in other places."

The lack of support from the United States, a traditional ally at times of global despotism, did not surprise Turaturanye. Only a year before, US troops had been killed in Somalia, and the government was in no hurry to become involved in another African dispute. Besides, Rwanda is a country of few natural resources, and as Turaturanye pointed out, "for Clinton, there was to be no return on his investments. What was he going to get in Rwanda?"

Soldiers from the RPF had already captured his region when Turaturanye joined their forces. He had seen so much already—houses burned with families inside them, people thrown into toilet pits that served as mass graves—and now maybe it was his turn to fight back. "I felt I had to do something," he said. "But I also felt protected. No one was going to chase me with a machete."

Three of his cousins, sons of a sister-in-law who somehow managed to survive although her husband did not, joined with him in enlisting. Their mother agreed to take care of Emmanuel's sister Amena. But even as a soldier, he never killed anyone. He could not. He fell back on the foundation his father had given him: "Love your neighbor as yourself. If you want to be treated well, why would you mistreat others? And God was my witness."

The trauma he had endured never left him. His emotional wounds were too deep and too fresh. He had terrible nightmares. "Oh my God, the nightmares," he says. In flashbacks, people chased him, constantly brandishing machetes.

His inner turmoil mirrored that of Rwanda as a whole. The country, its very soul ripped to shreds, had to rebuild from the ground up, starting with establishing a new constitution. Two public holidays were set aside to recognize and mourn the genocide. High school and college students alike are required to take a course that outlines the genocide.

The new government focused on helping its people to heal. Trauma therapy became widely available. Turaturanye did not hesitate to take advantage of these services. "The therapy really helped me to understand what I was going through," he said. In turn he trained as a counselor so he could help others.

He also went to college in Rwanda, saving the money to pay for his courses by skipping meals and ignoring the constant rumbling in his stomach. He earned one advanced degree in agricultural engineering and another in economics and management. He took a job as an agronomist agent for the government, helping people learn to grow healthy food.

But no amount of therapy or work as diversion could help him to reconcile the evil he had endured. The pastor's son gave up on God. He had no hope. He was angry. "I questioned God," he said. "If God existed, why did he not stop the murders?"

He has no idea where he found the money for alcohol and drugs, but somehow he did. Smoking marijuana was illegal, but he did not care. "I was an angry young man," he said. "Life was worthless. I wanted to die." He shook his head and said once again: "Life was worthless."

A VOICE SPEAKS

One day—Emmanuel swears this happened—he was standing around, smoking, when he heard a voice. "Emmanuel," said the voice, "what are you doing?"

He looked around but saw no one. His head spun once again, but still he was alone. Obviously, he concluded, he was losing his mind. "Emmanuel, what are you doing?" the voice asked for the second time.

The third time the voice spoke, it said: "Your dad Isaac is in heaven. You know how he did everything to make your life good. If he looked at you now, would he be proud?"

At that exact moment, he said, his life took a U-turn. He contacted his cousin, Jane, the only person he thought he could trust at that point. Jane had watched his downward spiral but had not passed judgment. When he told her about the voice he had heard, Jane looked up at the sky and asked Emmanuel to come to church with her the following day.

"The speaker that day was from Congo. He started preaching about the prodigal son," Turaturanye said. The message from the Biblical cycle on redemption hit home. Recognizing himself in the parable of the wasteful and dissolute son who falls into destitution,Turatanuye began to weep.

"That very day, I quit smoking. I quit drinking," he said. "One week after giving my life to Christ, I changed the group I was hanging out with. I started singing. I joined the choir. After two years I was playing music. Now I write music."

Indeed, as part of an oral history project to observe the genocide, he composed a song and sang it. His tune called "Just Having Good Time with the Spirit" can be seen on YouTube (https://www.youtube.com/watch?v=cEQsZpKmGV4).

Turaturanye was to hear from the voice, the Spirit, yet again. It was 2008 and he was serving as a choirmaster. Within his choir were people whose families had committed genocide, and people whose families had been killed in the genocide. This is when the Spirit told him he was a hypocrite, for through his music he was teaching forgiveness, the very notion he was unable to embrace himself.

The Spirit reminded him that the Lord's Prayer calls for forgiveness, then admonished: "I want you to do it." Turaturanye was angry. He started to cry. The voice repeated: "Do it!" The voice told Turaturanye he must return to the village where he was born and proclaim forgiveness.

"And that is when I started feeling inner peace," he said, because he did follow those instructions. "I felt alive, lighter. That is why I don't cry anymore. I found this grace, and it really transformed me."

This epiphany, this moment of true healing taught him another important lesson.

"Forgiveness is different from reconciliation," he said. "Reconciliation is between you and someone else. Forgiveness is within you. I started forgiving myself so I could find peace within myself."

His faith continues to sustain him, Turaturanye said: "I am a Christian. I have a personal relationship with Jesus Christ. To have that faith has really helped me."

TRIPLE REDEMPTION

Turaturanye likes to say that he was saved twice, once when he escaped the Hutu atrocities, and again when he found Christ. But there was a third moment of redemption, and that was when he met Danielle, the beautiful American woman who would become his wife.

It was 2008. Friends of his, Nathan and Pam, had opened an English-speaking school for the children of missionaries and NGO (nongovernmental organization) workers living in Rwanda. Turaturanye was hanging out at the school, in part to help with the music program, but also to encourage these newcomers to Rwanda to attend the English-speaking services at the Anglican church where he was both the organist and an unordained pastor.

Danielle, a traveling missionary, had arrived to serve as a teacher at the school. "I just saw her smile, and her beautiful golden eyes," Turaturanye said. "And oh man, I just felt something."

Evidently it was mutual. Danielle came to his church and began attending evening worship services. She didn't have a car, so he would walk her home at night. Sometimes he would take her hand. The relationship remained warm, but chaste, until Danielle moved back to the United States in 2010 to take a job with a nonprofit organization. When an opportunity to return to Rwanda cropped up soon after, Danielle jumped at it.

Finally, Turaturanye felt it was time to tell her how he felt. "It was a really long conversation," he remembered. When he at last told her he loved her, she replied, "Are you sure?" They began dating.

As she prepared once again to return to the United States in 2011, Turaturanye had a friend make a golden ring adorned with shiny rubies. He presented it to her in a Rwandan peace basket and asked her to be his wife. It was an intercultural, interracial partnership, and there were some large hurdles to overcome. On May 18, 2013, they became husband and wife. In the small church in the village where he was raised, Emmanuel and Danielle made sure that everyone was invited, even those who surely had taken part in the slaughter of Turaturanye's family.

"The same people who had surrounded my house, they were at my wedding," he said. "I embraced them."

A COOL NEW FAMILY

At first they lived in Rwanda. Things were not always easy. Days into the new year, 2016, Danielle and Emmanuel both lost their jobs.

"We got stuck. We had no severance pay," he said, and so "We prayed."

Emmanuel went to the US Embassy and was granted a ten-year visa to the United States. (He has since obtained a green card.) And so later in 2016 they moved to Danielle's native Portland. There were some immigration roadblocks: "It was a little complicated, because of my military background in Rwanda," he said. Also, his university degrees carried little weight in the United States.

But as they settled into life in Oregon, things began to fall into place. One of Danielle's cousins gave them a car. Danielle found a job with a nonprofit. Emmanuel received a work authorization permit.

Turaturanye considers himself lucky because "her family is really cool." Having lost nearly everyone in his own large family—upwards of

When Danielle and Emmanuel were married in 2013 in St. Etienne's Cathedral in Kigali, they summoned the spirit of forgiveness and invited even those neighbors who had murdered Emmanuel's family during the 1994 genocide. Photo courtesy of Turaturanye family archives

one hundred people, he estimates—he treasures the moments when his American nieces crawl into his lap and tell him how much they love their Uncle Manny.

"Her family," he said, "they love me and I love them."

Even from far across the globe, Emmanuel and Danielle stay in contact with his surviving sister and brother via Skype, WhatsApp, and other platforms. Emmanuel says that no matter how good his life is in Oregon, it is hard not to miss Rwanda.

"It is my home," he said.

Danielle and Emmanuel hope for children of their own one day. When the time is right, he will take them back to Rwanda and share with them the terrible history that he and his country endured. He will tell them the truth and hope that they learn from it.

But also, he vows, "I will tell them to love and respect every human being, no matter what their race or where they come from, no matter what their religion might be. Just love them, as a human being."

There are things, important things, that Turaturanye would like to tell the rest of the world. He would like people to understand, for instance, that "ignorance is preventable, but it is also contagious." He would like to make it known that as his home country reorganized, "one of the smartest things Rwanda did was to invest in education. Not just math and physics, but also teaching how to prevent hate crimes from happening."

Perhaps most important, he would like to talk about the toxic nature of anger. "Anger, let me tell you, anger does not exist on its own. It is like the second emotion, the thing that comes next. It is an iceberg. You only see just the top. But there are a lot of layers underneath."

Anger, he continued: "It just kills, and it destroys the soul." That is what he would like people to know, "if anyone can hear." But can people hear? Can they learn? Can the toxic tide of anger be turned back?

"People are still killing. There are still mass shootings," he conceded. "But I don't think it's too late to make a change. It's not too late to empower the younger generation to love and respect.

Abdulah Polovina. Photo by Sankar Raman

Hatidza Polovina. Photo by Sankar Raman

CHAPTER 6

With a Backdrop of Faith

Abdulah and Hatidza Polovina (Bosnia)

This story of deep faith and abiding love in the face of war, ethnic cleansing, and genocide unfolds in Sarajevo, in the heart of the Balkans, in the country of Bosnia and Herzegovina.

Surrounded by the Dinaric Alps and situated along the Miljacka River, the capital city of Sarajevo basked for centuries in its history of religious and cultural heterogeneity. Its wide variety of faiths earned Sarajevo such titles as "the Jerusalem of Europe," "the Jerusalem of the Balkans," and "the Damascus of the North." Sarajevo was among few European cities known to have a mosque, a Catholic church, an Orthodox church, and a synagogue, all within the same neighborhood.

Over the centuries, a city first settled in prehistoric times has experienced many invasions and transfers of power.

Christianity arrived in the first century. By the fourth century, the area was part of the Western Roman Empire. Celts soon made their way to the region, and Germanic tribes also invaded. Slavs followed, beginning in the sixth century. In 1136, Béla II of Hungary staged yet another incursion. In the mid-fifteenth century, the area by then known as Bosnia fell to the Ottoman Empire. Ottoman rule continued for four hundred years. Despite earlier settlements, Sarajevo lists its founding date as 1461. The city takes its name from the Turkish "saray," which means "palace" or "mansion." Some scholars argue that the addition of -evo changes the meaning to something akin to "palace plains."

With so many invasions from different parts of Europe, Sarajevo already had a multicultural flavor when, toward the end of the fifteenth century, Sephardic Jews ousted from Spain began arriving.

But the Ottoman influence was strong, and many local Christians began converting to Islam. The decision to switch faiths was not always rooted entirely in theology. Muslims held certain advantages in Sarajevo, paying lower taxes and holding higher social status than Christians. Muslims could also inherit property, a privilege not extended to Christians. With land ownership came certain political rights. By the mid-sixteenth century, Sarajevo had more than one hundred mosques, and within a few generations, most Bosnians were Muslim. Higher education also flourished. The first institution of higher learning was a Sufi philosophy academy established in 1537.

Ottoman rule in Bosnia began to crumble in the nineteenth century. Rebellions started in 1831; by 1875, it was a full-scale peasant revolution. This conflict forced the Ottomans to cede the country to the Austro-Hungarian Empire in 1878. Ultimately, the Ottomans lost most of their major holdings in Europe. Still, Sarajevo remained a center of the arts, architecture, and engineering. In 1885, Sarajevo was the first city in Europe—and only the second in the world after San Francisco—to install an electric tram system.

The fateful event on June 28, 1914, that sparked World War I thrust Sarajevo onto the world stage, when Archduke Franz Ferdinand of Austria and his wife Sophie were assassinated by a nineteen-year-old Bosnian activist named Gavrilo Princip. Another eventual consequence was the end of Austro-Hungarian rule in Bosnia and the creation of Yugoslavia. After the second World War, Sarajevo became the capital of the Socialist Republic of Bosnia and Herzegovina—contained within the Socialist Federal Republic of Yugoslavia.

All of this is germane to our love story, because not long after Bosnia declared its independence and received United Nations recognition in 1992, bombs once again began falling on Sarajevo. This time, the aggressor was neighboring Serbia. The three-year Serbian blockade of Sarajevo that began on May 2, 1992, was the longest siege of a capital city in the history of modern warfare.

Around 100,000 people were killed, and two million were displaced. In its aftermath, more than seventy people have been convicted by the United Nations of war crimes associated with the Bosnian war.

For a pair of young lovebirds, the war brought conscription, separation and eventually, a dramatic reunion via tunnels that snaked beneath Sarajevo. Family members and many friends were killed, children were born, marketplaces were bombed. At every turn, adversity intervened.

Still, love triumphed, even in a new land, far from the bombs and the battlefields of Bosnia.

LOVE IN THE MIDST OF MAYHEM

It was a simple wedding, and, but for the bombs exploding outside, a quiet one. She wore a plain gray skirt, a white blouse, and a white hijab befitting a young bride. He wore a fancy dress suit dating from the days before 1992, when the Serbs launched rockets at Sarajevo to begin the war in Bosnia. Shooting continued on the streets outside the basement where the wedding party had gathered. Their nuptial banquet was leftover fare from a military celebration the day before. Overjoyed at the prospect of a marriage in the midst of mayhem, several women from the Sarajevo Muslim community had somehow managed to gather a handful of red roses for the bride.

The ceremony was solemn. Afterward, once the guests had returned to their homes under the protective cover of darkness, the newlyweds shared a kiss—their first.

THE COUPLE MEETS

Abdulah and Hatidza Polovina met as high school students at Gazi Husrevbegova, a gender-segregated madrassa, or Muslim school, in Sarajevo. The school and its adjacent library were named for an Ottoman Empire governor of Bosnia, Gazi Husrev-beg. The library, founded in 1537, houses one of the county's most important collections of Islamic manuscripts. Gazi Husrev-beg, the governor, stipulated that "whatever money remains from the construction of the madrassa shall be used for purchasing good books."

Overjoyed at the prospect of a wedding while war raged in their city, neighborhood women gathered roses for the bride. Photo courtesy of Polovina family archives

Hatidza (pronounced *Hatija*) and Abdulah were sixteen years old when they met. Both were devout in their religious pursuits, but along with enlightenment, what Hatidza was seeking at that time was a boyfriend. She was not quite sure what this entailed, but she was pretty sure she wanted one. She offered a private prayer to God to send her a boyfriend who would be her destiny. A classmate pointed Abdulah out one day and asked Hatidza if she might be interested in him. As teenage girls are wont to do, she sized him up.

"I said, 'OK, he is nice, he is beautiful,'" she remembered. Now, all these years later, she cast a glance at her husband, a man whose dark eyes actually do twinkle. Abdulah's smile can range from impish to rakish, but it is always warm and engaging—so much so that when Abdulah smiles (which is often), it is hard not to smile along with him. His closely trimmed beard brings a focus to his face and helps detract from the fact that he is almost utterly bald.

"Oh, yes," she added. "He had hair then."

Boys and girls lived in separate dormitories and attended

gender-segregated classes at the madrassa. But there were occasions when all students gathered for special programs. The moment they met, Hatidza and Abdulah began talking. It was as if, she said, their spirits had been connected forever.

Love at first sight?

With not a heartbeat's hesitation, she said, "I think it was." Abdulah, less convinced, offered a shrug.

The strict rules of the madrassa were only the first of many obstacles their young romance would face. As the only residential Islamic academy of its kind in the country, the school was unique in Bosnia. Along with training future imams, the school made a firm point of enforcing morality. Dating, in the Western-world sense of that term, was inconceivable.

Lacking cell phones or other electronic communication devices, Abdulah and Hatidza traded illicit correspondence, slipping letters to one another like epistolary sweethearts from times gone by. Abdulah enlisted the trust of the fellow who delivered food to the girls' side of the school as his secret mailman. Every note he sent to Hatidza was signed with a heart. Once again, he demurred: "We were young. And we were crazy in love."

SEPARATION AND STRIFE

It was the practice for all students to be sent to their homes for Ramadan, the Muslim holy month. In 1992, Hatidza went back to Divič, her village in the eastern part of Bosnia, near Serbia.

Abdulah went home to the small town near Sarajevo where he and his mother had lived since his parents' divorce when he was five years old.

Then came a message from the school telling the students not to come back. Serbian forces had staged a surprise attack on Sarajevo. As part of their strategy, the Serbs cut off all vital services to the city.

"Nobody knew before then that war would start," Hatidza said. "When the war started, they disconnected everything. There was no radio, no telephones, no way to communicate."

When the war began in 1992, the Republic of Bosnia and Herzegovina, as the country was known from 1992 to 1995, was made up of about 44 percent

Muslims known as "Bosniaks." Orthodox Serbs accounted for about one-third of the population, followed by Catholic Croats (17 percent). Abdulah remembers a childhood where no one thought much about religious affiliation. Kids were kids. Young Muslim children did attend special weekend schools and after-school sessions, but general education took place in a fully integrated environment. Neighborhoods were mixed as well. Adults fraternized freely, regardless of where they worshiped.

Hatidza, too, thought little about religious differences when she was a child in her small town beside the Drina River. For instance, she did not know that certain surnames could identify certain religious groups.

"I had friends who were Catholic and who were Orthodox," she said. "That was OK. We were friends and it didn't matter."

All that changed with a concerted campaign of ethnic cleansing on the part of Bosnian Serbs led by Radovan Karadžić. The murderous Serb leader, trained as a psychiatrist, was so cutthroat that the Western media dubbed him the "Butcher of Bosnia." Karadžić in turn was supported by the Serbian government headed by President Slobodan Milošević, an equally treacherous leader who in 2006 suffered a fatal heart attack in his jail cell while on trial in The Hague for war crimes. Milošević died several months before a verdict in his case was due.

The anti-Muslim venom spread quickly. Soon after she returned from the madrassa in 1992 to spend Ramadan with her family, Hatidza ran into a Serbian girl who until that moment she had counted as a friend.

"She cursed my mom," Hatidza said, and made pejorative comments about Hatidza's hijab. "I was shocked."

Around 100,000 people perished in the three-year war. More than 2.2 million were displaced. Rape was a common weapon. By some estimates, 50,000 women were violated, most of them Bosniaks. Men, too, were tortured and subjected to violent sexual abuse. Their bodies were heaped into vast common graves.

"They forced fathers and sons to rape each other," Hatidza said, her voice calm but also cold.

Serb forces rounded up all the men in her village, including first Hatidza's father, and then her brother. Her father soon succumbed to the torture to which he and other Bosniaks were subjected. When the brother of one of Hatidza's childhood friends, a Serb, came to find Hatidza's brother, he was elated.

"He thought he would rescue him, but no, he beat him, almost to death," she said. The Serbian forces wasted no time finishing the job. "I lost my father and my oldest brother," she said. "He was just 29 years old."

DREADFUL TALLIES

Hatidza and the rest of her family did not know for sure of the fate of her father and brother until 2003, when a mass grave was uncovered. Her mother and sister provided DNA samples that proved that the remains of Hatidza's father and brother were among the dead.

During what became known as the Bosnian genocide, Muslim intellectuals and professionals became particular targets. Personal property and real estate were confiscated. Those remaining, mostly the women, were left with nothing, and no means of support.

"My mom, my two sisters-in-law and I started knocking on doors to see if anyone would accept us," Hatidza said. Megaphones were set up throughout the area, blasting messages designed to trick any Muslims who remained.

"Please come outside," the messages blared, according to Hatidza. "We have come not to harm you, but to save you."

But it was a lie. Serb soldiers grabbed one of Hatidza's childhood friends, ostensibly to serve as a cleaning person, but more likely for more nefarious purposes. Little did they know what they were up against.

"Her mom was really strong. She was so brave," said Hatidza. "She slapped the soldier and said, 'I want my child back.' They said, 'We will kill you.' And she said, 'Fine.' They gave her daughter back to her."

Just before the war broke out, Hatidza's other brother left for Austria in search of better work opportunities. He soon found employment in a butcher shop. In their own war-torn region, Hatidza, her sisters, sister-in-law and mother had all but run out of doors to knock on, seeking sanctuary, when they heard about one working telephone. As it happened, the owner was Muslim. The women waited in a long line before their turn for a call arrived. Talk fast, the phone's owner admonished. Miraculously, they were able to reach her brother in Austria.

"Come now," he told them. "Do not wait."

A blizzard of paperwork followed. Hatidza had no passport, no ID card, no proof of citizenship. They obtained some forms from the army, then traveled by bus to Zagreb, the capital of Croatia. They found temporary refuge in a mosque but were forced to exit abruptly when soldiers ordered them outside. They waited on the grass until her brother arrived to drive them to Austria. Hatidza still had no passport. She worried that without documentation, she would not be allowed into Austria.

"We were praying that everything would be all right," she said. "The guard at the border, he put his flashlight into the car. He counted us: one, two, three, four, five—then said, 'All right, go.'"

LIFE IN AUSTRIA

In Austria, so close to their native country, they found something of a normal life: no war, no bombs, no soldiers beating on doors. But since her brother had only a small studio to live in, all five women slept on the bare wooden floor. One day, while her brother was off working in his butcher shop, they heard loud knocking on the door. It was a group of police officers with dogs. The women did not speak German and the officers knew no Bosnian, but through elaborate hand gestures and other forms of universal expression, it became apparent that they were supposed to register with the local authorities.

Caritas, the international Catholic charity, gave them some help with the registration process. But they still needed money. Hatidza was just seventeen years old. She found work in Vienna and more important, she found a newspaper article that explained how to send letters to Bosnia. She wrote to Abdulah, telling him: I am alive, I am in Austria. After a month or two, a letter came back from Abdulah, sent via the Red Cross. One day, Abdulah even managed to place a phone call to Hatidza through a radio station.

Hatidza spent two and a half years in Austria before a long letter, three or four pages, arrived from Abdulah. In it was a proposal of marriage.

Abdulah insists he remembers few details of that particular piece of correspondence. In earlier letters, Hatidza had urged him to join her in Austria, where there was no war. But Abdulah, a member of the Bosnian army and a de facto imam to fellow soldiers, felt too connected to his country to consider a move. In peacetime, patriotism is a powerful force; in times of war, even more so.

"To leave would be to desert, giving up on my own people," he said. "I felt, 'I must stay here.' I could not leave."

Death was all around him, as was the devastation of a country that was part of his soul. By the end of the war, he had been wounded three times—once quite seriously. He blushes as he admits there may also have been some flirtations with some other women. But they were brief, he quickly adds, and besides, while she was in Austria, Hatidza had the chance to marry others.

"During the war, what can you do? You try to lead a normal life," said Hatidza. "The girls, they liked Abdulah."

Addressing the couple's romantic opportunities, Abdulah summoned his characteristic equanimity: "I had the chance, she had the chance," he said.

Hatidza makes no secret of her belief that their union was written in the stars. But when asked if their eventual marriage was predestined, Abdulah shakes his head: "I don't know." In any case, he said, something led her to embark on the dangerous journey back to Bosnia.

"Next thing you know, we get married," Abdulah said.

LONGING FOR ABDULAH AT HOME

Hatidza's memory of the proposal is more explicit. She was by then nineteen years old. Her country was at war, and it looked like the war would never end. She was desperately homesick. In Austria, she would search the radio for any trace of a transmission from Bosnia. When she heard her own language, she broke down and cried.

"It was my home, my memories, everything," she said.

Among the family clustered in Austria, there was discussion about whether it was prudent for Hatidza to return with so much danger and uncertainty looming. It was her brother—the surviving male and now "the man" of the family—who urged Hatidza to follow her heart.

"My brother told my mother and my sisters, 'Let her go,'" she remembers.

And so, "I went by bus, to be a bride."

Hatidza was one of only ten passengers on a bus that was otherwise crammed with packages sent by Bosnians in Austria to their families who had remained behind in their home country. Hatidza prayed constantly, asking God to give her a sign if what she was doing was right for her. Sarajevo was under siege. It was November, cold and dark, with no electricity. The only way into the city was through a tunnel the Bosnians dug under the airport. Hatidza, who is not a tall woman, recalls stooping to clamber through a passageway so narrow that the walls all but reached out to touch her. At last she emerged and was directed to a telephone. She called Abdulah.

"He could not believe I was there," she said.

Bombs were falling, seemingly everywhere. "Boom! Boom! Boom!" Hatidza said.

For Hatidza, the joy of her wedding was offset by the fact that she had no one to celebrate with. Not one person from her family was present. "It was full of people, but no family," she said. "It was sad for me."

How had her handsome husband scrounged a fancy suit in the middle of a war? Abdulah breaks into a smile that can only be described as infectious.

"Miracle!" he exclaims.

Their marital bliss was tempered by the sober reality of a country at war. They had no glass in the windows of their small apartment, only curtains to offer a veneer of privacy. The Serbs controlled the water, electricity, and gas for the city. Bodies often littered the marketplace. Even setting out from home to find food or water, Hatidza could not be sure that she would be able to return home. To take a bath, they had to heat water by fire. They collected rainwater to flush their toilet. One day Abdulah, as if he were expressing some mundane notion, told Hatidza that if he were to die in battle, she should go back to her family. Until then, she had not allowed herself to consider the possibility that he might be killed.

"It was hard, our new marriage, but it was also sweet," she said. "Sweet—and at the same time bitter."

Yet amid those harsh conditions, kindness and amity still managed to find their place. There was no television, no radio, no telephones—"only people," said Hatidza. Friends sat by candlelight when it was safe to visit.

"The atmosphere that people had between them, that was love, only love," she said.

Weeks after the warring parties signed a peace accord, Hatidza gave birth to the couple's first child, a son. Four more children would follow, all blessed with their mother's remarkable eyes. Draped in a soft lilac hijab trimmed with embroidery and sparkling stones, Hatidza's clear, cerulean eyes are the first feature one sees.

"The eyes," she agrees, acknowledging that she is aware of the effect of her own gaze. "The eyes are the window of your soul."

MAKING PEACE, MAKING A LIVING

Imams seldom earn extravagant salaries, and the years in Bosnia following the war were not easy. The rapidly expanding family lived in cramped conditions. Five people occupied what amounted to a one-room apartment with one small bathroom. They were poor. Abdulah found himself thinking: Peace—it is so hard. But Hatidza still clung to a fierce sense of patriotism.

"I told myself, 'I will never, ever leave my country again,'" she said.

Abdulah faced his own challenges. Many members of his congregation in Sarajevo had seen lives—their own and others—shattered by the war. It fell to Abdulah, their young imam, to persuade them that faith had any purpose at all. It was not easy, he said, to build—or rebuild—religion.

"The people were poor, hungry and tired of the war," he said. "They felt betrayed. In turn, I tried to help them realize that the only true friend we have in our lives, who always looks out for us, is the Almighty God."

His congregation in Sarajevo had further cause for disillusionment. In this case, the issue was semantics. After the war ended, experts and international diplomats sparred over what to call the concerted effort to eliminate Bosnia's Muslim population. More than 100,000 Bosnians had been killed. In a predominantly Muslim country, most were followers of Islam. Did this strategy of ethnic cleansing constitute actual genocide? Or should the casualties be categorized as war crimes?

The United Nations General Assembly deemed it genocide. So did the US Congress and, later, the Criminal Tribunal for the Former Yugoslavia.

But the European Court of Human Rights "expressly disagreed," arguing that "genocide, as defined in public international law, comprised only acts aimed at the physical or biological destruction of a protected group."

At another juncture, the International Tribunal for the Former Yugoslavia declared that it was "not convinced, on the basis of the evidence before it, that it has been conclusively established that the massive killings of members of the protected group were committed with the specific intent . . . on the part of the perpetrators to destroy, in whole or in part, the group as such."

The linguistic dispute over how to describe the systematic killing of Muslims, including her own father and brother, sends Hatidza into a polite form of apoplexy.

"I don't know what is going on with the human brain anymore," she says. "It looks like we are not human beings anymore."

Her voice takes on a tone of intense frustration: "The genocide, what happened in Bosnia, you can definitely say it was genocide because it was planned." As for those who doubt the intent behind the atrocities: "I think that was Satanic whispers that they got."

And yet, she points out, mass killings aimed at targeted groups continue, even today. Her husband chimes in: "Burma, Syria, Yemen. And so it continues."

A NEW LIFE IN AMERICA

In 2000, five years after the Dayton Accords were signed, ending the 3.5-year Bosnian War, Abdulah was invited to Seattle to preside at the funeral of a cousin who had died there. The ceremony coincided with the month of Ramadan, and Abdulah also officiated at those observances. Ramadan is a time for believers to make personal changes, and by the time he returned to Bosnia forty-five days later, he had been offered a job as imam to the Bosnian community in Seattle.

Hatidza was not happy. But Abdulah wore her down, sprinkling his entreaties with talk about a better life, better opportunities for their children, and new adventures for their family. He talked about how friendly Americans were. In Seattle, he told her, he felt relaxed, connected. Maybe a move to Seattle was their destiny.

"Somehow he persuaded me," she said. But, she cautioned him, "I said yes, but even if I said yes, my heart says no."

On the way to the US embassy to seek entry papers, Hatidza prayed that officials there would refuse to give her a visa. The prayer worked, temporarily, because a clerk disputed a number on her documents. Then Abdulah showed the woman her error, and the visa was granted. Hatidza decided that someone who outranked the embassy official, Abdulah or herself was pulling the strings on this decision. "God knows what is good for you," she said.

But there were challenges. Hatidza had no idea where Seattle was. She knew little about the United States. Her English was rudimentary at best. The day after they arrived in Seattle, an earthquake shook the city. Let's go home, Hatidza thought.

The family entered the United States as religious workers, the lowest category on the immigration scale. They could not hold jobs outside the mosque or madrassa. Once again they were poor. They were shocked by the high cost of basic goods in the United States. Things had been tough in Sarajevo, Hatidza thought, but she had lived a better life there than in Seattle.

She enrolled in English as a second language (ESL) classes and soon enough, learned about and passed the exam that gave her a US high school equivalency certificate. Meantime, as they applied for permanent resident status, she once again prayed that it would not be granted. Five years after arriving in Seattle, they received green cards, and then US citizenship. Finally Hatidza let herself receive the hospitality of the people around her.

"You begin to feel, 'This is really my home,'" she said.

Abdulah, too, took advantage of the chance in America to further his education. He earned an associate's degree from a community college, then a bachelor's in Islamic studies from Cloverdale College in Indiana, then a second bachelor's degree, this one in comparative religion, from the University of Washington. Next he earned a master's degree in transformational leadership from Seattle University, where he was the first Muslim ever to enroll at that Catholic theological institution. He began giving speeches in churches, and meeting with intercultural and interfaith groups around the Pacific Northwest. In 2015, he accepted the call to serve as imam at Portland's Bosnian Educational and Cultural Organization (BECO—also known as IBECO, for Islamic Bosniaks Educational and Cultural Organization).

Abdulah delivers a sermon during Friday prayers at the Islamic Bosniaks Educational & Cultural Organization (IBECO) mosque in Portland. Photo by John Rudoff

Their children are thriving, in no small measure, presumably, as a result of the moral and spiritual guidance they receive at home.

"I teach my kids that after all I went through, if I was not a strong believer, I would not have made it," Hatidza explained. "Always, in the hardest situations in my life, I had God with me. I teach my kids that they must put God first, that they must respect everyone, and that they cannot judge."

The family lives above the store, so to speak, in living quarters above the BECO mosque in southeast Portland. Their community hovers around two hundred members. Hatidza works as a sterile processing technician at Oregon Health & Science University, also in Portland. Abdulah has a part-time job as well.

War and its wounds taught him the important things in life: hope, freedom, family values, and the desire to live peacefully. But as a Muslim leader and as an American, what Abdulah was unprepared for was open discussion during the presidency of Donald Trump of "a Muslim registry" as an actual policy platform.

In an open letter to his congregants, he wrote: "Muslims have resolved not to become casualties of the disaffection and bigotry that made Donald Trump's election possible. We are part of what made America great before his election and we will work to ensure that the nation's light remains bright—even if the bulb seems to be flickering." And he continued: "American Muslims have found their peace here in the USA. We started our families, our businesses, and we have rebuilt our lives here. America is our home."

Hatidza worries that her children are growing up with little knowledge of their history, their culture, and their many relatives in a distant country.

"They do not know my family," she laments.

But several years ago, she went back to Bosnia, alone, and stayed for close to three months. Just see, her husband told her, see for yourself which is the better life. When she returned, she told him she did not feel they should move back.

Rudwan Dawod. Photo by Sankar Raman

CHAPTER 7

A Country in Near-Constant Conflict

Rudwan Dawod (South Sudan)

A US State Department advisory from February 22, 2021, minced no words in warning against travel to South Sudan. Echoing a Centers for Disease Control notice about the perils of infection from the coronavirus, the State Department cautioned that "violent crime, such as carjackings, shootings, ambushes, assaults, robberies, and kidnappings, is common throughout South Sudan."

Further, the bulletin advised, "Armed conflict is ongoing and includes fighting between various political and ethnic groups. Weapons are readily available to the population."

In truth, it would be difficult to name a moment in recent history when South Sudan—or for that matter, Sudan, from which it gained independence in 2011—was not in some state of turmoil. Indeed, a 2012 article in The New Yorker magazine that characterized Sudan as "catastrophically troubled" since the moment of independence called the country "a forced union of mismatched parts."

South Sudan is lush, almost tropical. Its inhabitants are Black Africans who are mostly Christian or animist. The population in the northern region of Sudan, an arid desert, consists mainly of Muslims of mixed African-Arab descent.

The First Sudanese Civil War began in 1955, the year before the flags of Great Britain and Egypt were lowered in the capital city of Khartoum, marking Sudan's independence following nearly sixty years of joint rule. Half a million people died in the north-south war that lasted until 1972.

Peace was short-lived. The Second Sudanese Civil War, pitting the government of Sudan against a militia group from the south called the Sudan People's Liberation Army, raged from 1983 to 2005. Six years after that war ended, there was jubilation in the streets of the capital city of Juba when South Sudan received independence. But the new republic felt little relief from strife. Spiraling tensions were heightened by poverty and dire food shortages. In Juba, violence erupted in the streets late in 2013 when South Sudan's president accused his own vice president of an attempted coup. Peace agreements, according to diplomatic observers, were routinely violated or ignored.

Meanwhile, in Sudan's westernmost region, the twenty-first century brought more than a decade of "genocidal counter-insurgency efforts" directed by Khartoum, according to reports by several human rights groups. Darfur is Sudan's largest region, somewhat larger than the state of California. Darfur was the traditional home to around eighty tribes and ethnic groups, according to the United Nations Office for the Coordination of Human Affairs (OCHA). One of the region's primary tribes is called the Fur; the very name "Darfur" translates to "Home of the Fur."

The Darfuri city of Nyala and Khartoum are 761 miles apart. The single highway intended to connect them remains unfinished.

While the northern part of Sudan dominated the country's economy and controlled its political machine, the people of Darfur chafed at what they saw as decades of marginalization and economic neglect on the part of Khartoum.

Years of skirmishes exploded into civil war in February 2003 when a group known as the Sudan Liberation Movement (and formerly known as the Darfur Liberation Front) launched an assault against the Sudanese government. Harsh retaliation came swiftly. Armed militia known as Janjaweed stormed in, often riding on the backs of camels. Villages were burned. Thousands were killed.

As the assaults against Darfur's largest tribal populations continued, then US secretary of state Colin Powell deemed the situation a "genocide." Powell's statement in 2004 was the first time the United States had labeled a conflict genocide while a crisis was still in progress. Then secretary general of the United Nations Kofi Anan called the situation in Darfur a "humanitarian emergency of catastrophic proportions."

The Sudanese government lists ten thousand casualties in Darfur. Estimates of the dead from human rights groups and other observers range from 200,000 to 400,000. Out of a total population of 6.2 million, more than 2.5 million inhabitants of Darfur have been displaced.

To the north, in a region whose history traces to the time of the pharaohs, political tranquility also has proven elusive. Nubian kings ruled Sudan until the fifteenth century. Arab nomads moved in, and in 1898, the British took control in a joint agreement with Egypt. Just over thirteen years after Sudan gained independence in 1956, a coup d'état installed Col. Gaafar Nimeiry as prime minister. Nimeiry swiftly abolished both parliament and political parties.

All this turmoil has played out in one of the world's poorest and least developed countries. One-third of the Sudanese population squeezes by as subsistence farmers, according to the United Nations' Food and Agriculture Organization. An inadequate water supply adds to the challenge of raising crops such as cotton, peanuts, sesame, sorghum, and sugarcane. Along with exacerbating food scarcity, the wars in Sudan have also limited the population's access to health care and education.

The first successful drillings for oil in Sudan took place between 1975 and 1980, according to the Republic of Sudan's Government Oil Ministry. But the country's unstable political situation at first thwarted development. After oil production began in earnest in the 1990s, oil became one of the country's largest exports.

The United States established diplomatic relations with Sudan in 1956, the year of Sudanese independence. But in 1967, following the Arab-Israeli War, Sudan broke off ties to the United States. Five years later, relations between the two countries were reestablished. Then, in 1993, the United States designated Sudan a State Sponsor of Terror and closed its embassy in Khartoum. Relations were resumed and the embassy was reopened in 2002, the same year that President George W. Bush signed the Sudan Peace Act. The measure condemned violations of civil rights on all sides, including the Sudanese government's record on human rights and the aerial bombing of civilian targets.

At various times, the United States imposed sanctions against Sudan. But the penalties were lifted in 2017, according to the US State Department. Over the years, the United States has steadily provided humanitarian assistance to Sudan. A State Department bulletin from January 2021 stated: "The United States government will continue to focus development assistance on programs that help ensure women, youth and marginalized communities are able to participate meaningfully in building Sudan's democratic foundation and emerging economic opportunities."

The back-and-forth connection with the United States was not dissimilar to the persistent political whipsawing within Sudan. Bubbling unrest was nearly constant, even under the iron hand of Omar Hassan Ahmad al-Bashir, the army colonel who took command of Sudan in a military coup in June 1989. Al-Bashir's thirty-year grip on Sudan was marked by executions of top military leaders who challenged him. Al-Bashir also imposed Islamic law, banned independent newspapers, and imprisoned political opponents. Al-Bashir controlled the country, according to the 2012 New Yorker article, through "tactical repression and gamesmanship."

In 1993, al-Bashir appointed himself Sudan's president. When he ran for election three years later, no one opposed him. Sudan had become a one-party state.

Despite the wars and deprivation that ravaged his country, al-Bashir remained in power. Late in 2018, massive protests erupted after the country's inflation rate soared to 70 percent, and the government tripled the price of basic goods. When opposing groups joined forces to form a single coalition, the government responded by arresting more than eight hundred opposition figures. At last, in 2019, massive sit-ins in front of the military headquarters resulted in the overthrow of the al-Bashir government. Key to the revolution that unseated al-Bashir were neighborhood committees—small groups of civilians working together.

According to Human Rights Watch, military and civilian leaders in Sudan signed an agreement to share power in August 2019. Still, clashes between the government and different factions in Sudan continue. A New York Times report from that time asserted that hundreds of thousands of Sudanese were living in displaced persons camps.

While awaiting trial, al-Bashir was held in the same Khartoum jail that had housed thousands of political dissidents during his thirty-year regime. In December 2019, a Sudanese court convicted him of corruption, receiving illegal gifts and possessing foreign currency. At the time of his arrest, millions of Euros and Sudanese pounds were found in al-Bashir's residence.

Citing al-Bashir's age, seventy-five at the time, the presiding judge said he would be sent to a facility for older prisoners for the duration of his two-year sentence. Al-Bashir had been indicted by the International Criminal Court (ICC) in 2009, charged with war crimes and crimes against humanity. Charges of genocide, on grounds that he had tried to eradicate much of Darfur's tribal population, were added later. In 2021, Sudan agreed to turn al-Bashir over to the ICC, along with two other former Sudanese leaders. Al-Bashir has been transferred to Khartoum's high-security Kober prison, where he remains as discussions continue over whether his ICC trial will take place in The Hague or in Sudan.

Asserting that their client was in poor health and citing the need for better medical treatment than the prison could provide, al-Bashir's lawyers managed to have the deposed leader transferred from prison to a hospital late in 2022. But film footage from December of that year that showed al-Bashir dressed in casual attire as he strolled around his hospital ward and greeted visitors as if he were a gracious host raised questions about the actual status of al-Bashir's health.

On December 5, 2022, a group of Sudan's military and political factions signed a Framework Agreement (FA) with the goal of facilitating the country's transition to civilian government. An earlier effort to move toward civilian government failed when the same military leaders who had signed the earlier accord staged a violent coup.

Volker Turk, the United Nations High Commissioner for Human Rights, hailed the 2022 FA as "an important first step" toward political stability in Sudan. At the same time, a UN spokesperson, Stephane

Dujarric, cautioned that any lasting settlement in Sudan must include "the broadest array of Sudanese stakeholders, including women, youth and civil society."

A FOOTHOLD ON TWO CONTINENTS

He is a husband, a father, and—at the time of our interview—a dedicated Amazon employee. But Rudwan Dawod is also an impassioned freedom fighter, determined to see democracy prevail one day in his native Sudan.

Who knows? he muses. Maybe one day he will even run for office in Sudan. Doing this would require Dawod, his wife Nancy, and their daughter Sudan Nyala to relocate from Eugene, Oregon, to the country Sudan was named for. The family has traveled extensively in Sudan, where Dawod and Nancy first met. The Dawods share a joint commitment to Rudwan's home country.

Sudan, Africa's third largest country, is also the third-largest country in the Arab world. Before the secession of South Sudan in 2011, the Republic of Sudan was the largest country, both in Africa and in the Arab world.

About 43 million people live in this nation in northeast Africa. Sudan shares borders with Egypt, Libya, Chad, the Central African Republic, South Sudan, Ethiopia, and Eritrea. To its northeast, Sudan hugs the banks of the Red Sea. Natural resources abound, including an alphabet's roster of minerals, from asbestos to zinc.

Repression in Dawod's native country remains widespread. According to Reporters Without Borders, Sudan ranks as number 172 out of 180 countries in terms of freedom of the press. Public gatherings—peaceful assembly—continue to be suppressed. Unrest has been a near-perpetual condition in twenty-first-century Sudan. As recently as September 2022, a United Nations report documented numerous civilian deaths in Sudan, as well as "widespread human rights violations without repercussion." The UN also reported extensive cases of sexual abuse, with some victims as young as eight or nine years old.

SO MANY ARRESTS

If modern-day Sudan offered a frequent user's card for political prisoners, Rudwan Dawod would certainly qualify. The duration of his

The Dawod—Rudwan, Sudan, and Nancy—at home in Eugene. Photo by Sankar Raman

incarcerations varied, but the longest took place in 2012, when Nancy was at home in Oregon, and pregnant. That, he says, was the hardest of all, being away from Nancy at such a key time.

On his most recent stay in Sudan, he was imprisoned on four separate occasions.

"Each time it was different," he said of his many prison sojourns. "It was crazy every time."

In his most recent prison stint, Dawod found himself in a tiny cell, maybe 3 meters by 1.5 meters. There were no windows and only a primitive toilet. Each day, tiny pieces of bread were passed through small holes, the day's ration for however many prisoners were in the cell.

Typically, Dawod said, that number was thirteen. But sometimes, eighteen prisoners were squeezed into the squalid space. Sleeping presented a major challenge. The prisoners squashed next to one another on the floor in tight formation, alternating head-to-toe, then toe-to-head.

"When you breathed, either you breathed on someone's feet or on someone's face," he said.

The overhead light glared twenty-four hours a day.

At various times, Dawod has been charged with spying—an offense punishable by death in Sudan—and other offenses. He bristled when asked if he and his most recent cellmates had been convicted of the same crime.

"We don't consider what we did a crime," he said. "We were all freedom fighters, all peaceful protesters. We were activists. We knew each other. Adversity breeds camaraderie, he pointed out: "Whoever you meet today (from that time), they would be like a brother."

EARLY YEARS

Dawod was born in east Sudan in 1982. His native city of El-Gadarif—also called Gadarif and sometimes spelled Gedaref—lay about 250 miles from Sudan's capital, Khartoum. Tall mountains surrounded the city on three sides. Although Gadarif was not in the Darfur region, most of the inhabitants were of Darfuri origin, Dawod said.

But starting when he was ten years old, Dawod and one of his brothers went to live in Darfur, in the western part of Sudan, with their grandmother. Their grandmother was getting older and welcomed their company and their help. The boys tended her goats. They made the long trek to get fresh water for the family and the animals. They loved their life in Darfur, and when their father wanted to move his sons back north with the rest of the family, the boys asked to remain with their grandma.

"In our culture," Dawod said, "it is very common to give one of your children to your mom as a gift." And so the boys were given to their grandmother.

It was the 1990s, a time Dawod remembers when Darfur was peaceful, "completely different from what it became," he said. "This place was so beautiful. Everything was so good. Until the Sudanese government interfered in the feuds in early 2000."

Around the world, history textbooks written for schoolchildren have a habit of glossing over cultural unpleasantries. Dawod said he knows now that "the South Sudanese people were always oppressed. But we didn't learn that from history books or TV."

Instead, "most of the Sudanese perceived the South Sudanese as bad people, supported by Christian countries, who always wanted to take over our country," he said. "We didn't realize they were fighting for the right to be equal citizens."

Dawod was just a schoolboy, and the struggle between the northern and southern parts of his country—the emerging civil war—was confusing. People from the south of his country were portrayed as inferior, since they were not Arabs, he said. The distinction was harsh.

Arabic was Dawod's first language, but he learned it with a noticeable accent because it was not the first language of his parents. Dawod worked to lose his accent because it invited discrimination, even beating, from other children.

"In Sudan, it was Arab versus Black culture," he said. "It was just a whole brainwashing process."

As the strife between north and south turned into all-out civil war, Sudan's central government took a page from conflicts around the globe and added religion to the mix, Dawod said. The country's official religion was Islam, the faith Dawod himself practices. But many in the south were Christian.

"The government added the religious element to make it sound like they were infidels," he said. "It was not really a religious war, but the government of Sudan made it sound like a religious war to recruit more people and to build more anger. It also sounded like a war between Arabs and against Blacks. The government was trying to organize the whole of Sudan by forcing the Arab culture against the African culture."

Dawod, with his very dark skin, felt conflicted. "I felt some secret pride in my identity as a Black person, as an African," he said. "But I couldn't really talk about it."

THE MILITARY

Sudan had firm rules about military service. Before enrolling at a university, all students were required to receive military training for forty-five days. The ensuing one-year service requirement could be completed at any time while the students were in college. Once Rudwan finished high school in 2000, he headed off to military camp for his forty-five days of training. The experience turned out to be transformational.

The central government needed to mobilize the entire nation, and "the camp's purpose was to brainwash you even more and to prepare you for the war against South Sudan," Dawod said. "You got brainwashed. You got radicalized, basically. It was jihad, and why this was more important than anything, even mom and dad."

The government referred to this process as "intellectual training," and in most cases, it worked, Dawod said. "Some, especially the young boys I went to camp with, became jihadists."

There was one exception at camp, a trainee named Santino. Dawod gravitated to him immediately. At the conclusion of indoctrination lectures, trainees were expected to respond with enthusiastic applause. But Santino, said Dawod, "he was always so numb, not reacting like the rest of the trainees."

Santino was slightly older than most of his fellow trainees. "I was short, he was tall, like most of the South Sudanese," Dawod said. They developed a bond of trust. "I felt I could talk to him about what I had been feeling for many years."

And both knew, said Dawod, "that what we were being taught here was completely wrong."

Santino talked about his own background, as a South Sudanese, as a Christian. For Dawod, this unleashed feelings he thought he had quashed.

"From an early age, I remember the South Sudanese who were housemaids. They came to the house to wash clothes. They were not treated fairly," he said. "They were called names. It was common to use the N-word."

But someone like Santino, Dawod said, "he was aware that he was not less than the rest of the Sudanese people."

Santino and Dawod lost touch as the military moved them to different assignments. Rudwan went to Khartoum, while Santino remained in

Darfur. "But I can still see his innocent face," Dawod said. "Santino," he went on, "I just appreciate the time I spent with him."

In Khartoum, Dawod joined a technical unit of the military. Two years later, he was ordered to join the Sudanese forces fighting in South Sudan. He refused. He had completed his mandatory service and knew that because he was perceived as a Darfuri, he had no future for advancement in the military.

POLITICAL AWAKENING

Dawod's political activism began sometime around 2005, after he had enrolled at the University of Juba. Originally the school had been in South Sudan's capital, but because of the war, the whole administration had moved north, to Khartoum. Dawod joined the student wing of the Sudanese Congress Party, called Congress of Independent Students.

Dawod, calling himself a progressive, viewed Islam as a religion, not a political ideology. He advocated a secular nation, "where everyone could coexist." And so he became a leader of a new youth movement called Grifina. In Arabic, the term translates to "we're fed up." Grifina based its platform in opposition to "war, corruption, dictatorship, injustice and discrimination against minorities." Grifina was Sudan's first youth nonviolent movement.

Under Dawod's leadership, the group set out to educate the Sudanese public, especially young people, about the rights and methodologies of nonviolent resistance. Grifina staged educational campaigns that included public forums, art exhibits, and mukhatabat, or street talks.

It was an uphill battle. "Nonviolence is not that popular in Sudan," Dawod said. "Violence is rooted deep in our culture in Sudan. Sudan's people are just fighters. We are warriors."

Domestic violence in his country is especially problematic, Dawod said. "To me, I can't isolate the violence that is happening in families—how we raise our kids, how husbands treat their wives—I don't isolate that from civil war. Many people believe that with violence, you get what you want," he said. "It has been proven in Sudan that violence works."

Initially, their new movement had recognition issues. "At first there was no support," Dawod said. "People did not see us as serious."

Dawod had his own struggles as well, “because I came from Darfur, and Darfur is like the center of violence in Sudan. This regime does not listen unless you have a military movement.”

At the university, Dawod thrived. He learned about different ideologies. He met new people who shared his views. He felt validated.

“My friends who were going to the university, they were what inspired me,” he said. “I could relate to them. Whatever I said, they would get it. The level of conversation was completely different. I felt I belonged.”

One advantage to enrolling at Juba was that it was among the few Sudanese schools that had a dual system of studies in English and in Arabic. Most of his compatriots, he said, had to learn English after they got to the United States or another English-speaking country.

In his first year, Dawod became part of the student union. He received training about leadership and debate. It was an honor. The school had 20,000 students, and only about forty were elected each year to the student union.

Dawod found his political voice. He spoke at protests and in public discussions. The crowds loved his message. The government was trying to paint the resistance in Darfur as nothing but a bunch of criminals, he told his audiences. Dawod had a different message: “What I told them was, these guys are not criminals. You are not criminals. We know what is going on.”

Dawod knew it was dangerous to speak out, and he knew people from the government were watching his house.

On one especially emotional day, Dawod learned from a friend that the friend’s village in Darfur had been destroyed by government troops. The friend’s entire family had been killed.

“Not just his family, his entire village was wiped out,” Dawod said. In his speech that day, “I pointed at him and told the audience about his story.” The friend’s family had no connection to the military on either side, Dawod explained. “They were killed because of their ethnicity.”

Sadly, his friend’s loss was not unusual. “In every village in Darfur, you will find war casualties,” Dawod said, “people who lost their homes, their savings, ladies who got raped.”

Just recently, in the South Darfur city of Nyala, two of his childhood friends were killed, Dawod said. "They were brothers. We used to call them the twins," he said.

Officially, the civil war death toll is 350,000. "But that number was reported three or four years ago," Dawod said. "Unfortunately, the killing has never stopped."

LOVE WALKS IN

In 2006, Dawod joined a protest at Juba University because the student union had been suspended. He and his fellow student union members were all expelled. Students began rallying in support of them at universities throughout the country.

In 2009, he moved to South Sudan and became involved with a non-profit organization called Sudan Sunrise. The US-based group was dedicated to building schools and also to promoting reconciliation, education, and community building. Among the group's founders was Manute Bol, the late NBA player who was a native of South Sudan. A recent newsletter from Sudan Sunrise declared, "Compassion spreads faster than COVID."

While working on a school-building project in South Sudan, Dawod met an American volunteer named Nancy Williams.

"First we became friends," he said. "And then we fell in love."

Their union faced many cultural roadblocks. Nancy was slightly older than Dawod. She had been married before. She was white, born in Wisconsin and raised in Oregon. Dawod was committed to remaining in Sudan to help his country. He was a student. He had no assets to speak of.

"I just saw all these obstacles," he said. "I could not see her living in Sudan, and I could not live anywhere but Sudan. I love Sudan."

In Sudan, Dawod explained, "the matter of getting married is a family decision. You have to get the whole family's approval."

Those conversations were awkward, starting, Dawod said, with the fact that "They were shocked when I told them I had found a nice lady from America."

His uncles, part of the family council, opposed the match because Nancy was Christian. They told Dawod they would not consent to the match unless she became Muslim. But his father said, "Son, you love her. Go ahead."

They married in Sudan in February 2010. The following September, after Dawod had received the requisite papers to enter the United States they had a second ceremony in Springfield, Oregon.

The couple had agreed that Dawod would settle in the United States, but that each year, he would return to Sudan. Dawod had warned her, "The path I am taking, it is very challenging." On a 2012 visit to Sudan, Dawod was arrested once again while organizing what he called a peaceful protest for Grifina. His father and three of his brothers were arrested with him.

"None of us was prepared for the prison time, the torture," he said. "That was one of my worst arrests."

Back in the United States, Nancy was eight months' pregnant. She was determined to have her husband beside her when their child was born. Nancy worked diplomatic channels, and Dawod was released from detention. He returned to Oregon two weeks before Sudan Nyala was born.

TORTURE AND THE PATH OF NONVIOLENCE

According to Rudwan, violence is so prevalent in his home country that it is even a part of the Sudanese spoken word. The language, he said, has many words to express brutality. This makes it difficult to preach a doctrine of nonviolence, Dawod said. But as his political consciousness was growing, Dawod had studied nonviolence extensively. In particular, he read the works of Dr. Martin Luther King Jr., Mahatma Gandhi, Nelson Mandela, and the late US congressman John Lewis. In the process, he said, "I fell in love with the US civil rights movement."

He and others from Grifina were preparing for a large march on July 3, 2012. He was about to start leading a chant of "Freedom!" when government security agents showed up.

"They picked me up, threw me on the ground, then tied my hands and legs," he said. "At least twelve people were arrested at that moment. They were beating us all the way to the police station. Then they covered our eyes when they tortured us so we could not see their faces."

Dawod could not fight back. He felt doubly helpless because he also could not protect his seventy-two-year-old father, who had been arrested at the same time.

"My dad, surprisingly, he was so proud of what I was doing that he lectured our torturers. He told them: 'You are not real men. I am proud of my son.'"

In retaliation, the officers isolated Dawod, throwing him into a smelly, postage-stamp of a windowless cell.

"When I asked to pray, they said, 'you are not even Muslim,'" he said. For three days he remained in that squalid cell, and then was transferred to a different prison. That arrest lasted 45 days.

Dawod was charged with spying for the United States. The offense carried a possible death sentence, or a prison sentence of at least fifteen years. At his court hearing, he was surprised to see a throng of supporters, mobilized from afar by Nancy and from within Sudan, by Grifina. Dawod looked around and saw Sudanese activists from all over the world. One contingent that had come from the US embassy was especially imposing, Dawod said: "A bunch of foreigners coming to court in a big armored vehicle."

In his weakened state from torture and imprisonment, "When I saw so many people there in court for me, I got extra strength," he said.

After several trials, he was acquitted. Sudanese newspapers reported that he was an American, trying to overthrow the Sudanese government through violence. Back in the United States, he joined the Democratic presidential campaigns of both Barack Obama and then Hillary Clinton. On January 20, 2017, he returned to Sudan.

"I had to leave," he said. "I could not imagine living in Donald Trump's America."

GANDHI ON FACEBOOK

On every trip to Sudan, Dawod comes equipped with dozens of cell phones and other technology to hand out to opponents of the government who share his passion for nonviolence. He says social media has made it possible to spread the message as never before, as if, he suggested, Gandhi had taken to Facebook.

"With Facebook, we knew the future was ours," he said. "Finally we had a platform."

Twitter (now known as X) has also been a social movement godsend. The Sudanese government-controlled radio, television, and newspapers, Dawod said, but was slow to realize the threat of the internet.

Dawod hands out cell phones and notebook computers, allowing his followers to become "citizen journalists," countering government propaganda with their own first-hand observations.

In the final years of al-Bashir's long reign, Dawod and others in Grifina struggled with how to damage his carefully sculpted image as a respected, charismatic leader. Then they hit on the idea of humor, creating political cartoons in his image.

"We made fun of him, and it went viral," he said. "And there are no laws that prohibit this kind of action."

Al-Bashir may be out, but his successor, Lt. Gen. Abdel Fattah al-Burhan, is no great champion of democracy, according to Dawod. He and his Grifina comrades continue to recruit, focusing on young people, and striving for diversity. In most Sudanese political groups, he said, "there isn't any sense of nationalism. We wanted to create that."

Giving women equal footing in the movement is also unusual, Dawod said. Grifina encourages women to deliver speeches, then uploads them to social media. He said some young politicians also have joined up with Grifina and the Sudan of the Future campaign. That campaign, he says, adheres to a fiercely democratic philosophy.

"Anyone who wants to run, he can come up with a plan. We will all support one another," Dawod said. "Losers support winners. We will all unite behind one candidate. The people will choose who will represent them, not the elite."

BACK IN THE US OF A

Even the most committed political activist needs to feed his family. Dawod returned to Oregon in early May 2020 and found a job at an Amazon warehouse near Portland. At first he made the one-hour-each-way commute via bicycle; eventually he bought a car. His body is apparently a constantly self-charging battery, for in order to maintain his toehold on two distant continents, he sleeps very little.

"But a very deep sleep," he points out.

Before the confinement that came with the coronavirus pandemic, Dawod often spoke at US universities and high schools, through Sudan Sunrise. Now he has transferred to online events. He works with a network, Friends of Sudan, to tell people in the United States about his native country.

"Here in the US, I don't think people really know a lot about Sudan," he said. "Some people don't even know where Sudan is. We are trying to change that."

Fears about al-Qaida and other forms of Islamic radicalism hamper that effort, he conceded. Dawod does not dispute the dangers of such groups.

"Now, since Islamist groups are not in power, we are afraid they will use assassination and bombing to destabilize Sudan," he said. "That is where the US and other countries can help Sudan."

Along with nonstop political activism, Dawod is an unabashedly proud father. He reports that his daughter, born in 2012, is trilingual, speaking English, Arabic, and the Spanish she has learned at her Spanish-immersion school in Eugene. Sudan Nyala has marched in protests, often standing at the front of the crowd to lead the chants.

"She is a young activist," Dawod said. "We don't want to choose her path in life, but it seems she is doing just that."

Family discussions are likely to include such topics as systemic racism. Dawod noted: "In the US, it is really deep."

But he sees glimmers of change. Oregon today feels very different from the place where he arrived eight years ago, Dawod said. Specifically, "You feel like you are more welcome here, as a person of color. To me, to witness that, it is really amazing."

A MESSAGE FOR HIS PEOPLE

If Rudwan Dawod has one message for the people of Sudan, it is this: Sudan can become truly democratic "only if we are united, and only if we do it through nonviolence. I hope the military leaders will put down their weapons and work together. I hope we have no more war."

Dijana Ihas. Photo by Sankar Raman

CHAPTER 8

Music to Soothe a City's Soul

Dijana Ihas (Bosnia)

According to the American Music Therapy Association, the discipline of music therapy involves the "clinical and evidence-based use of music interventions . . . by a credentialed professional."

Well, they may not have been licensed mental health professionals, but the musicians who formed the Sarajevo String Quartet were credentialed from here to there. All had played string instruments since childhood, and in a country where conservatory education carries glittering prestige, all had superb training. All played in a variety of orchestras throughout Bosnia's capital city. They were the kind of experienced performers who might as well have known Mozart or Beethoven personally, so familiar were they with the works of those musical giants.

On April 6, 1992, forces from neighboring Serbia attacked Sarajevo. It was the start of a nearly four-year assault on a citadel of culture in central Europe. Bombs fell relentlessly, often targeting popular gathering spots, such as markets, libraries, city squares or places of worship. Residents of Sarajevo knew that Serbian snipers might strike at any moment. The Serbs cut off vital services to the city. There was no electricity and no running water. Dwelling spaces were lit by candles.

The four musicians who marched across the city to deliver free performances throughout the blockade had not set out to make a courageous statement. Rather, when they agreed to perform a single concert in the bombed-out synagogue where one of the players worshiped with his family, at least one quartet member—viola player Dijana Ihas—wondered if anyone would come. Who would be crazy enough to risk venturing out to hear music when every street was filled with danger?

It was late June 1992, two months after the siege of Sarajevo had begun. As the musicians approached the synagogue, they heard sirens warning that bombings were imminent. The string players set up their music stands and agreed: If no one came, fine, they would just play for their own families and then go home.

But as the quartet performed that day, a steady stream of listeners trickled in. They had put out forty or so chairs. By the concert's end, all the chairs were filled, "perhaps one hundred people," Ihas said. Some in the makeshift audience were standing, leaning against the synagogue's ruined walls. When the concert ended, no one wanted to leave. Many people came forward, Ihas said, to thank the musicians and to tell them this was the best thing that had happened to them since the start of the blockade.

Music therapy has measurable benefits, according to its practitioners. For instance, music therapy can help slow body rhythms. Heart rates can grow steadier. Brain stimulation can occur. Moods can alter, usually for the better. The escapism offered by many forms of music can help to relieve stress. Or, to borrow from the seventeenth- and eighteenth-century dramatist Thomas Congreve, "Musick has Charms to soothe a savage Breast, To soften Rocks, or bend a knotted Oak."

And so the four musicians became soldiers of a sort—cultural warriors—intent on soothing their city's battered soul. Instead of weapons, they carried stringed instruments and sheafs of musical scores. During 1,425 days of attack on Sarajevo, they performed 206 concerts—essentially, one every seven days.

"Everywhere people needed a sense that they were still human beings, we played," said Ihas, the group's youngest member and its only female musician. "We never said no."

When two of their original players were killed, one by a grenade and one by a sniper, new musicians took their places. Ihas performed throughout her pregnancy—literally, while labor pains were raging. In fact, her son was born less than an hour after an important concert had concluded.

After her two colleagues were killed, Ihas's family begged her to leave not just the quartet, but also to get out of Bosnia.

"I honestly did not have any special reason to stay, except that I felt it would be dishonest to leave my country when my country needed me most," she said.

The sirens became a kind of background noise for the musicians. They kept on playing, determined to show that bombs could not destroy their city's spirit.

AND THE QUARTET PLAYED ON

> Outside the monster raged with flaming nostrils. But inside there was tranquility. The melancholy notes of Albinoni's adagio drifted into every corner of the room, and out through the windows where they were consumed by the thunder of the explosions echoing through the city. The concert was beautiful. The musicians might have been playing in New York, Paris or Rome. Serb shells were ripping apart their city and their lives, but their souls were their own. Dijana's face was serene, her hands sure and strong on the gleaming body of the viola.
>
> — *From Sarajevo Roses: War Memoir of a Peacekeeper by Anné Mariè du Preez Bezdrob*

Throughout Sarajevo, once the siege began on that early April day in 1992, residents of what was for centuries a proud and splendid city had no heat, no electricity, and no running water. Food was scarce. When the bombs went off, sometimes for twenty-two hours a day, occupants of entire apartment buildings rushed to their basements. Above ground, in their own dwellings, they had no windows, only plastic sheeting where once there had been glass.

By some estimates, twenty-seven fatal shells fell to each square acre during the years of persistent attack, the longest siege of a capital city in the history of modern warfare, three times longer than the Battle of Stalingrad in World War II.

But even for the bomb blasts, even for the bloodshed, still they had music.

Again and again they played—206 concerts in the years their city was effectively imprisoned: two violinists, a viola player, and a cellist who made up the venerable Sarajevo String Quartet. They performed on the front lines, in bombed-out schools and hospitals, in civic buildings, theaters, concert halls, and the ruins of houses of worship. Several times each week, they walked for miles to rehearse by candlelight.

Buildings could be destroyed, the members of the quartet realized, but spirits could not be broken. In simple terms, said Ihas, "it became a mission."

WAR CONCERTS, THE BEGINNING

The concerts began not long after Serbian forces began shelling Sarajevo. The first violinist asked his colleagues if they would be willing to perform at his synagogue—or rather, what remained of his synagogue following a bomb blast. This is when Ihas secretly wondered who in the city would show up.

The medieval city of Sarajevo had been an ancient stronghold for the arts in central Europe, bursting with galleries, museums, and packed theater houses. Seats at the opera seldom went unoccupied. At least one of four professional orchestras performed nightly.

Who, Ihas wondered, would attend an outdoor concert when bombs or grenades might drop at any moment or when a sniper might suddenly take aim? Who thought a few measures of Mendelssohn or Mozart were worth dying for?

Sure enough, as the musicians were walking to the temple, they heard those sirens warning of an impending bombing by the Serbs. The foursome paused to discuss whether they should continue. The second violinist said he had to go to the temple because his wife would be there. There was no further discussion. Of course they would all go.

From the volume of the blasts, they could tell the bombs were near the city. But the four musicians and their spouses set up the chairs in the synagogue's atrium. They began to play. Slowly, as the quartet performed Mozart's "Eine Kleine Nachtmusik," people drifted in from the street. When they had rested their bows after a half-hour of playing, their audience questioned them: When will you play again?

"That is when we realized this could really be something that we could offer to our city in this time of crisis," Ihas said. "When people came, despite the bombing, and sat through the concert, I felt this was more than music. I felt I had a responsibility to my country to do something, and the tool with which I can do it is music."

Music, she realized that day in the bomb-damaged synagogue, was "a symbol of human spirit," and stronger than any of the bombs descending on Sarajevo.

Within months, the first violinist, Momir Vlacic, was killed by a grenade. Just a month later—October 1992, to be exact—a sniper claimed the second violinist, Kamenko Ostojic. New musicians replaced them. This is when Ihas's family began begging her to leave, fearing that she would be next in what seemed to be a systematic attempt to silence the quartet. She refused. "How do you leave the country that gave you everything, which was very generous to you, which gave you music, and therefore, your life?" she explained.

Ed Vulliamy, a correspondent for The Guardian, attended a concert in Sarajevo's blacked-out National Theater during the quartet's tenure as a trio. The musicians were playing Joseph Haydn's String Trio Op. 8 No. 6.

At one point, during the andante, a mortar crashed close to the theater. The walls shook so hard that Ihas's music stand and score fell over. The audience waited in silence until the music stand was righted and the first violinist lifted his bow.

"The trio played on," Vulliamy wrote.

Throughout the war, the quartet's cellist, Miron Strutinski, kept a small notebook, recording the date and location of each performance. With each concert, the quartet was offering hope to the embattled citizens of Sarajevo, Ihas said. "Of course it was risky," she conceded. "But the passion for music was greater than that risk."

The members of the quartet were well aware of the risks they were taking each time they set off on foot to perform in public. Beyond the actual music, Ihas said, the four felt a sense of greater purpose when they played.

"You are providing hope for all those people," she said.

Anné Mariè du Preez Bezdrob, a United Nations peacekeeper in Sarajevo at that time, described a Sarajevo String Quartet concert in her book *Sarajevo Roses: War Memoir of a Peacekeeper*. The title refers to the craters left throughout the city by the impact of mortar or artillery shells.

"With their unique sense of the ironic," she writes, residents of the Bosnian capital named these hollows "Sarajevo Roses" because the depressions resembled giant flowers with scattered petals.

Because the city was under curfew, concerts took place by daylight. Tickets were free, and seats seldom went empty. At a July concert at the old Chamber Theater in central Sarajevo, du Preez Bezdrob remembers feeling uncomfortable because the windows had not been secured with adhesive tape. Accompanied by the background thunder of exploding shells, "nobody batted an eye, neither the audience nor the musicians, who didn't miss a note and serenely continued playing their well-rehearsed Mozart, Gounod and Bach."

Even as some in the audience began to leave, perhaps "eager for the false security of their own homes," du Preez Bezdrob writes, "the quartet kept playing, as though nothing was amiss, their faces calm and composed, their practiced hands unwavering."

This stoic determination, said the peacekeeper, "was the essence of survival in Sarajevo. To complete what you'd set out to do was a victory; to give up and run for cover meant moral defeat."

WAR ITSELF, THE BEGINNING

From 1945 to 1992, the Socialist Republic of Bosnia and Herzegovina was one of the six federal states that formed the Socialist Federal Republic of Yugoslavia. In February 1992, following the breakup of the former Yugoslavia, the multi-ethnic Socialist Republic of Bosnia and Herzegovina declared its independence. In May of the same year, the Republic of Bosnia and Herzegovina was admitted as a member state of the United Nations.

But the Bosnian Serbs, led by Radovan Karadžić and Slobodan Milošević, rejected the move. Intent on establishing a greater Serbia, Milošević and others wanted Bosnia's land.

Ihas bristles when the assault on her country is called a civil war. Rather, she contends, "It was an invasion by a foreign country (Serbia) of an internationally recognized independent country (Bosnia). Serbia wanted the land to expand their territory into what they called 'Greater Serbia.' The problem was that the land was inhabited by Muslim people. The most convenient way of getting rid of the Muslims was by killing them." Keep in mind, she adds, "I am not Muslim. I just speak of what I saw and experienced. An objective reality of that war."

The Serbian attacks were marked by bitter fighting, random shelling of cities and towns, and ethnic cleansing. Mass rape also was common. At least 100,000 people died during the war. Another 2.2 million were displaced. Between 12,000 and 50,000 women were raped.

The invasion by Serbian troops and the subsequent years of battle came as a surprise, said Ihas: "Nobody could imagine that this war would happen in the middle of Europe."

If the world, and by extension the United States, fell under a siege of sorts by the coronavirus pandemic, Ihas chafes at the comparison. During the pandemic, she could put her mask on and venture out, knowing that "nobody is going to kill me." No such assurance was possible during the Bosnian War.

Food shortage had never before been a problem in the sophisticated city of Sarajevo. Two years into the war, the deadliest single attack took place when a 120-millimeter mortar shell fell on a crowded Sarajevo marketplace called the Markale. The first of two Markale massacres at the neoclassical building filled with food stalls killed sixty-eight men and women. Another 144 were wounded.

Ihas and her three colleagues were performing for a group of government dignitaries when the massacre occurred. Ihas was seated so close to the prime minister that she noticed a tear roll down his cheek when his press secretary crept up to whisper something in his ear. Unaware of what had just happened at the city's central marketplace, Ihas marveled that the head of her country's government could be so moved by the music of the Sarajevo String Quartet.

THE YOUNG MUSICIAN

Her family was tiny, just Dijana, born in 1969, and her mom, Stojanka Sturika, in a one-bedroom apartment in Sarajevo. Her mother and her

Hungarian-born father divorced when she was so young that she has no memory of all of them living under one roof.

Her mother worked in a furniture factory and cleaned houses on weekends for extra income. One client, the trombonist for the Sarajevo Philharmonic Orchestra, sometimes gave her tickets to the opera as a gratuity. Ihas's mother was engulfed in the splendor of the productions, but what really astonished her was when the performers took their final bows and were showered with bouquets from the audience.

"She was so excited and amazed to see that there are professions on earth where you could get flowers," her daughter said.

The type of communism practiced in the former Yugoslavia, according to Ihas, was more like social communism. The country was known, after all, as the Socialist Federal Republic of Yugoslavia. As early as 1948, not long after the end of World War II, some Soviet leaders denounced their Yugoslav counterparts as "dubious Marxists," and at times the form of socialism practiced in Yugoslavia was called "Titoism." Yugoslavia assumed a neutral role during the Cold War, and in the 1950s and early 1960s, Yugoslavia traded openly with both the East and the West—becoming, at one time, the most prosperous communist state in Eastern Europe.

Yugoslav citizens enjoyed greater liberties than others in the Eastern Bloc and former Soviet Union. Ihas doesn't remember ever being hungry. On the contrary, "you could go to a supermarket and find twenty kinds of beef," she said. "Not only meat, but twenty types of vinegar—are you kidding me?"

Education flourished, with many new universities established in the post-World War II years. Literacy at one time reached 91 percent. Medical care was free. The system meant that a single parent, working in a furniture factory, could send her daughter to a stellar music school.

Under the Yugoslav system at that time, students attended conventional schools as in other Western countries. But instead of heading home when the final bell rang in the afternoon, children in Sarajevo could go to a second sort of school, for training in ballet, music or languages. After six years of this specialized instruction, students became eligible to enter a high school that specialized in their chosen field. After that, in Ihas's case, came the music conservatory.

Starting when she was just six years old, Ihas had lessons in violin, piano, music theory and solfeggio, the six-tone scale of frequencies used in ancient sacred music such as Gregorian chants. "Do, re, mi, fa, si," she sang, in perfect pitch.

During those early years, Ihas's mother, still in her blue factory uniform, would somehow manage to slip away from work twice a week to sit in on her daughter's violin lessons. At home, her mother would put Ihas in the bathroom for an hour each day to practice her triplets. Never mind, said Ihas, that "she had no idea what triplets were."

Every day, after her regular school and then after her music school, Ihas practiced for two full hours. By the end of sixth grade, she knew music was what she wanted to do with her life.

To attend the specialized high school, Ihas and other aspiring musicians were required to stand for a rigorous entrance exam. In front of a roomful of people, a pianist played a melody. Each student was then asked to sing it back. Next came rhythmic hand claps. The student had to clap back, mimicking the rhythm. And so forth. When the exam concluded, a teacher would announce in front of everybody whether a student was qualified, and if so, for which instrument.

Ihas was overjoyed when her verdict was the violin. The school gave her mother—the furniture factory worker—six months to acquire one.

FIRST VIOLIN, FIRST VIOLA

When they entered a small music store in Sarajevo, Ihas was mesmerized. Hundreds of violins and cellos covered every inch of the place, even hanging from the ceiling. But Ihas's mother went blank when the proprietor asked what size violin they were interested in.

Ihas was still a little girl. The proprietor brought out one instrument that was one-quarter the size of a traditional violin, and another that was one-half sized. Both were priced well out of their range.

"Don't you have something for a little less?" her mother asked.

Illogically, the three-quarter-sized violin he produced was less expensive than either of the two smaller models. And so Ihas went home with the violin she played until she reached high school.

The tightly controlled government meant that working parents such as Ihas's mother had few worries about the after-school welfare of their children. At ten years old, Ihas said it was safe for her to ride a bus from one side of town to the other—for example, if she wanted to attend a concert featuring one of the many acclaimed performers who visited her city. Students paid no entrance fees and were encouraged to go backstage to meet the musicians. So there she was, ten years old, shaking hands with perhaps the most famous violinist in the world at the time, Yehudi Menuhin.

Ihas still thinks that the violin she grew to love—technically, too large for such a young child—may have paved her way to the viola. When her teacher suggested she switch to the still-larger instrument, Ihas was thrilled. Many of those after-school concert outings had been to hear chamber music groups. Ihas listened carefully. The mellow timbre of the viola, she realized, was the closest to the sound of the human voice.

Ihas's father had long since returned to his native Hungary, where he had remarried and established a new family. His sister, Ihas's aunt, offered to look for a viola for Dijana. When she found one that was affordable and of a suitable size, the question was how to get it to her niece. Though she seldom saw her father, Ihas said "he actually traveled all day and all night" to bring the handmade instrument to his daughter in Sarajevo.

Ihas has since studied with some of the world's most renowned viola teachers. But her first viola instructor in Bosnia, she maintains, outshines them all. There was something magical about the way he immersed his students in techniques, long before the music they were playing actually demanded those refinements.

For instance, from day one, her teacher had her learning vibrato, the rapid, pulsating change of pitch that adds expression to musical notes. Her teacher began by showing her how to move her wrists, without even holding her viola. To this day, Ihas employs similar teaching methods with her own students.

THE ARTISTS' CLUB

Ihas's studies at the Sarajevo Conservatory lasted four years. The work was demanding, but as she noted, even in communist countries, young people like to have fun. Once again, the government devised a structure that allowed for kids to be kids—within certain strict limitations.

"Everything is organized," Ihas said. "In communist countries, that is how they control your mind."

After-school activities became government-sponsored, alcohol-free youth clubs centered around different areas of interest. Ihas naturally gravitated to the gatherings that focused on the arts. But there were also political education classes, and for an entire year, Ihas took a class called "Defense." Assignments in that class included practice shooting in open fields.

"Not handguns," Ihas said. "These were the guns you would use if you were in the army."

How did she do in that class? "Very well," Ihas said.

It was also around this time that Ihas took up yoga and transcendental meditation. Tall and almost impossibly thin, she continues both practices today and makes no secret of how important both disciplines have been to her, ascribing "everything I have accomplished in my life to my spiritual practice." Ihas is also a strict vegetarian.

In that happier time before the war, the lively city of Sarajevo was known as the musical mecca of the former Yugoslavia, Ihas said. Beyond shooting drills and political studies, groups from the youth clubs also attended rock concerts.

"We would have these major, major concerts," she said. "We had the Rolling Stones, everything. It would happen every school week." At the arts group, she found herself admiring the paintings of a young man named Mirza. Ihas was enthralled by his use of color. Mirza, in turn, was captivated by the willowy musician who admired his works. Soon enough, they were seeing one another. But Mirza was Muslim, "which was totally not okay with my Catholic family."

Any parent of any teenager knows that the best way to ensure a wedding is to oppose a child's chosen love interest. Rather than breaking off their relationship, as Ihas's family wanted, the two got married. Mirza's Muslim family adored their new daughter-in-law. But Ihas's mother slammed the door on both of them.

"She was very disappointed in me," Ihas said.

Dijana with her infant son, Abellar Nizar, named for the twelfth-century poet and philosopher, Peter Abellard, and for a Persian word meaning "someone who sees beyond." Photo courtesy of Mirza Ajanovic

Even in the middle of a war—or maybe especially in the middle of a war—there's nothing like a baby to patch up family fissures. With their mixed-culture marriage, Dijana and Mirza chose a name, Abellar Nizar, to connect both traditions when their son was born in 1994. Abellar was a paean to the twelfth-century philosopher, theologian, poet, and musician, Peter Abelard. Nizar derives from a Persian word meaning "someone who sees beyond." The child came to be known by his middle name.

"He needed to be baptized," Ihas explained. "So OK, let's baptize him. My entire Muslim family came to Sarajevo Cathedral in the middle of the war to get him baptized."

BIRTH AMID THE BOMBINGS

Ihas was only twenty when she was hired as a viola player in the Sarajevo Symphony Orchestra. As was common for talented musicians in Sarajevo at that time, she also played with several other groups. Not long after the war began in 1992, the viola player for the Sarajevo String Quartet told Ihas he was going to retire. He suggested she apply for the job.

Within months of their first wartime concert at the synagogue, the quartet became known as the go-to group for musical healing as the city's heart was shattered by bombs.

"Known to the point that we would walk on the street and ordinary people would recognize us," Ihas says.

Midway through the war, in hopes of fostering the Bosnian spirit of identity, the quartet was asked to present a concert featuring only Bosnian composers. Ihas was nervous. She was very pregnant at the time, and since many of the works to be performed were contemporary, the music was complicated and required extensive rehearsals.

She also worried that, as the youngest member of the group and as the sole female, her colleagues might fire her if she did not agree to perform. The concert was set for July 16, three days before Ihas's baby was due. After losing two fellow players to war violence and after playing in other treacherous situations, she figured she could finesse this one.

But babies do not always listen to doctors who declare due dates. Her contractions began the night before the concert. "All I could think of was, 'This cannot happen,'" Ihas said.

Her husband scoured the neighborhood for someone with a car and found a neighbor who happened to be a policeman. The neighbor agreed to drive Ihas and her husband to the concert. He said he would wait and then drive them to the hospital after the concert ended.

"Sure enough," said Ihas, "we start playing, and there are my contractions. There are moments when the pain is stronger than my mind."

But the audience, filled with government dignitaries, was oblivious, aware only of the patriotic power of the music.

When the concert concluded, the musicians were asked to stay for an interview. Ihas, barely able to stand, said no. The first violinist asked why she could not stay.

"I am right now going to the hospital to have this baby," Ihas replied.

The first violinist dropped to a chair, open-mouthed, as if he were the one about to deliver a child. The concert ended at 5 p.m. Forty minutes later, Ihas's son came into the world.

Motherhood and music: Ihas had a newborn. Still she continued to traipse through the city to rehearse. Still she continued to play with the quartet.

"At the beginning of any crisis, human beings tend to be in a state of survival," she said. "Then you have two options. Either you give up and die, or you have an option to say, 'I am going to survive, let's see what happens.'" At some point, she continued, "you decide, am I going to sit inside, or am I going to carry on? You are aware of the risks, but you do

The three-year Siege of Sarajevo was well into its second year when Dijana Ihas carried her viola past the rubble for another concert. Photo courtesy of Mirza Ajanovic

it anyway. After a while—for me it was around 1993—you actually start thriving."

THE TATTERED COAT

The Bosnian War raged on. After the treaty that ended the conflict in 1995, international artists such as the Irish rock group U2 began traveling to Bosnia for concerts. Diana, Princess of Wales, attended a benefit for child victims of the Bosnian war staged by opera megastar Luciano Pavarotti in Modena, Italy, in 1995. Shortly before her death in 1997, Princess Diana also visited Bosnia as part of a mission to rid the country of land mines.

During the war, however, Ihas said the sole international artist to perform in Bosnia was the famed Indian-American conductor Zubin Mehta. Mehta led the Sarajevo Symphony Orchestra as they played Mozart's "Requiem" at Sarajevo's rubble-strewn National Library. Ihas, three weeks away from delivering her son, played as the fourth-chair viola.

Word of the string quartet made its way to Great Britain. A charity called Hazelwood House that touted its link to Princess Diana—falsely, as it turned out—invited the group to come to the United Kingdom for a series of concerts to raise awareness about the crisis in Bosnia. The sponsoring group promised that all expenses would be covered, and the musicians would be paid for their time.

Ihas said she would not make the trip without her baby son. A stalemate ensued because the United Nations aircraft that was to fly them out of Bosnia required all passengers to wear heavy, bullet-proof outerwear that was not available in infant sizes. Eventually, a compromise was reached. Ihas would hold Nizar in her lap and place the heavy jacket over both of them.

In the third week of March 1995, on the day the group was to depart, family and neighbors of the players bade tearful farewells to the musicians, wondering if they would ever see these artists again. An armored vehicle came to pick each player up. It was cold and miserable, with heavy snow falling. Every kilometer or so, the vehicle would stop so soldiers could check to make sure the passengers were who they said they were.

Finally, they reached the rubble of what had been the airport terminal. There was no roof left, and for six hours the snow that had turned to heavy, frigid rain fell on the players as they sat on the floor, waiting to take off. At last, officials sent them back home. Two days later, they went through the same thwarted routine again.

On the third try, the quartet once again spent five or six hours huddled in the debris of Sarajevo International Airport. This time, they were led aboard a UN aircraft that also had no seats. Once again, they sat close to one another to stay warm.

The flight to Zagreb in Croatia lasted just twenty minutes. But what greeted them there might have been a scene from another planet. All four musicians underwent something called "shock from silence," because during 3.5 years of near-constant explosions in Sarajevo, they had not experienced silence.

When Ihas took her seven-month-old son into their hotel room, she switched on the lights. Immediately, reflexively, the baby began to wail in terror.

"This child had never seen electricity," she said.

To quiet him, she took him out for a walk. Close to the hotel she spied a grocery store whose front window held a bounteous display of fresh fruit. Ihas had almost forgotten such delicacies could exist.

"I thought, 'How on earth is this possible? Twenty minutes by plane.' In Sarajevo, there is nothing, and here there are blueberries," Ihas said.

Back at the hotel, she went to wash her hands. Once again, her son began to scream. Never before had he heard the sound of running water.

The following day, the musicians sat for their visa interviews. When the standard question came up—"Do you plan to return to your own country?"—the other three were dumbfounded when the group's cellist said no. Ihas never saw him again, although in time she learned he was able to join relatives in Canada.

In London, a cellist named Nigel Blomiley agreed to sub for their missing player. The quartet was put up in a townhouse in South London, adjacent to the headquarters of the sponsoring charity. There was no interpreter and no one in the group spoke much English.

"They told us we would play seventeen different concerts in many cities, and at the end of the tour they would pay us," Ihas said.

The coat Ihas was wearing dated from before the onset of the war. The fabric was nearly threadbare, and the lining was in shreds. Ihas had mended it too many times to count. Now she was done with that old thing. With the prospect of some money and some time to shop in London's famous stores, she promised herself a new coat at the end of the tour.

Ceremoniously, she handed the coat to a housekeeper and asked her to throw it out.

ON TOUR, THE UNITED KINGDOM

Along with no interpreter, the host group had not thought to provide childcare for Nizar. At their first concert, a woman in the audience volunteered to walk him outside. As she played, Ihas tried to concentrate on the music, not the piercing cries of her baby son.

Every morning, the musicians had breakfast waiting for them at their lodgings. Cigarettes were passed around, and in due course a translator arrived. Juggling the conflicting schedules of rehearsals and her son's naptime, Ihas always skipped lunch. She had just enough time to pack Nizar and her viola into the van each afternoon at three o'clock to travel to that day's concert venue.

On Good Friday, three days before the group was scheduled to leave London, their hosts said they would be paid the following Monday. At last, the musicians had some time to explore London—and for Ihas, to do some shopping at the Easter sales. Only she was broke and could not buy anything.

At their final breakfast, their hosts presented them with an invoice charging them for transportation, every meal, their visas—even the cigarettes that they thought had been graciously offered to them. In a feat of mathematical gymnastics, the musicians' expenses exactly equaled the amount they were to have been paid. In other words, they were about to go home just as broke as when they had arrived.

As they prepared to leave, Ihas asked the housekeeper if by any chance she still had her scruffy coat. Luckily, the housekeeper said yes.

Her voice heavy with irony, Ihas noted that the tour had been called "Don't Forget Bosnia." Three-plus years into the war, it seemed, "the world got tired of Bosnia."

ON TOUR, NORWAY

The group returned to Zagreb and played several more concerts before heading to Norway, where they were to be the first-ever international group to perform on Norway Independence Day. Their appearance was intended to be a way to honor Bosnia and the prospect of Bosnian independence.

From the very first moment, the two musical tours could not have been more different. At the Oslo Airport, Ihas discovered that her luggage had been lost. But the translator—the translator!—who met them at their hotel assured her all would be well. The concert organizers told them they would stay for seven days and play one concert, for fifteen minutes, for which they would each be paid 1,000 Deutsche Marks (about $1,200 USD).

Walking Ihas to the airline office to file a claim, the translator again told her not to worry about her lost luggage—the sponsors would provide everything she and her son needed in the meantime. The airline expressed profound regrets and handed her a check for $1,500. The translator later brought her a bag stuffed with supplies, right down to a dress to wear for the concert and fancy shoes to match. When Ihas's suitcase finally showed up, she offered to return the check to the airlines. Oh no, she was told. You must keep this as compensation for your inconvenience.

Finally it was time for that new coat—and maybe a few other additions to her wardrobe as well. She laughed as she admitted: She might have done a little shopping at H&M in Oslo.

A SORT OF PEACE

With the signing of the Dayton Agreement in December 1995, the Bosnian War came to an official end. But splitting the Republic of Bosnia and Herzegovina into two states was only one way in which the accord accentuated ethnic enmities rather than assuaging them. Tensions between factions in the region boiled to the surface almost immediately, Ihas said.

"In Bosnia, for five hundred years it didn't matter what your last name was," said Ihas, whose surname was unusual in her country because it came from her Hungarian father.

But right away, the fact that her son shared his Muslim father's surname became a problem. Humanitarian groups that poured into Sarajevo to distribute diapers, milk, and formula were organized mostly around religious lines. Ihas, a Catholic, went to the Catholic-sponsored group for supplies and was rebuffed because of the boy's Muslim name. At the Muslim-based aid organization, the child's Catholic baptismal certificate was grounds for refusal as well.

The Dayton Agreement, however, had made specific provisions to allow Bosnian children born in mixed marriages to relocate to Croatia with their parents.

"I said to my husband, 'I cannot stay here. You do what you want,'" Ihas said.

The only person Ihas knew in Croatia was one of her former violin teachers. She contacted him, explaining that she needed a place to stay, but had only what little money she had made in Norway. In turn, her former teacher contacted his own father, an elderly man who walked with a cane and lived in a little town called Duga Resa.

With an agreement that she would buy the food and cook, Dijana and her son settled into a small room in the old man's house, only to discover that at night, the basement became a nightclub for Croatian soldiers. Ihas had seen enough during the war to be terrified. The room she shared with her son had no locks, so every night she barricaded it with a chair.

Three months later, her husband was able to join them. Ihas went to Zagreb to apply for asylum in the United States. A full year later, they found themselves on a charter plane, flying first to Milan, Italy, and then over the Atlantic Ocean. Ihas saw that among their fellow passengers, most came from what she called "disadvantaged" backgrounds. Her heart went out to them.

"To this day, I ask myself, 'What happened to those people? If I, with a college degree, had so many difficulties, how have they managed?'"

At John F. Kennedy International Airport in New York, Ihas felt she had stepped into an absurdist drama. She felt insignificant, unable to speak English and lacking any ballast.

"In your home country, you have a homeland, you have a story," she said. Here, suddenly, she had nothing.

Their small group of refugees marched through the airport, following a woman who led them with a blue plastic rose attached to an umbrella. Ihas had a cousin in Orange County, California, and together with two other Bosnian families they were led to a plane to take them to the West Coast.

Ihas began talking to another young couple with a child. They said they were going to a place called Portland, Oregon.

"We had never heard of this place—Portland or Oregon," Ihas said.

BEING AN IMMIGRANT IN AMERICA

That is what Ihas would like to title the Orange County chapter of her odyssey: "Being an Immigrant in America."

From the outset, life was difficult. Ihas and Mirza spoke no English. They could not afford a car, and in any case, neither had a driver's license.

Their life as a family had traumatic beginnings. All Ihas wanted to do was to make a better life for all three of them.

They took adult-education classes in English. Dijana took a job as a nanny. Mirza found occasional work painting houses. Through a Croatian doctor to whom they were referred, Ihas befriended an organist for the Los Angeles Philharmonic. For their first Thanksgiving in America in 1997, the organist brought them to his home in Los Angeles to celebrate with his family.

Through him, she began getting small freelance jobs as a viola player. But the sprawling quality of the Southern California basin and its spider's web freeway system sometimes confused Ihas to the point of tears. She got lost constantly and once arrived sobbing at a rehearsal in San Diego. She began to see that if she wanted to advance as a musician—and especially if she wanted to be able to support her family—she needed more academic ammunition. A fellow musician in one of the orchestras where she was freelancing advised her to look into the master's degree program at the University of Southern California.

"So here I am, no clue what the University of Southern California even is," she said.

She looked through the university's website and found two viola professors. One of them, Pamela Goldsmith, agreed to talk to Ihas if she would come for an interview at her home in Studio City.

"Where?" Ihas wondered. And then luckily a friend from her adult English classes agreed to drive her to the San Fernando Valley community where Goldsmith lived.

The interview went well. Goldsmith said Ihas could play in the university orchestra in exchange for weekly lessons with Goldsmith. But then a friend from another of the orchestras Ihas was playing with told her that a public school in Mission Viejo needed a string music teacher. The pay was $150 per month—not much, but the first semblance of a stable income Ihas had been offered since arriving in the United States.

In the meantime, Ihas and her husband had gone their separate ways. This is a fissure she prefers not to discuss.

Soon it became clear to Ihas that teaching would offer her a steadier income than her frenetic life as a freelance orchestra minstrel. Another public school approached her about setting up a chamber music program. Goldsmith suggested she consider the music program at the University of California, Irvine (UCI).

Thomas Cockrell, the UCI orchestra director, swiftly became a mentor to Ihas. His wife was Romanian, so he understood something about the politics of Central and Eastern Europe. Ihas was admitted to the master's program at UC-Irvine with a full scholarship. Cockrell even managed to bend the requirement that Ihas pass the mandatory English-language proficiency test.

Cockrell's wife, Yvonne Creanga, taught viola and chamber music at UCI. She was also an immigrant, having defected from Romania on a visit to the United States when she was eighteen. Her daughter was the same age as Nizar, and she and Ihas struck up a friendship that continues today.

From the outset, Creanga said by telephone from her home in Tucson, Arizona, what struck her about Ihas was "her very, very focused and dedicated work ethic, her passion to become a better musician." Ihas, already an accomplished musician, showed nothing but "humbleness," Creanga said. Ihas always wanted to learn from the best. "The standards she imposed on herself, you do not see that often," Creanga remarked.

UCI set Ihas and her son up in graduate student housing and enrolled Nizar in the university-sponsored daycare program. Ihas was floored by how kind people had been.

"I strongly believe that Americans are just the most wonderful people," she said. "Not having difficult lives molds people into people who are willing to help, not to have envy."

LEARNING BY DEGREES

As she continued to do work with music students in Orange County public schools, Ihas decided she needed yet another degree, this one in music education. The two best master's degree programs for her in that field were at Florida State University and the University of Arizona. Ihas was accepted at both.

But her ex-husband balked at blessing a move for his young son all the way to Florida. So did the judge who heard his complaint. And so, "that is how I ended up moving to Tucson and finishing my second master's."

Two master's degrees and a bachelor's from the Sarajevo Conservatory were not enough. Ihas knew that to make a stable life for herself and her son and to continue a career in music education she needed a doctorate. This time, she thought first about where she wanted to live and more importantly, where she wanted to raise her son.

On the West Coast, it came down to two schools: the University of Washington and the University of Oregon. The day she visited Eugene, it was pouring. She didn't care. It was green and welcoming, and she could see living there with her son. Besides, she added, "I loved the viola teacher."

Turns out there was more to love on campus than the viola teacher. While studying for her PhD, Ihas met her second husband. Michael Denny, who died in late 2023, was a professor of jazz guitar who performed with Mary Wells, Eartha Kitt, Della Reese, and many other well-known artists.

As it happened, one of the country's best high school orchestra-education programs was in nearby Salem. Ihas took over the program, and for three straight years the Sprague High School Orchestra won top awards in statewide competitions. She took the orchestra to New York, even playing a concert in Carnegie Hall.

Then along came an email in 2014 announcing "a job opening at some school I never heard of in my life, Pacific University." Ihas's interest was piqued because the university in Forest Grove, Oregon, wanted someone to launch a string-music education program for public school students.

HEART STRINGS

The offer fell into the category of too-good-to-refuse. Among other benefits, the university offered tuition relief for faculty children. After graduating from Pacific, Ihas's son, a cellist, earned a master's in screenwriting from Chapman University in Southern California.

Headed by Ihas, the Pacific University String Project provides stringed-instrument music education for children from second to twelfth grade. Pacific University music students act as teachers. Many of the students served by the project come from economically challenged backgrounds.

“I am very passionate about providing equal opportunity music education for disadvantaged kids,” Ihas said. “Two-hundred-and-forty students who would never be able to play musical instruments except for this program.”

In a sense, Ihas is returning the favor given to her when she began studying music in first grade in Bosnia. Her friend Yvonne Creanga, in Tucson, said this is part of an unwritten, but deeply understood impulse for many immigrants.

“People have helped me, so you pay forward,” Creanga said.

In 2018, the Pacific University String Project was named the outstanding string project of the year by the American String Teachers Association. Ihas herself was selected as Oregon’s Music Educator of the Year in 2021. In bestowing that distinction, the Oregon Music Association called Ihas “a world-class violist, an outstanding conductor and a devoted music educator.”

Mimi Zweig, a professor of music at Indiana University and director of that school’s String Academy, playfully calls Ihas “a walking encyclopedia of string pedagogy.” Ihas has “traveled the world to become as knowledgeable as possible about everything that has to do with string playing,” Zweig said by email. Just as important, Zweig wrote, Ihas puts that information “to invaluable use in her current position.”

Throughout their marriage, Ihas and Denny maintained a commuting marriage, with weekends together in Eugene or Forest Grove. In the summers, Ihas often returns to Bosnia to care for her mother’s grave. Ihas has never stopped being grateful to her mother for guiding her into a life of music.

“To this day, she is my hero,” she said.

Despite the deprivations of war, despite the hardships she and her family endured, Ihas also harbors gratitude to the nation where she grew up. “I was privileged to be raised in a country that valued education and made high-quality education accessible to everyone,” she said. “In my own little way, I want to provide that opportunity for others.”

Music, Ihas maintains, is more than a kind of accessory to life.

“It’s a necessity,” she said. In wartime and in times of peace, music “helps us keep our dignity and keeps us feeling human.”

Baher Butti. Photo by Sankar Raman

CHAPTER 9

An Ancient History, a Rocky Present, an Uncertain Future

Baher Butti (Iraq)

For denizens of a country founded officially in 1776, the history of the ancient region now known as Iraq is almost impossible to fathom. Caves in the region have yielded skeletons dating from 60,000 to 80,000 years ago. Some appear to have been buried with flowers, suggesting rituals associated with civilization. What is certain is that civilization in what has come to be known as ancient Mesopotamia encompassed the Neolithic period and the Bronze and Iron Ages.

Archeologists refer to Mesopotamia, among the predecessors of the country of Iraq, as the cradle of civilization. The Sumerian people who occupied the region as early as the sixth century BC built a half-dozen city states—walled cities containing a ziggurat, the rectangular stepped tower that may have inspired the biblical story of the Tower of Babel.

The Sumerians originated urbanization, and possibly urban density as well. One of those city states, Uruk, had a population of between 40,000 and 80,000 residents, most likely making it the largest city in the world at the time, around 2800 BC. "Uruk" may be an early homonym for the country's ultimate name, Iraq.

If the ancient Sumerians did not actually invent the wheel—and many scholars believe they did—they likely were the first to harness it. Sumerians, savvy enough to live in the fertile region of the Tigris and

Euphrates Rivers, are also credited with developing the plow. The sixty-minute hour and sixty-second minute method of timing that the world uses today were also creations of ancient Sumeria.

What other innovations trace to Mesopotamia? How about mathematics, astronomy, astrology, and recorded law? The world's first writing system traces to this region, in the fourth century BC. Sumerian cuneiforms were wedged-shaped clay tablets originally used to record business and financial transactions. Gradually the cuneiforms grew into repositories for written history. For instance, there was the King List, a clay tablet that cataloged the region's rulers. Apparently the authors of the King List took some liberties, however, as one king was said to have lived for more than 43,000 years.

A less-fictional entry may have been a female monarch named Kubaba, said by the King List to have taken the throne of the city of Kish around 2500 BC. Kubaba's previous occupation is described as "tavern keeper." That depiction, of course, is subject to interpretation.

Speaking of spirits, the Sumerians also were early aficionados of a malty beverage said in some records to be vital to "a joyful heart and a contented liver." This early precursor to Bud Light was so thick it had to be drunk through a straw. Perhaps signifying the importance of this elixir, the Sumerians even had a goddess of brewing named Ninkasi. Ninkasi's father was the king of Uruk. Her mother was the goddess of procreation.

The Sumerians were avid traders who may have traveled as far as what is today Afghanistan in search of lapis lazuli, a lush blue stone they treasured. They also were storytellers. The Epic of Gilgamesh is a 3,600-line Sumerian poem that follows a king named Gilgamesh as he battles a forest monster. Some historians contend that the fictional Gilgamesh was based on an actual ruler, also named Gilgamesh.

The city states of Mesopotamia did not always get along, and in fact, often battled one another. Sadly, regional conflict is another legacy that has persisted through the ages. The area has been conquered by the early Persians, Greeks, Romans and then, once again, the Persians. At various times the Turks moved in. So did the Mongols, who sacked and burned the city of Baghdad.

Set astride the Tigris River, Baghdad was established as a caliphate capital following the Arab-Islamic conquest of the mid-eighth century AD. By the ninth century AD, Baghdad was known as the center of the "Islamic Golden Age." By the height of the Middle Ages, prior to the Mongol invasion and the arrival of bubonic plague, Baghdad's population had soared to more than one million.

By 1534, Iraq had become part of the sprawling Ottoman Empire. With some sporadic interruptions, this dominance continued until World War I. When the Ottomans chose to side with Germany, the British moved in with the Mesopotamian Campaign, capturing Baghdad in 1917. In 1920, the newly formed League of Nations awarded England a mandate to rule Iraq, known thereafter as Mandatory Iraq.

British rule did not go smoothly. Hoping to establish stability in the familiar form of a monarchy, British leaders named King Faisal to head an Iraqi throne in 1921. Faisal was already King of the Arab Kingdom of Syria. He was born in Mecca and raised in Istanbul. One of his endorsements as a potential sovereign of Iraq came from T. E. Lawrence, known popularly as Lawrence of Arabia. A weakened sense of Iraqi nationalism was not helped when, lacking an anthem to play as Faisal took the throne, a band struck up a British favorite, "God Save the King."

After Faisal died of a heart attack in Switzerland in 1933, his only son ascended to the throne. King Ghazi was a notorious playboy whose own rule ended when, fueled with copious amounts of alcohol, he wrapped his sports car around a Baghdad utility pole in 1939. Summarily, Ghazi's only son, Faisal II, succeeded his father as king. Faisal II was three years old at the time.

Along with other members of the royal family, King Faisal II died in a bloody coup known as the 14 July Revolution of 1958. For the next twenty years, Iraq struggled under a series of military and civilian governments. Among the conflicts was the 17 July Revolution, a bloodless coup in 1968 linked to the Ba'athists, a pan-Arab socialist movement that began in Syria. Among those celebrating the 1968 Ba'athist takeover was a young Saddam Hussein, who rode through Baghdad in triumph atop a tank.

Saddam did not take a conventional route through the ranks of the military. Rather, he was a hired henchman for politicians who often organized counter-demonstrations to disrupt gatherings of political opponents. After an attempt on the life of the then ruler of Iraq, Gen. Abd al-Karim Qasim, Saddam fled to Egypt, where he spent four years in exile. While imprisoned for nearly two years for political murders or attempted killings, Saddam was elected deputy secretary general of the Ba'ath party. Upon his release, he was named head of national security.

In July 1979, Saddam succeeded Gen. Ahmed Hassan al-Bakr as president. The move marked the start of a despotic rule that continued for close to a quarter-century. In 1980, Iraq invaded Iran. The eight-year conflict resulted neither in reparations nor in border changes.

In 1988, Iraqi bombs and lethal gasses killed five thousand villagers in the territory of Kurdistan. In 1990, Iraq invaded Kuwait. The following year, the United States moved into the region, entering the Persian Gulf War, also known as Operation Desert Storm. In 2002, Saddam claimed a 100 percent victory in a presidential referendum.

Corruption and political repression were rife throughout the Saddam years. Many political opponents were killed; many others just disappeared. Kidnappings were common. Tyranny and fear were the ruling principles.

On March 20, 2003, a US-led coalition invaded Iraq. Hussein fled—only to be captured by US forces in December 2003, after he was found hiding in a hole near his home in Tikrit. Tried by a court in Iraq, Saddam was executed by hanging in December 2006.

But all has not been calm in post-Saddam Iraq. Sectarian tensions continue. The presence of al-Qaida has grown. Unemployment is high, especially among young Iraqis. Public services—health care, education, utilities—are poor. Corruption is rampant. Despite abundant oil reserves, poverty is widespread. Torture is a routine (if unofficial) part of the country's criminal justice system. Arrests are arbitrary, and protesters, activists, journalists, and others who might be openly critical of the government are often known to disappear.

In October 2021, Iraq held parliamentary elections. Following a year of deliberation, the Iraqi Council of Representatives selected Abdul Latif Rashid as the country's new president.

In recognizing the new regime, a statement from the US State Department cautioned: "As Iraq's political leaders form a new government, we encourage them to bear in mind the will of the Iraqi people, who voted for a government responsive to their needs. The United States urges all parties to refrain from violence and to resolve differences amicably and peacefully through the political process."

Iraq sits at about the same latitude as the southern United States. Almost two-fifths of the country is desert. Iraq—bordered by Turkey, Iran, Jordan, Syria and Kuwait—is about the same size as the state of California, and with close to the same population, about 40 million. The future of this proud, ancient nation remains uncertain.

THE ELUSIVE NATURE OF HOME

Sometimes, even now, Dr. Baher Butti asks himself if it was cowardice that drove him from his native Iraq. But no, he reminds himself. Day after day, reason wrestles with homesickness for space in his soul. His activism, his political affiliation, his profession as a champion of mental health and his family history had made him a marked man.

Butti—sixty years old at the time of our interview—descends from a family of prominent Iraqi journalists, intellectuals, and political activists. During Iraq's monarchy period, his grandfather published one of the country's most popular newspapers. The name of his periodical, Al-Bilad, translates to "The Country." His father, both a journalist and a leftist, was twice imprisoned for what he printed—or refused to print. Baher Butti's uncle Faik was a leader in the opposition to Saddam Hussein.

During the final years of Hussein's regime, Baher Butti himself had published controversial articles. As a psychiatrist, among the topics he took on were the rights of the mentally ill and the virtues of freedom and democracy. He met regularly with fellow intellectuals—technocrats, as he called them—who opposed the dictator known throughout the country by his first name, Saddam, and also feared the religious fundamentalism that was gripping their nation.

Butti and his wife, Balsam, were among Iraq's Christian minority. As the Shia Muslim faction gained power in post-Saddam Iraq, social strictures increased. His wife, a physician specializing in obstetrics and gynecology, had been asked at work to stop wearing fitted dresses and to start wearing a hijab. A cousin of his wife was killed because he owned a liquor store. Balsam Butti herself narrowly dodged death when shells from a 2003 bombing at Baghdad's airport highway landed beside her car.

Kidnappings for ransom were epidemic, with professionals the prime targets. The Dora section of Baghdad, where the Buttis lived, was wracked with violence. In May 2005, their seven-year-old daughter Ula was badly injured when a car bomb exploded in front of her school bus in central Baghdad.

Along with their daughter, Butti and his wife had two sons, Fadi and Sarmad. In 2006, he visited his brother in the United Arab Emirates. His brother told him that Baher's name had shown up on a list of individuals in Iraq threatened with assassination. There was no choice but to leave, Butti decided.

"I had to think of my family," he said. "This is the issue," he said. "Staying in Iraq, I am sure I would have been killed. I just didn't know which one of them was going to kill me, the al-Qaida or the pro-Iranians."

"COUP AFTER COUP"

Baher Butti was born into a middle-class, Christian family in Baghdad in 1961. Throughout his childhood, he remembers almost nonstop political chaos: "coup after coup" until Saddam Hussein took over in 1979. Among his earliest memories are jailhouse visits to his father, imprisoned when the country's military regime took exception to something published in his newspaper, Al-Bilad. One of the imprisonments was especially memorable to the young Baher because the family was Christian, and his father was released on Christmas day.

His father, Baher Sami Rafael Butti, was known as Sami, a name that translates to "Semites." Sami Butti ran the family newspaper from 1957 to 1963. Toward the end of 1962, he was sent to jail. Before he was incarcerated, Butti's father faced a judge who gave him an ultimatum: Either change the principles of the newspaper or go to jail.

“My father said, ‘Sorry, I cannot change the principles of the newspaper,’ ” Butti said. “And he went to jail.”

In February 1963, Al-Bilad was shut down by the country's pan-Arabist government. Just two months after his release on Christmas day, Sami went to jail again. Meanwhile, instability at the highest levels of government continued. Iraq's modern history is filled with peoples' uprisings, revolutions, and military takeovers.

The Butti family occupied a position of intellectual distinction in Iraq. Speaking from his home in Hillsboro, Oregon, a Portland suburb, Butti pointed to a bookshelf containing volumes written by his uncle, Faik Butti. Butti's newspaper-publisher grandfather became the second Christian in Iraq to hold a Cabinet position when he was appointed minister of literature.

After his second imprisonment, Sami Butti—a graduate of the American University of Cairo—became a teacher of chemistry. Baher Butti's mother was also a teacher. Among their neighbors and acquaintances were Christians, Jews, Muslims, and Kurdish people, “very culturally diverse.”

At his church-run elementary school, one-fifth of his classmates were Muslim, Butti said, adding, “There was no discrimination that we felt.” In general, he said of Baghdad in the 1970s, “It was nice.” He paused for a moment, then added “a nice life as long as you stayed away from politics.”

Butti was a strong student, seldom naughty. But of course, he noted: What else would you expect from a son of two teachers? According to the Iraqi system at the time, high school grades determined not only college entry, but field of study. Medicine was considered the pinnacle, and Butti's parents knew that with his excellent record at Baghdad College high school, their son would qualify for this concentration. Butti, however, had other plans. He wanted to study architecture, he told his parents.

“So my father played a trick on me,” he said. As he filled out his college applications, “he said, ‘OK, put architecture first, then medicine.’ He knew my grades would send me to medicine.”

Butti grew up in a house with a big library filled with novels and books about politics and philosophy. His interest in psychology began in adolescence when he devoured those same books. A seminal title for him was George Orwell's *Animal Farm,* which he read in English.

His classes at the all-boys Baghdad College were in English. The school was founded in 1932 by Jesuits from Massachusetts. Typically, about half the student body was Christian and half was Muslim. Some Jewish students were also enrolled. In 1969, the Iraqi government expelled the Jesuits who had been running the school.

While he was at the school, a student union was formed, "which was of course led by the Ba'ath Party." The Arab Socialist Ba'ath Party, founded in Syria in 1947, sought to unify the Arab world, ideally as a single state. The party spread throughout the Arab world, gaining its strongest footing in Syria and Iraq. The party espoused Ba'athism, meaning "Renaissance," or "Resurrection."

A group of young communists also tried to entice Butti to their membership. Butti did not join either, preferring to toe "the middle ground." He remembers how angry his father became when he saw the pro-communist literature the communist club recruiter had given to Baher.

"Those books, he tore them away from me and yelled at me," Butti said. "He knew I would be in danger if anyone saw me with them." His father's fears were far from baseless. In 1978, Butti said, "one of my friends, he was a communist—he was not accepted at college. He had to leave Iraq. He went to Britain. That was the penalty."

Officially, Saddam Hussein became Iraq's president on July 16, 1979. In fact, Butti said, "Saddam was in power since the coup of 1968." His ascension to his country's highest office followed closely on the heels of the Iranian Revolution, in which Shah Mohammed Reza Pahlavi was ousted from power. In his place rose Ayatollah Khomeini, who declared Iran an Islamic republic. As avowed enemies of the Shah, Saddam and earlier Iraqi leaders had hosted Khomeini in exile for more than ten years. But once Khomeini and his loyalists took control in Tehran, Khomeini took aim at his former protector, with Khomeini calling upon Iraqi Shia' Muslims to turn on their own government—thus extending his Islamic Republic to Iraq. Khomeini and Saddam became bitter antagonists. Both were men, moreover, of absolute power.

"Disagree and you will be executed," Butti said of Saddam.

Conflict between Iraq and Iran stretched back for decades. Barely a year into Saddam's presidency, he declared war to stop the assaults by the Khomeini regime on Iraqi borders. Iraqi troops invaded the western border of neighboring Iran. The Iran-Iraq War, sometimes also called the First Persian Gulf War, lasted eight years, concluding with a ceasefire brokered by the United Nations. Khomeini later described his acceptance of the ceasefire as "worse than poison."

The war ended without border changes for either country and with no reparations. Casualty figures vary, but at least 500,000 Iraqi and Iranian soldiers died in the war. At least 100,000 civilians perished as well.

In Baghdad, Butti said, "Around 1979, we started having explosions in public areas" that he said were launched by the Islamist Shia' party, partly supported by Khomeini's regime. In short order, these events came to seem normal. "You see, we got used to it," Butti said. "In the Middle East, you get used to violence."

MEDICAL SCHOOL AMID THE BOMBING

In 1978, Butti fulfilled his parents' expectations when he entered the College of Medicine at Baghdad University. Its location next to the Ministry of Defense put students, faculty and patients at risk when the Iran-Iraq war broke out. Medical students like Butti did double duty as unofficial security guards, patrolling the halls of the school.

One evening, just as darkness was descending, Butti and his fellow students realized that an Iranian fighter plane was circling the area. Of course, he realized, the plane was probably trying to bomb the Ministry of Defense. But was the pilot using light from within the hospital to guide him? Butti and his classmates took it upon themselves to darken the medical complex.

"We ran through the hospital. I ran on the floors I was responsible for, knocking all the lights out with my shoe." He admitted that the image might sound comical but stressed that it was quite the opposite. "I am telling you like it was a funny story. It was not."

Students at the medical school were divided into alphabetical groups. As it happened, one person in his group was a young woman whose first name was Balsam. Half the class was female. But Butti, for his part, had gone to an all-male high school and was shy around the opposite sex. He of course took notice of the attractive female in his group but was too bashful at first to do anything about it.

"I did not get personally introduced to her until the second year," he said.

That was the same year he joined the Ba'ath Party, a move he describes as a "pragmatic choice." Once again, his father had been right to warn him away from political involvement when he was younger. A review by Lisa Blaydes, an associate professor at Stanford University, of more than ten million digitized pages of Ba'ath Party records housed at Stanford's Hoover Institution showed that Ba'ath Party monitoring of political activity by high school students was not uncommon. Blaydes also found that the party thrived on the circulation of rumors and propaganda. One widespread rumor, for example, held that President Bill Clinton's mother had been born in the Iraqi city of Mosul. (In fact, Virginia Clinton Kelley was born in Bodcaw, Arkansas.)

BA'ATH PARTY

In Iraq, the Ba'ath Party helped propagate the cult of personality that surrounded Saddam Hussein. When he took office as president of Iraq, Saddam also held the titles of chairman of the Revolutionary Command Council of Iraq, prime minister, and secretary general of the National Command of the Arab Socialist Ba'ath Party. Blaydes also found in her research that Saddam and the Ba'ath Party made sure that terror was a prevailing force in Iraqi society.

"As long as you were not opposing the regime, you were safe," Butti said.

So for Butti, joining the party was a practical step. "I didn't like what was happening, but I thought it was better to be inside than outside."

His classmate, Balsam Matti, was also part of the Ba'ath Party at the medical school. "We were called 'followers,'" Butti said. When Balsam withdrew from the party, it fell to Butti to try to persuade her to rethink her decision. But first, he had to introduce himself.

"I went up to her and said, 'I am Baher. Hello,'" he said. "And she looked at me and said, 'And?'"

This less-than-auspicious beginning turned out to be the start of a slow, cautious courtship.

"Iraq is very conservative," Butti explained. "To go out with a man, a woman is called slutty."

Nevertheless, by their third year in medical school, they were recognized as a couple. That Christmas, Baher invited Balsam to a party at his family's home. Two of her brothers came along as "escorts," by which Baher meant "guards." In the middle of their sixth year, the fix was in when Balsam's mother took matters into her own hands and arranged an engagement party. (Never mind that they were not yet officially engaged.) Two months after they finished medical school in 1984, Baher and Balsam were married. Although both families were Christian, there was a small theological hitch.

"My family is Syriac Orthodox; her family is Catholic," Butti said. By tradition in Iraq, a couple typically marries in the groom's house of worship. Just to be sure, Butti's new mother-in-law brought the Catholic archbishop to the ceremony. Their marriage began with bilateral benedictions.

"The Orthodox archbishop blessed me, and Balsam's archbishop blessed her," Butti said.

AT WORK, AT WAR

After a three-day lakeside honeymoon, the newlyweds went to work at hospitals run by the Ministry of Health. Following a year of residency, Butti was called up for mandatory service as a medical officer in the Iraqi army. Shortly after the Iraqi invasion of Kuwait in August 1990, Butti was released from service, allowing him to pursue his specialty in psychiatry.

The following January marked the start of the Gulf War's massive air campaign. Butti was on duty at a hospital housing 1,200 patients with chronic mental illness when he heard a sound he recognized from his military service at an air base. Butti knew a missile was headed their way.

He summoned a command from his military duty and shouted: "Fall to the ground!" to his colleagues and anyone else who was nearby. "Fortunately, that missile hit a septic tank."

Mental health care was "undeveloped" at that time in Iraq, Butti said. The field of clinical psychology was not even recognized. By 1999, Butti had become the director of the city's only mental health hospital. The working environment was tense in those final years of Saddam Hussein's rule. As is often the case in repressive regimes, spying was common, and trust among colleagues was thin. When a picture of Saddam Hussein hanging in a nurse's room disappeared, suspicions went wild. Was this an intentional act of disrespect to the nation's leader? Was it a simple mistake?

An investigation followed. Butti's former chief nurse accused him of protecting the nurse who had ripped the picture off the wall. Butti managed to protect himself by proving that the picture had been cut from a newspaper, an act that in and of itself was against the rules. Still, he was removed from his post by a security officer who in turn had been bribed by a staff member whom Butti had penalized previously.

Or, as he put it, "removed from my post, not sent to jail." So the bad news was, he lost his job. The good news was, he didn't end up in prison. "Too many things happened in the 1990s," he remarked.

The years leading up to the 2003 invasion of Iraq by the United States were tense. Harsh economic sanctions imposed in 1990 by the United Nations Security Council—four days after Iraq attacked Kuwait—had severely affected Iraq's economy. Iraq's health care system was badly hampered, as the sharp limitations on foreign trade resulted in a paucity of medical supplies. Disease and infant mortality increased. The cost of everyday goods, such as food, shot up, while at the same time, supplies of such goods shrank. Salaries shrank, even for professionals.

"When the sanctions happened," Butti said, the family had three children and two paychecks. Still, "it was living on the edge." By day, the two physicians had government jobs. By night, they worked at private clinics.

As UN sanctions tightened, neighboring Iran became one of Iraq's top trading partners, according to Suzanne Maloney, vice president and director of the foreign policy program at the Brookings Institution in Washington, DC. Although deep hostilities persisted following the prolonged Iran-Iraq War of the 1980s, the two countries shared not only a nearly thousand-mile border but also certain cultural and religious ties.

Butti watched his country crumbling around him. Butti was a

psychiatrist at Baghdad's al-Rashad psychiatric facility, and as it became clear that war was coming in early 2003, he grew fearful that Saddam might deploy weapons against his own people. Butti prepared a bottle of antidepressants for his own potential use.

Saddam, said the psychiatrist, "was stuck in his own grandiose delusions."

When the US attacks on Iraq started in 2003, bombs began exploding in the Buttis' neighborhood in the southern end of Baghdad. Their trim, ranch-style house was located near an oil refinery, a key target for US airstrikes.

"The neighborhood got bombed," he said.

Men took to patrolling the neighborhood at night, when so many of the bombings occurred. One night, Butti was out on such an ad hoc neighborhood guard mission when a friend invited him in for a beer. Suddenly, the two heard an enormous explosion close by. Butti's instinct as a doctor was to rush out and tend to any casualties. But his friend held him back—and then came the second big blast.

The people who were on the highway, where Butti would have been had his friend not stopped him, were injured, and some were killed. After that, Butti and his family went to live with his in-laws in the northern part of the city.

Insisting that Iraq was a storehouse of weapons of mass destruction, the United States was intent on ending the regime of Saddam Hussein. On April 9, 2003, that mission succeeded. On December 13, 2003, Saddam was captured while hiding in a hole near his hometown in Tikrit. In a trial before the Special Tribunal, Saddam was convicted of crimes against humanity for his role in a 1982 massacre that claimed the lives of 148 Iraqi Shi'ites. He was executed by hanging on December 30, 2006, at Camp Justice, a joint Iraqi-US military base in a suburb northeast of Baghdad.

But taking down Saddam only plunged Baghdad into further chaos. Looting was rampant. Buildings and houses were burned. Widespread corruption permeated the city. And as the United States disbanded the Iraqi army, forces from al-Qaida, the Islamic State, and pro-Iranian militias gathered strength.

Looters who descended on Butti's hospital stole drugs and whatever else they could get their hands on. Sewing had been a rehabilitation activity; the looters grabbed the sewing machines.

"People were in such poverty and despair," he said. "At the hospital, even the electrical plugs were taken."

What Butti called "intentional destruction" was seemingly everywhere.

"The museum was ransacked. Baghdad was burning. National treasures were burned. Yes, everything was stolen or destroyed," he said.

Factionalization pitted Iraqis against one another. Butti remembered a pharmacist at his hospital. He was Sunni, and our hospital was in a Shia area," he said. "And he was assassinated."

With some classmates from Baghdad College, Butti helped set up a group aimed at "psycho-social" rehabilitation with the formal name of the Baghdad Rehabilitation and Development Group. Among themselves, Butti and his colleagues called it The Bridge. In Butti's view, much of his country was suffering from a sort of mass case of post-traumatic stress disorder—except that there was very little "post" about the traumatic stress Iraqis were undergoing. By the end of 2003, chaos and violence continued in Baghdad.

"The pro-Iranians were assassinating important people," Butti said, such as "the dean of the medical school and an artist who sang a song for Saddam."

Kidnapping for ransom continued as a growth industry, Butti said. Sometimes the payment of a hefty ransom meant the return of a loved one. Other times the kidnappers took the money and ran, killing their victims anyway.

"Fortunately," Butti said, his voice heavy with irony, "psychiatrists (in Iraq) don't make much money."

Butti was among a handful of doctors who made exchange visits to other countries, starting with a visit to England in 2004. His friends there urged him to stay. And then his second-grade daughter's school bus was bombed. Seven-year-old Ula's entire face was covered with bandages when Butti reached the hospital. Today, he said, she still has scars on her lips and one arm.

He was heartbroken. His own little girl had nearly been killed. "And still I didn't leave Iraq," he said.

AN IRAQI "ENEMIES LIST"

When Butti visited his brother in the United Arab Emirates in 2006, his brother pleaded with him not to return to Iraq. That was when Butti learned that his name was on a list of five hundred people targeted for assassination. Butti knew that the lists were real, and that people whose names appeared on these lists were considered enemies of the state. The lists were essentially sentences of death.

"That rose the red flag for me," he said.

Along with writing anti-Iranian articles, Butti was a co-founder of the Iraqi Minorities Council. In 2004 he ran for the Iraqi parliament in 2004 as part of a national alliance representing Iraqi factions headed by a Sunni tribal leader named Nawaf Aljarba. Butti ran as a representative of the alliance's Christian faction. Even before he declared his candidacy, his proposal to establish something called the Gilgamesh Center for Creative Thinking had roused unwanted attention.

"A great number of Iraqi people are suffering a great deal because of the severed communication with the civilized world," Butti wrote in his proposal. "They suffer from lacking the ability to communicate with others, they have lost the hope in the future, they suspect anything foreign, they are not sufficient in their professional performance, they don't feel enough responsibility toward the society, they lack the power to experience freedom, they don't comprehend the correct performance of democracy, they cannot deal with group working. . . . Rebuilding what the war has destroyed is a simple effort if compared with the task of rebuilding the distorted human person."

Fundamentally, after so many years of wars and coups and countercoups, Iraqis had lost the ability to trust one another, Butti maintained.

"The trauma was always there, one way or another, for most of the people," he said. "We just lived with the trauma."

With the narrow ray of hope brought on by Saddam's ouster in 2003, "the technocrats, some of us, started trying to use this as a window for democracy." The bombings, the violence, the lootings, the killings: "Everything gets triggered again and again," he said. "It's just continuous."

When he wrote in his Gilgamesh proposal that Iraqis lacked "the power to experience freedom," Butti said he was referring to "this theme of creative chaos" that wracked his country.

"The national identity got into a kind of coma," he said.

Pivoting to the language of his profession, Butti wrote in a paper called "Roots and Reflections: The Lesson of History" that his country experienced a massive identity crisis. "Roots and Reflections" was published in *What They Carried*, a book written and illustrated by US photographer Jim Lomasson.

"The identity crisis of Iraqis started in 2003 when the national identity collapsed and sub-identities took over," Butti wrote. "This is because the fall of the regime was accompanied by dissolving the Iraqi state itself."

In 2006, Butti did manage to open a small facility aimed at improving psycho-social health. The al-Janna Center was financed by donations from a newspaper after none of the Iraqi officials he turned to would support his idea. Butti envisioned a place where lectures would alternate with poetry readings and computer classes.

But then came that 2006 visit to his brother in the UAE and his encounter with his name on a list of potential assassination victims.

He returned to Baghdad. His sons stayed behind to finish school, but Butti, Balsam, and Ula packed up. Two weeks later, they relocated to the UAE to stay with his brother. Butti brought his mother, Adeeba, with them. A lingering sadness for Butti is that he has not been able to return to the UAE since he sought asylum in the United States. His mother died in the UAE in 2009, "and I don't know where the cemetery is."

AN INVITATION

Late in 2005, Butti was interviewed in Baghdad by a reporter for National Public Radio (NPR). Thousands of miles away, in an unimaginably distant place called Portland, Oregon, a cultural psychiatrist named Dr. David Kinzie heard the broadcast. Kinzie had worked on mental health issues in Malaysia, India, and Vietnam, among other places. He founded the Intercultural Psychiatry Program at Oregon Health & Science University (OHSU), and had treated refugees from Cambodia, Bosnia, Somalia, and Guatemala. As director of the Intercultural Psychiatric

Clinic, Kinzie also had made a study of the effects of the terrorist attacks of September 11, 2001, on refugees who had experienced earlier traumas.

Butti's description on NPR of the pervasive sense of trauma in Baghdad rang true to Kinzie. He contacted Butti and invited him to attend the 2006 conference of the World Association of Cultural Psychiatry in Beijing.

Butti took a circuitous route to China, flying from the UAE to Jordan, and then on to Beijing. The return trip hit a roadblock when the UAE denied Butti an entrance visa. He was stuck in al-Salt, Jordan. His sons, having finished school in Baghdad, went to Syria when Jordan denied them entrance. Months passed, and then Dr. Kinzie contacted Butti once again. This time, he was inviting Butti to speak about the psychological and psychiatric consequences of war at OHSU.

With sponsorship from IPP and OHSU, Butti applied for asylum in the United States.

"I tried to teach people humanitarian attitudes, especially in my field of psychiatry, as an anti-stigma movement to defend the human rights of the mentally ill," Butti wrote in his asylum application. "I served my patients as a director of the only mental hospital for chronic long-stay patients in Iraq. Still, I was subjected to the effects of the dictatorship and tyranny of Saddam that caused corruption and injustices."

His work in mental health and his activism had put him at risk of grave harm. "Being a civil community activist," he wrote, "especially in the field of human rights and rights of minorities, these are not accepted by fundamentalists and extremists of all factions. Insurgents would target even humanitarian organizations if the organization receives international help, as it would be considered an ally to the Americans."

By 2009, Butti's entire family was reunited in Portland. Butti helped start an Arabic-language clinic within OHSU's Intercultural Psychiatric Program. Today he works at the Intercultural Counseling Center of Catholic Charities of Oregon. Butti marvels continually at the welcome he and his family have received.

"I even stayed at Dr. Kinzie's house for a few months," he said.

At a state senator's town hall, he met an activist named Kayse Jama, who founded the Center for Intercultural Organizing, and who is now an Oregon state senator, representing Portland. He met then mayor Tom

Potter of Portland at a meeting at Portland City Hall focusing on envisioning the city's future. After so many years of repression in Iraq, and so much fear swirling around any potential encounter with government leaders, he was struck by the openness of US elected officials.

"That was the moment when I realized people [in the United States] can make decisions for themselves," without fear of recrimination, he said. "I always say that if you are going to be outside your own country, you'd better be in America. Democracy is real. You are still allowed to speak here. You will not be assassinated."

ACTIVISM IN AMERICA

Arriving in the United States, Butti knew he immediately wanted to engage in activism. That impulse may have represented a form of compensation, he conceded—"a way of making up for my loss." Butti founded the Iraqi Society of Oregon in 2008, and at the time of our interview served as co-chair of the New Portland Policy Commission in the City of Portland.

To be sure, there were compromises. To be licensed to practice in the United States, foreign physicians must pass rigorous exams. Butti, by then in his late forties, decided that he did not need the title of medical doctor in order to work in mental health. But he continued his work as a counselor, acting as a sort of de facto psychiatrist without the title and trappings. In any case, he was helping people, and thus fulfilling the goals he had set for himself in Baghdad.

"I didn't feel that my identity was my degree," he said. As an intercultural counselor, "I am serving the people. As a mission in life, I am serving people of all levels."

Hoping at first to practice in Oregon, his wife did make several attempts to pass the rigorous medical licensing exams required for doctors who have been educated abroad. Every time, the clinical final exam tripped her up. Today she works as a medical interpreter, what Butti calls "a new way to channel her medical knowledge."

His sons both graduated from Portland State University. His daughter has plans to become a nurse. Both sons live close to their parents in Hillsboro. One son is married; the other is still a bachelor.

"No grandchildren yet," Butti said, poking fun at himself, "just a dog."

The family worships at St. Ignatius of Antioch Church—Portland's Syriac Orthodox Church. But even in a sacred setting—maybe especially in a sacred setting, Butti is not above challenging the authorities. Making fun of his outspoken tendencies, he said, "as usual, I am in a dispute with the priest."

Butti stays in touch with Iraqi colleagues via social media. He wrestles still with concerns about the fate of his country. When he gets too treacly, his friends step in. If he gets too nostalgic about Iraq, "they scold me. They say, 'OK, come here and get killed.'"

Recently, an opportunity to work at a university in southern Iraq came up. His loyalty to the land of his birth tugged hard at him. Butti considered applying for the job, "but I was unable to do it because of fear."

Though seldom allowing himself the luxury of true optimism about Iraq's future, Butti does not rule out the possibility one day of a productive relationship between the United States and his home country.

"We are hoping that this year something will happen," he said. But he sees political roadblocks: "The passivity of Obama (toward Iraq), that did not serve the Iraqi people. Trump, you just didn't know what he would do next. For Biden—well, he voted for the war and supported a plan to divide Iraq. But then it seems he changed his mind. We are watching. There are signs that there is going to be a change. But we do not know when, or how much. Small bites, they are happening."

For now, Butti is focusing on improving the intercultural experience in America. He keeps his sense of humor, laughing at the sometimes-heated discussions that unravel when he is at work at Catholic Charities of Oregon. He knows he is sometimes seen as the resident radical, and when he shoots his mouth off maybe a little too much, someone will say, "Oh, ask the Marxist."

"And that is when I shut my mouth," he said.

But he knows that he can speak now without fear of retribution. "At least we can put our voice out," he said.

"That is what I like about America."

A PART OF HISTORY

His ardent embrace of America's democratic principles does not fully cushion the blow of severing ties with Iraq. Starting with his grandfather, the newspaper publisher and Minister of Literature, Butti's family played a significant role in the modern history of an ancient country. Staking a claim to history matters, Butti said.

"It is something," he said, "for the family to keep the history, to be remembered. It is important for me, a family thing."

And so Butti takes pride in having been featured as part of a permanent exhibit at the Oregon Historical Society called Experience Oregon. The organization's website calls the seven-thousand-square-foot exhibit depicting the state's cultural diversity "the cornerstone of our museum."

Among the displays is a poster-sized photograph of Dr. Baher Butti, founder of the Iraqi Society of Oregon (http://www.iraqisocietyoforegon.org/). The interfaith, intercultural organization was founded to help newcomers from Iraq integrate into local communities, and to promote greater mutual understanding.

"Following the US invasion of Iraq in 2003," the accompanying legend reads, "thousands of Iraqis found refuge in Oregon. Like other refugees, they have endured by working collectively and building a cross-cultural sense of identity."

For Butti, his representation in the exhibit is both an honor and a kind of psychological homecoming. His new life, he said, now feels affirmed.

"I have this history rooted in my root home," he said, speaking of his family's long legacy in Iraq. "And now I am rooted in the history of my new home. I am not in Iraq. I am in Oregon. And now I am in the history of Oregon."

With this poster in the Oregon Historical Society, he continued, "I feel my mission in life to carry the legacy of my family history."

Psychiatrists over time have often focused on the meaning of "home." Just how does one anchor oneself? When does "home" mean not just a dwelling or a set of relatives, but a state of mind? Does "home" mean a sense of safety and security? "Home," does the very word imply geographic familiarity—hills or mountains or deserts or rivers or oceans that convey an instant sense of affinity?

For Butti, this is yet another reason that Oregon has come to feel like home.

Iraq, his home country, is a land of two rivers, the Tigris and the Euphrates. How fitting, he said, that he should find himself residing at the confluence of the Willamette and the Columbia.

"And now we are in the land of two rivers," he said. "I achieved the mission of my family in the new chapter of my life."

Dr. Baher Butti at home in Hillsboro, Oregon. Photo by Jim Lommasson

Evelyn Banko. Photo by John Rudoff

CHAPTER 10

A Vibrant Jewish Presence Is Snuffed Out

Evelyn Banko (Austria)

More than eight hundred years of Jewish life in Vienna saw prolonged periods of persecution punctuated by decades when Jewish residents of the Austrian capital made great strides in business, education, and the arts. A turning point came with the reign of Emperor Franz Joseph, who in 1867 gave Jewish citizens the same civil, political, and religious rights that other Austrians enjoyed. It is hardly a coincidence that during this same time frame, Vienna blossomed as a major European cultural center. Jewish artists and intellectuals such as Gustav Mahler, Arnold Schoenberg, Alfred Adler, symbolist painter Gustav Klimt, and the philosopher Martin Buber played key roles in Vienna's late cultural growth in the late nineteenth and early twentieth centuries.

According to the Jewishvirtuallibrary.org, a "Jewish renaissance" that started in Vienna in 1848 lasted up to World War II. Three out of the four Austrian Nobel Prize winners during this time were Jewish. More than half of Vienna's doctors and dentists, and more than 60 percent of the city's lawyers were Jewish. Jews made up just 3 percent of the Austrian population, but in Vienna, that figure was 10 percent.

Throughout the 1930s, many Jews had assimilated into Christian society. By 1938, the Jewish population in Vienna numbered around 185,000. Family memoirs from that period describe an active café society among many Jews.

Also among the prominent Jewish residents of Vienna was Sigmund Freud, widely viewed as the father of the field of psychoanalysis. The house at Bergasse 19 in Vienna's Alsegrund district where Freud lived for forty-seven years and produced most of his writings is now a museum. Freud was able to flee Vienna in 1938, escaping first to Paris and then to London.

Before 1938, Vienna was home to twenty-two synagogues and more than fifty Jewish houses of prayer. There was a Jewish museum, along with Jewish schools, libraries, sports clubs, political associations, newspapers and magazines, and charitable organizations. One of the largest such charitable groups was the Jewish World War I Veterans' Association.

But as the Nazi party took hold in neighboring Germany, anti-Jewish sentiment was on the rise in Austria. Neither Jews nor Roma were allowed to vote in a plebiscite in April 1938, in which 99 percent of voters enthusiastically supported a union with Germany. Anti-Jewish legislation swiftly followed, forcing many Jews from their jobs.

Tanks and troops led by German Chancellor Adolf Hitler—an Austrian by birth—rolled into Austria on March 12, 1938. To a Vienna crowd that showered him with thunderous applause, Hitler declared: "As leader and chancellor of the German nation and Reich, I announce to German history now the entry of my homeland into the German nation."

Harassment of Jews in Vienna became rampant. Jews were subjected to public insults and humiliation, forced to scrub sidewalks or clean public toilets. Jewish-owned businesses were vandalized. Non-Jewish neighbors thought nothing of hurling anti-Semitic invectives at Jews they had once greeted on the street as friends and neighbors.

In 1938, Austria also became home to a notorious Nazi concentration camp called Mauthausen. The camp, not far from the city of Linz, was located near an abandoned stone quarry. Inmates were forced to carry heavy stones up 186 steps to the camp, a passageway so steep and treacherous that it became known as "the Stairway of Death."

Then came Kristallnacht—"Night of Broken Glass"—November 8–9, 1938. Civilians joined with members of the Nazi party to form mobs that rampaged the city, while police offered no intervention. Many businesses known to be owned by Jews were torched, and all but one of the city's synagogues and Jewish houses of prayer were burned to the ground. Though the interior of the remaining synagogue was destroyed, the

Nazis and their supporters did not burn the whole building because it was too close to Nazi headquarters in the Hotel Metropole. Kristallnacht also brought the arrests of hundreds of prominent Jews.

Close to three-quarters of Vienna's Jews managed to escape, many to the United States. Visitors to Vienna today cannot help but notice the "Solperstein" commemorative cubes embedded in many sidewalks. "Here lived . . ." followed by the name and life and death dates of a Jewish victim of the Nazi extermination. "Solperstein" translates to "stumbling stone," an ironic twist on an old expression from Nazi Germany. If one stumbled over a protruding stone, it was said, "a Jew must be buried here."

For many years, Austria adhered to an uncomfortable ambivalence about its complicit role in the treatment of Jews during World War II. But beginning in 1995, the Austrian government started to introduce legislation that provided benefits to Austrian victims of the Nazis. The National Fund for Victims of National Socialism was soon followed by a 1998 art restitution law. Working in tandem with the United States, Austria to date has returned more than 32,000 art objects to their rightful owners, according to a report by the US Department of State. These efforts continue. As recently as 2010, Austria set up a Fund for Jewish Cemeteries.

FLEEING HITLER'S HATRED, FINDING A HOME FAR AWAY

The sanctuary of the First United Methodist Church in Southwest Portland is a cavernous space, and on August 16, 1958, the pews bulged as Evelyn Diamant became the bride of Richard Banko. Her parents, Joseph and Frieda Diamant, looked on with love and pride as their only child exchanged a kiss with her new husband. Richard was not Jewish, but far from feeling concerned that Evelyn had neither married a man of their Jewish faith nor solemnized her vows in a synagogue, their daughter said the Diamants may have felt some sense of relief.

"They didn't want me to grow up Jewish," Evelyn said more than fifty years later. "They were afraid of anti-Semitism."

The Diamants had good reason to be afraid. The couple had lost nearly all their own relatives to the Nazi Holocaust. They were afraid because

Frieda and Joseph Diamant, Evelyn's parents, in 1933. Photo courtesy of Banko family archives

before they fled Europe they had suffered indignities on account of their faith. They were afraid because in Germany their passports had been stamped with a large pink "J." They were afraid because they had witnessed first-hand the contagious fire of fascism—when hate can escalate with terrifying speed.

Years later, living in Portland, Oregon, Evelyn's mother was in her nineties and had become somewhat forgetful. One day, she asked her daughter why she hadn't been raised Jewish.

"Because you were afraid," Evelyn answered.

THE DIAMANTS' DIAMONDS

Born in Vienna in 1936, Evelyn Banko is now a widow herself. She lives in Lake Oswego, a suburb about eight miles south of Portland. Her late husband taught special education students in Oregon City schools. Evelyn, an elementary school teacher, began teaching second grade students at Sumner School in the Parkrose neighborhood of Portland when she was twenty-one years old. Her long teaching career went on to take her to the Parkrose School District, and elsewhere in Portland, at Grout, Robert Gray K-8 School, and Hayhurst Elementary School before she went into Teacher On Special Assignment (TSOA) work. As an instructional specialist, she worked with schools in the Wilson High School District.

On her left hand, Evelyn's engagement ring sparkles with a diamond her mother spirited out of Vienna when she, her husband, and their toddler daughter escaped in 1938, just months after Hitler's troops stormed in and claimed Austria as part of Germany. The stones were valuable, Frieda Diamant reasoned, and might come in handy once they made their way to the United States.

Like the Diamants themselves, the diamonds took a circuitous route to their eventual home in Oregon. After the Nazi takeover of Austria, the Diamants had learned of an exit route through Latvia. Frieda Vielgut Diamant, known as Fritzi, had no trouble taking the stones out of Vienna. In Latvia, she planned to sew the loose stones into a belt. But friends in Riga warned her that someone might alert guards about Fritzi's jewelry. What if they abducted Fritzi in order to steal the jewels? What would happen to little Evie if her mother disappeared?

From Vienna, the family made their way to Latvia. When the Russians overtook that country—along with Lithuania and Estonia—Russian authorities told Fritzi that she could only take as much jewelry as she could wear.

In Riga, the Diamants waited for the necessary paperwork—an affidavit of support and visas—that would allow them to travel. The first set of papers routed them through Sweden. But when the Germans took over neighboring Denmark—through which they would have to pass in order to reach Sweden—that plan became unworkable. The next path was through Italy. But with the Italians on the side of Hitler's Germany, that course became too dangerous as well. Finally, from Riga they boarded a train that took them to Moscow, Siberia, China, and Japan, until—after an odyssey of more than two years—they reached the Pacific coast of the United States.

Fritzi had grown up in privilege. Her Viennese uncles had many houses, some along the Danube River. They took her on vacations to

Italy and around Austria. They had domestic help. Evelyn doubts that her mom ever set foot in a kitchen while she was growing up.

"My mother didn't know how to clean, how to cook," Evelyn said. "She knew nothing about housework."

Fritzi was twelve years old when she met sixteen-year-old Joseph. They married after Joseph finished his training as an engineer and started his own business. One of Fritzi's uncles gave them an apartment, rent-free for three years, as a wedding present. While they were in Austria, Fritzi never worked outside the home, and when their daughter came along, she became a full-time mother.

Fritzi played cards and loved to frequent Vienna's famous coffee houses. They lived in comfort. Joseph ran a business that imported and sold automotive parts. There was some irony to this because, as Evelyn later noted, "Dad didn't know anything about cars or tires."

Joseph doted on his wife and loved to buy jewelry for her.

But for the Diamants, as for other prosperous Jews in Vienna, things changed fast when German troops rolled into Austria on March 12, 1938. Cheering crowds greeted Hitler's forces as they crossed the border. Some waved Nazi flags. Others offered the straight-armed Nazi salute.

The Anschluss—the official name for the annexation of Austria into Germany—had personal significance for German Chancellor Adolf Hitler, the Austrian-born Führer of the Nazi government.

"I announce to German history now the entry of my homeland into the German Reich," he declared as he and his troops reached Vienna.

The campaign against Viennese Jews began overnight. Jews were rounded up and forced out of the city. Houses and shops were plundered. Anti-Jewish laws were put in place. Jews could not own a business nor hold most jobs. They were not permitted to ride public transportation. Jewish children could not own bicycles or go to school. Suddenly, non-Jewish friends who in earlier times would have greeted their Jewish acquaintances on the street, hastily crossed to the other side when they spotted someone Jewish.

Joseph realized he needed to get his family out of Austria—and ideally, out of Europe. The United States, traditionally a beacon of hope for immigrants, offered the best prospect as a safe haven. But the United

States had tough immigration quotas. These restrictions, introduced in the isolationist period that followed World War I, limited the number of people who could enter the United States from any one country. Under US policy, immigrants applying for visas also were required to produce affidavits from US citizens. One affidavit was expected to support the applicant's moral character; the other, to attest to financial stability.

After the Anschluss, Joseph tried to liquidate his business so the family could leave. As tensions spread among Vienna's Jewish community, both he and Fritzi decided to go to an Umschulung, a retraining program that focused on trades and manual labor. Joseph, who had always had an artistic streak, learned to design belts and purses. Fritzi learned to sew on leather and left the Umschulung with a document certifying her as a qualified seamstress.

THE ROAD TO RIGA

In seeking an escape route out of Austria, the Diamant family joined what amounted to a mass migration. Between 1938 and 1940, according to the US State Department, approximately 117,000 Jewish people fled Austria to countries around the world. They were the fortunate ones, as about 65,000 Austrian Jews perished in the Holocaust, US State Department records show.

The Diamant family already had passports—stamped by now with the pink "J" that identified them as Jewish—and through his attorney, Joseph learned the family could obtain tourist visas to travel to Latvia. Then, in August 1938, a friend who had joined ranks with the Nazis warned Joseph that if he returned home that night, he would either be arrested and deported to a concentration camp, or possibly killed. Joseph stayed away, returning five days later to gather up Fritzi and little Evie.

There had been payoffs, enabling them to obtain visas and tickets for the trains. Others were not so lucky. As Fritzi later told Evie, they strode past people waiting in line as they boarded the train for Riga, the capital of Latvia.

By nature, Joseph was gregarious. On the train, he befriended a man who connected the family with a lawyer in Riga. The Diamants became friends with the attorney and his family, and in their two years in Riga, celebrated Jewish holidays at his home.

Other relatives had joined the Diamants in Riga, and together they set up a small business, making belts and purses that they then sold to stores.

Evelyn remembers little of the drama—or the anxiety that gripped her parents and other Viennese Jews. In fact, she remembers nothing about Vienna. Many decades later, when she and her mother made a pilgrimage to Austria, it was as if Evelyn were seeing the city for the first time.

Of course, she was just two when the family made their hasty departure from Vienna. Her memories of Riga are those of a child. For instance, she recalls running down a staircase and bumping into a boy at the base of the stairs. In the impact, he scratched her nose. The scar stayed with her for many years.

Life in Riga was comfortable at first. But with war raging all around it, Latvia could not long remain immune from its impacts.

"We knew it was going to be either the Russians or the Nazis that came in, and for us, very luckily, it was the Russians," Evelyn said during a 2008 interview recorded at the Oregon Jewish Museum and Center for Holocaust Education (OJMCHE).

"There was no fighting at all," she said. "They took over Latvia, Lithuania and Estonia and just marched in, and all of a sudden, it was part of Russia." Again, the memories of a child: "The only thing I remember about that is that all of a sudden, this man's picture was in every single store window, and of course it was Stalin. And his picture was put in all the stores in Latvia."

Word filtered down that fifteen hundred people would be allowed to leave Latvia. Among that number were twenty-three Jewish refugees. Fortunately, the Diamants were included on the roster of those permitted to leave. Joseph Diamant was put in charge of the group. Just before they were to leave, the Russians escorted Joseph, an engineer, and a physician named Dr. Norbert Fell into an interrogation room. They kept them all night, offering enticements for them to remain in Russian-held territory. It was clear, according to his daughter, that "they didn't want educated people leaving the country" when war with Germany was imminent.

At the last minute, the interrogators relented. Joseph and Dr. Fell were allowed to leave with their families. But the Russians added a strong caveat. In her OJMCHE interview, Evelyn said the interrogators told her father, "'We're going to let you go to America; we have a lot of people in the United States and if we ever come to you this is going to be our secret password and we expect you to help us.'

"And of course, my dad said yes, he would, just to get us out of the country," Evelyn said. The implicit understanding, according to Evelyn, was that if pressed, her father would be expected to spy for the Russians.

Finally, "at the last minute," Evelyn continued "they said to him, 'OK, you are all ready to go.'" The next morning, the Diamants boarded a train out of Latvia. It was August 1940. Evelyn was four years old. Their first stop after Riga: Moscow.

THE LONG, LONG RIDE

On the long train ride, the bond between Joseph Diamant and Dr. Fell tightened. Their families grew closer as well. Dr. Fell's wife Jenny formed a fast friendship with Fritzi. Evie fell into games of chase, up and down the train's long aisles, with Alice Fell, four years Evie's senior. Many years later, Alice Fell would write a memoir, *Becoming Alice,* under her married name, Alice Rene. Evie did not know that she would be included in the book—along with a photograph—and identified by the pseudonym of Trudy Feldman. Evie and Alice remain close today.

The Diamants and the Fells decided on that trip that wherever they would end up in the United States, they would go together. On the train ride, Fritzi asked Jenny Fell to wear one of her diamond brooches, to make her own glittering accessories appear a little less flashy.

The Trans-Siberian Railroad that would take them to China ran only on certain days, so the two families spent three days in Moscow. Joseph Diamant and Norbert Fell took it upon themselves to go to the German Embassy and ask for money. They were rewarded with a cache of rubles, "worthless money," as far as the Germans were concerned.

Joseph Diamant divided the money among the small group of Jewish refugees he had been appointed to lead. Everyone went out to go shopping, only to discover, Evelyn said, that "there was nothing to be bought in any of the stores. The stores were absolutely empty. And not only that, but every single night, people would line up in front of all the office buildings."

Someone from the refugee group who spoke Russian asked what the lines meant. It turned out these were homeless people, waiting to sleep in empty offices after they were closed for the day.

Evie and her mother were walking down a Moscow street when they saw "some Jewish man" selling shoelaces. The man spoke in Yiddish. Again, from the OJMCHE interview: "And he said to my mother: 'Don't stay here. Get out of this country. If I were selling this shoelace for one kopek more than what they tell me to, they would kill me. This is a terrible place to be.'"

The Trans-Siberian Railroad comes by its name honestly. The ride across Siberia was long and cold, Evie said. Everyone aboard was thirsty because there was so little water. The Diamants drew stares of envy because they had thought to pack pillows and down comforters for the trip. Food on the train was scarce and "very, very salty"—a steady diet of canned red caviar. Armed guards were stationed outside each train car.

Here is something else Evelyn remembers from that long journey: To enter Japan, they needed a visa. Because Japan was an ally of Germany, the only Japanese consulate that was open in Europe was in Germany. When the visas came back to the Diamants, they were stamped with the eagle that symbolized the Nazi regime. Although neither of her parents had been given middle names, their new visas assigned them middle names. Just in case there was any confusion about their ethnicity, the Germans had supplied middle names from the Old Testament, making the visas out to Joseph Israel Diamant and Frieda Sara Diamant. Evelyn was also given the name of Sara.

The Nazis' renaming policy began in the 1930s. People of the Jewish faith in Germany were deemed a "race," as distinguished simply from followers of a religion or culture. Nazi officials began requiring Jews to adopt names from a list issued by the German government. The list contained 185 male names and 91 names for females. In 1939, the policy was tightened yet again. Any Jewish man in Germany whose first name was not on the approved list became Israel, and any Jewish woman without an approved first name became Sara. The protocol was a further example of how Germans stripped Jews not only of their jobs and possessions, but of their given name—and in that sense, of their very identities.

Evelyn also remembers that when the train passed through military installations, heavy metal bars descended on the windows. Evelyn was a kid; she was curious: What was out there? But her mother warned her not to look out the windows or she could be killed.

As the train inched toward Manchuria, all the passengers stepped off, carrying their baggage. They walked across the invisible border separating Siberia and Manchuria and boarded their next train.

Next came two days in Harbin, China, a city whose harsh weather has earned it the moniker "Ice City." At last, the train pulled into the coastal city of Dalian (also called Dairen), a port claimed by the Japanese after the Russo-Japanese War (1904–1905). The Diamants and the Fells had arrived just in time for both a typhoid and a cholera epidemic. Evelyn remembers that everyone she saw was masked.

WELCOMING ARMS

At every stop in China, someone from the Hebrew Immigrant Aid Society (HIAS) would greet the small group headed by Joseph Diamant. HIAS was founded in a storefront in lower Manhattan in 1881 with the purpose of helping Jewish immigrants fleeing pogroms in Eastern Europe. As the years passed, the persecution continued and refugees sought sanctuary, HIAS established outposts around the globe.

"And they would give us money for food, and tell us a place to stay," Evelyn remembered in the OJMCHE interview. "Whether it was a nice hotel or a gymnasium floor or whatever, but we had somewhere to stay."

In Dalian, Evelyn said her mother spotted a house where a European family was living. Fritzi looked wistfully at the family's grand chandelier and linen tablecloth, wondering if she would ever again enjoy the luxuries she had taken for granted in Vienna.

Next came Kobe, Japan, where the families awaited the Japanese ship that would take them at last to the United States. They sailed in August 1940, one of the last Japanese ships to sail to North America before the Japanese attack on Pearl Harbor.

The voyage was dreadful. Their quarters, such as they were, were on the ship's lowest deck, "like steerage," in Evelyn's memory. They slept in small bunks and were already suffering from seasickness when a typhoon hit. Only her father and two other male passengers escaped the wretched nausea.

"They were the only people that, through that whole voyage, went up to the restaurant and got food," Evelyn said.

At last the ship made port in September in Vancouver, British Columbia, Canada. All told, the journey from Riga had lasted six weeks. The Diamants actually had relatives in British Columbia. But Canada was at war with Germany, the country that issued their passports, so they were not permitted to leave the ship.

In Seattle, the Diamants and the Fells were given the choice between settling in San Francisco or Portland. They chose the smaller city, figuring there would be more opportunities. Besides, they had looked at a map, and the Cascade Range reminded them of the Austrian Alps.

Joseph Diamant turned forty three days after they arrived in the United States in August 1940. Evelyn contracted whooping cough while they were in Seattle, so she was housebound at the boardinghouse they were sent to in Portland. Every day she looked longingly at the children playing across the street. She could hardly wait to join them. When she was declared well enough to go out, she ran across to play—and could not understand one word the other children were saying.

"Mommy," she yelled to her mother, in German, "I don't understand anything."

In German, Fritzi yelled back, "I don't either."

But Evie picked up her new language quickly, and soon enrolled at the Fruit & Flower preschool, then located in downtown Portland. Even before Joseph could find work, Fritzi landed a job as a seamstress at the precursor to White Stag sportswear, Hirsch-Weis. As a refugee, Fritzi earned $9 a week, $3 less than non-refugee employees. Evie remembers that her first "new" clothes in the United States were actually used clothes provided by a service agency from Portland's First Christian Church.

Soon enough, Joseph found a job—as a janitor. "Here's my dad, with a college education, working as a janitor," Evie reflected. "That's how completely their lives were uprooted."

Joseph's next job was as a service station attendant. This was another irony, Evie pointed out, because her father knew nothing about cars. "But you do whatever it takes," she said. Her father's entrepreneurial spirit took hold, and before long he decided to try to open his own service station. He contacted Texaco and learned that a new station was planned at the corner of Southeast 17th Avenue and Holgate Street. Despite his poor English—and his equally pitiful ignorance about cars and trucks—Joseph jumped at the offer to lease the station and manage it.

"So here's my dad, who's never fixed a flat tire in his life, and never did anything with a car, all of a sudden fixing flats, changing oil, doing all these things in the service station," Evelyn told OJMCHE.

Fritzi found a nearby house to rent on Reynolds Street, just off Milwaukie Avenue in Southeast Portland. Maybe two or three weeks after they moved in, people started showing up to walk through their home. When Fritzi called the agent who had rented them the house, she learned that the owners actually wanted to sell it. The Diamants took a few deep breaths: maybe they could make the purchase. Joseph borrowed some money from a customer at the service station, and suddenly they were homeowners.

On December 7, 1941, Japanese forces attacked Pearl Harbor, marking the US entry into World War II. Joseph had been fighting competition from two other service stations close to his own. When the managers from those stations joined the US armed forces, business at Joseph's station expanded. He worked seven days a week, often twelve or fourteen hours a day. Within six months they had paid off their loan.

Evie started kindergarten at Brooklyn Elementary School. At the end of each school day she would walk to her dad's service station and stay there until her mother got off work at 6 p.m. from Hirsch-Weis. Many evenings, the little family walked across the street to the Semaphore Restaurant for dinner. If Joseph spotted a car pulling up to his station, he would rush across to help his customer, then hurry back to finish his meal.

They had a house. They had two good jobs. Their daughter was happy in her new school. Through a customer at the Texaco station, Joseph found a new job selling automotive ignition parts—another irony, because it was much like his former job in Vienna.

"We probably had a better life than a lot of immigrants," Evie said.

WHAT'S IN A NAME?

Evie was so young that she does not know quite when or where it happened, but soon after they arrived in the United States, someone suggested that they should Americanize their names. This, of course, was a familiar experience at New York's Ellis Island, where immigrants often emerged with newly sanitized, "all-American" identities that bore no resemblance to their original names. But the Diamants had entered the country through Seattle, not Ellis Island. Instead of "Diamant," they were advised, they should use the American version: "Diamond." But Joseph was adamant that they should not trade the final "d" in their last name for a "t."

Why? "I don't know," said Evelyn. "Because it was his name."

But there was a compromise: Trade the final "a" in their surname for an "o." And so the Diamant family became the Diamonts.

"Also," Evie said, "they told my mother that Frieda and Fritzi were too German-sounding." It was, after all, 1940 and the United States was nearly at war with Germany. Her mother agreed to a change but insisted that she wanted to keep "F" as the first letter of whatever name she adopted. From then on she was known as Florence.

A CLOSE COMMUNITY

Perhaps because it was not large, the community of Jewish immigrants in Portland was very close, Evelyn said. They formed a group called the Friendship Club that met monthly until at least 1960. They gathered at the Neighborhood House, or sometimes at the Jewish Community Center. Evie remembers parties to celebrate Purim, a festival celebrating the survival of Persian Jews in the fifth century BC. They invited speakers to address the group, held dinners, and once, Evie remembers, even performed an opera.

Some of the families became so close that Evie referred to them as her aunts and uncles. She had left Austria too young to remember any of her biological relatives, and in any case, most had perished in the Holocaust.

In the absence of a biological family, she said, they created a new kind of family.

Still, Evie knew no one outside the Friendship Club who was Jewish. In elementary school, she was the only Jewish child. She never encountered bias, but her parents decided nonetheless "it would be better if they didn't tell people we were Jewish."

So she had an ecumenical childhood. She attended B'nai B'rith camp, but also went to a Christian camp. She went to Bible school with her best girlfriends. Years later, when Evie finally began speaking about her family's experience, one of her oldest friends expressed amazement.

"I always wondered why you left Austria," said the friend, who had no idea that Evie was Jewish. She and Evie had gone to Bible school together.

Yet the family pored over a weekly publication called *The Aufbau* that catered to German-speaking Jews. The journal, founded in New York City in 1934, listed writers such as Thomas Mann and Hannah Arendt among its contributors. Even Albert Einstein wrote for *The Aufbau*. But its main appeal in the Diamant house were the lists it published of Holocaust victims and survivors. Fritzi Diamant never stopped hoping that she would find the names of her father and brother on the survivors' list. But that never happened.

Just once, after the family settled in Portland, Fritzi went into a synagogue.

"She told me she walked in, and all she saw were the faces of her dead relatives," Evie said. Except for funerals and other occasions, Fritzi never went back to a synagogue.

SEEKING FAMILY HISTORY

Joseph's sister Hilda, her husband and Joseph's niece, Vera, and nephew, Walter, were sent to Jasenovac in the Slavonia region of Croatia, one of World War II's largest and most notorious concentration camps. The United States Holocaust Memorial Museum estimates that between 77,000 people and 99,000 people—Jews, Roma, and others—were murdered at Jasenovac from 1941 to 1945.

Walter's mother, father, and sister died in the camp. But Walter was an electrician, and his captors needed his skills. He managed to survive until close to the end of the war, when upwards of two thousand prisoners stormed the guards.

"About eighty escaped and Walter was one of them," Evelyn Banko said. "He was picked up by the communists in Yugoslavia and brought back to health." Walter eventually settled in Israel.

In the United States, Fritzi Diamant tried and tried to cut through the red tape that was preventing her brothers, Max and Walter, from joining them. "But of course, all the immigration laws made that impossible," Evelyn said.

Fritzi's brother Max was not so lucky. Max Vielgut was sent to four concentration camps. He died in 1945 at Buchenwald just weeks before the camp was liberated.

In the early 1980s, after the death of her father, Evelyn and her mother made a sort of sentimental pilgrimage to locate family members who had dispersed around Europe and elsewhere. They went to England to visit Fritzi's favorite cousin's daughter, and then to Paris, "just because it was Paris."

And then the Diamants went to Vienna.

"My mother took me around to the apartment I had lived in as a child, my dad's office and all the places that were familiar to her," said Evelyn. "I honestly don't think I have any memories (of those places) at all, just vague memories until we got to the United States. Everything I know is what people told me."

The same overseas trip took Evie and her mother to visit relatives of her father who had survived the war and settled in Israel. One relative was a cousin of Evie's father who had been sent from Vienna to Shanghai—alone—as a seventeen-year-old girl. "They had to get her out because she was in so much danger," Evie explained. Eventually the rest of her family was able to join the cousin and her parents in China, and after World War II came to an end, they joined the hundreds of thousands of Jews who sought new lives in Israel.

The family lived in the beautiful city of Netanya, beside the Mediterranean Sea. For Evie, the surprise was when her father's aunt presented her with her own parents' wedding invitation.

"They had brought it from Vienna and then to China and then to

Israel," Evie said. "Can you imagine?"

For Evie, the wedding invitation was a small treasure—a tangible connection to the life in Vienna she could scarcely remember. The visit to Israel also meant a lot to her because some of her relatives there remembered her as a baby in Vienna. The memories they shared helped her round out a picture of a childhood she had left behind when she and her parents abruptly fled Vienna.

A MATTER OF LUCK

As she grew interested in her own family's story, as well as the experiences of others who survived World War II in Europe, Evelyn became a speaker at OJMCHE. She is convinced that beyond the evil politics that engineered the deaths of six million Jews and others, survival or its alternative came down to luck.

"For everybody, something involved luck. Either bad luck or good luck," Evelyn said. The Diamants were fortunate. Quick thinking and some lucky breaks helped them escape.

"The rest of my family, it was all bad luck," she said. "My immediate family, all of them died in the Holocaust."

In fact, the memorial wall of a synagogue in Prague lists twenty-three Diamant family members who were killed in concentration camps. In Vienna, the new Shoah Wall of Names Memorial—officially inaugurated on November 9, 2021—has at least twenty-three more names of her family.

Evelyn Banko was married and the mother of two children when she began digging into her family's history. She remembered that her mother had managed to bring a large box with them when they came to America. In it were family photographs, even her father's baby pictures from 1900 and her mother's first pictures from 1904.

While his grandmother was still alive, Evelyn's son James often visited her at her apartment in downtown Portland. James went through every photograph in the box with his grandmother and wrote the name of each person on the back of each photo.

Evelyn also found letters from her Uncle Max written on tissue-thin blue stationery. Max's handwriting was elegant, and he wrote in tiny script,

Evelyn and Richard Banko with their children, Michelle (now Michelle Banko Lancaden) and Joseph, at their home in the Hillsdale section of Southwest Portland. Photo courtesy of Banko family archives

on both sides of the pages. After so many years, the ink had bled through, making the letters difficult to read. Evelyn presented Max's letters to the Holocaust Memorial Museum in Washington, DC, and, in return, they later gave her a book with all the letters reprinted in legible form.

"The other day, for some reason, I just picked up the book and read the letters," she said. Evelyn also discovered an article from a historian who had written an article about Max titled "A Viennese Jew Trapped In Vichy France."

In the large rectangular box that her mother had kept, Evelyn was also surprised to discover a cache of letters from her grandparents. Many were censored, and as she noted, it is possible that some of the correspondence never got through.

"The letters talked about the weather. The weather is terrible, the weather is getting worse," she said. But "the weather" was a code phrase: "'The weather' was, of course, the Nazis," said Evelyn. All the letters stopped in 1942, "because that was when everybody was picked up and taken to the camps.

From their safe perch in America, the Diamants held out hope that the hatred that had killed their family members might have faded with the years. To celebrate their fiftieth wedding anniversary, Joseph and Fritzi went back to Vienna.

"My mother knocked on the door of the last apartment she lived in," Evelyn said. Fritzi explained that the home had once been theirs. The warm greeting they had hoped for did not take place. Evelyn continued, "The woman who opened the door wouldn't even talk to her, just slammed the door."

To stave off boredom in his retirement, Joseph Diamant had taken up baking. The rich chocolate cakes of his homeland were his specialty. The day before he died of an aneurysm on June 6, 1981, Joseph brought a homemade Sacher Torte to a party Richard and Evelyn were having for other special education teachers. He drove himself to the Bankos' house, and before he left for home, made a point of sitting and talking with Evelyn for an unusually long time. The next day, he was gone.

Fritzi Diamant died fourteen years later. Her stomach was bothering her; something was not right. Evelyn drove her to an emergency room. Fritzi's mind had slipped a little, Evelyn said, but not so much that she didn't compliment her granddaughter Michelle on her outfit shortly before she closed her eyes for the final time.

SPEAKING OUT

In 1991, an Anne Frank exhibit was scheduled to open at the First United Methodist Church in downtown Portland. Evelyn's friend, Janie Rosenbaum, decided to invite as many people as she could to speak about their Holocaust experiences.

Evelyn was a bit perplexed. "I had never even thought about speaking," she said. "At the time I was still (working) for the school district," by then in an administrative capacity. Besides, as she pointed out, "I was not a hidden child. I was not in a camp. I never suffered in any way. I was very lucky."

Still, she asked for and received permission to speak, provided her appearances did not interfere with her schedule at the school district. The ad hoc Holocaust-survivors' speaking circuit introduced Evelyn to people she had never met, such as a minister who helped liberate a concentration camp at the end of the war. She became friendly with survivors Eva and Les Aigner, realizing later that she had once gotten her hair done at Eva's salon on Southwest King Street.

Another friend, Miriam Greenstein, had never even told her own children that she had survived Auschwitz until she saw a swastika painted at Cleveland High School.

Because she was so young when she and her family escaped the Nazis, Evelyn focused her talks on the toll that prejudice and hatred take on humanity. "I think my talks were always more education-based," she said. "As a teacher, I thought it was so important that we get to the schools." Evelyn worried, for instance, about the growth of gangs in Portland and elsewhere—groups that often include and exclude on the basis of race or ethnicity.

"I thought it was so important to talk about acceptance," she said.

In 2019, Oregon became the twelfth US state to mandate Holocaust and genocide education as part of the public-school curriculum, from kindergarten through high school. As a teacher in Portland for thirty-plus years, Evelyn Banko was overjoyed by this development.

"When I talk to the kids, I say that this happened almost eighty years ago, so why is it important now?" Evelyn says. "I tell them that if we don't learn to get along with people, and we don't show humanity to others, we're never going to have peace in the world."

Evelyn admonishes her young audiences to keep their eyes and ears open for subtle—or maybe not subtle—signs of prejudice.

"I tell them, 'If you see people making fun of someone, or if you hear a joke that is not appropriate, say something,'" she said. "And then I always say, 'And when you are eighteen, be sure to vote!'"

Telling these stories—hers and the experiences of other survivors of cruelty and despotism—is important for more than historical value, Evelyn contends. "I tell the story of how someone can have a normal life, and all of a sudden it falls apart, because of hate," she said. "If more people stood up and said, 'This is wrong,' it might not happen."

But her biggest message is this: "Don't be a bystander. Pick what you can do. But don't just stand there and let it happen."

THE PAYOFF AND THE FUTURE

Even the most idealistic educator knows it is virtually impossible to reach every student in a room. So when a lesson does get through, it's as magical for the teacher as it is for the student.

"The nicest thing is the letters I get from students," Evelyn said, smiling into the Zoom camera while her fourteen-year-old dog, Wrigley, slumbered beside her. Sometimes, in pre-pandemic times, students would recognize her on the street or in a store and thank her for her lessons about the Holocaust.

"You never know who is going to be the person who remembers what, or what is going to be the thing that is remembered," she said. "But to reach even a few, it's worth it. If I can change one person's life, reach one person who was going to be in a gang, or be mean to a friend, I've done my job."

In the future, Evelyn said the work of teaching about the Holocaust will fall to the children and grandchildren of the survivors. In the lexicon of the Holocaust community, this group is known as "Second Gen" or "Next Gen." "They tell the story of their parents or their grandparents," she said. This is important, "As we survivors age and can no longer speak, our children and grandchildren will continue our message."

For those who did somehow survive, "we feel that we need to give back," Evelyn said. "That is one of the reasons we speak out. We just feel we are here for a reason. We need to give back."

But there are big questions about human cruelties and atrocity that no one can answer, Evelyn said.

"Why does this keep happening? I don't know. I don't know how anybody can answer that. You watch it from country to country. You feel almost like people haven't learned the lesson."

To help convey the larger lessons illustrated through her family's experiences, Evelyn is at work on her own life story. The finished product will go online, and students will be able to interview her virtually. In other words, the lessons will continue.

Saron Khut. Photo by John Rudoff

CHAPTER 11

War in the Time of Childhood

Saron Khut (Cambodia)

It might seem surprising that it is only relatively recently that US researchers have begun studying child immigrants who are survivors of wars. The topic is so rich, so filled with the complexities of conflict and the exigencies of endurance.

Then again, maybe it is not so surprising, considering the challenges the study subjects present. Kids are tough to follow, after all. They change as they grow, and they do both quickly. They move around, making it difficult to track their addresses. The youngest who arrive as refugees often are the quickest to learn English, sometimes to the detriment of their native tongues—and often at the expense of memories lodged in the language they learned at birth.

If success is defined in terms of a comfortable adjustment to a radically new life, the most successful child survivors of war who relocate to the United States are those who assimilate. Key to this process, according to "Resilience & Recovery After War: Refugee Children and Families in the United States," a 2010 paper published by the American Psychological Association, is a sturdy sense of resilience.

"While the circumstances of their war experiences, their journeys to the United States and the conditions in which they find themselves as new arrivals greatly vary," the paper explains, "children displaced from war zones endure a tremendous amount of trauma, stress and adversity that can impact their functioning and development.

"These children and their families also demonstrate profound strength and resilience in their survival strategies, coping mechanisms and abilities to adapt within what are often completely unfamiliar environments," the paper continues.

The American Psychological Association defines resilience as the process of successful adaptation "in the face of adversity, trauma, tragedy threats, or significant sources of stress." Doctors Steven and Sybil Wolin, a husband-and-wife team who have made a long career of studying resilience, concede that children are often hurt by the hardships they have endured. But as they strive to overcome these adversities, they often gain strength, the Wolins maintain. The resilience that sustains these children is a kind of emotional smorgasbord, made up of qualities such as insight, independence, relationship-building, creativity, humor, and morality.

As it happens, these same qualities might provide the artistic tools for a sketch of Kacrna Saron Khut. The Portland restaurateur was only four or five years old—his actual birthdate is uncertain—when his father was taken from their Cambodian village by Khmer Rouge agents of Pol Pot, the dictator who dreamed of turning his country into an agrarian, socialist utopia.

In the process, Pol Pot's regime decimated the economy, the educational system, and the spirit of Cambodia. Between 1.5 million and 2 million people perished in a genocidal reign that lasted from 1975 to 1979. Many were executed. Others died of starvation or malnutrition. Disease was rampant, claiming many, many lives. Under Pol Pot, some Cambodians were literally worked to death. The dictator and his forces made special targets of intellectuals and educators, such as Kacrna Saron Khut's father.

The literature of resilience also cites family cohesion as an important element in allowing children to flourish despite grave misfortune. When his mother was sent to labor in the grounds that became known as the "killing fields," thanks to their stunning death tolls, Kacrna Saron Khut became the de facto parent to his two younger sisters. Somehow, the children managed to remain in physical proximity to their grandmother. Saron, as he is known today, set out on his own to find their mother. He succeeded, and throughout the war, the family somehow was able to stick together.

Along with currency and private property, the Khmer Rouge abolished religion. Since at least the fifth century, Buddhism had been the dominant faith in Cambodia. A 1989 Cambodian government document reported that under Pol Pot, more than 25,000 monks were killed, and nearly two thousand temples were destroyed. Some temples that were allowed to stand were used to house pigs. Pali, the language of the Buddhist scripture, was banned.

Yet some monks managed to survive. Seeking a safe place for her son and his sisters, Saron's mother found a monk so beloved in his village that residents were willing to shelter him and protect him from the Khmer Rouge. The monk became a kind of surrogate father for Saron. In fact, it was the monk who urged the boy to drop his formal first name. The monk told him the name, Kacrna, sounded too upper-class and thus might entice the Khmer Rouge. (Kacrna translates to "merciful.")

"It means you are higher class, which we were not, but that is what my dad named me," Saron said. The monk told Saron he needed to change his birth name: "He said it was too fancy." The new name, the monk told him, rhymed with his mother's name.

In turn, the boy called the monk "Uncle," a term that at once connoted respect and a sense of family.

Nothing about what happened to Cambodia or its people under Pol Pot could be considered fortunate. But the Buddhist values that Uncle helped instill in his young charge may have bolstered his resilience.

Self-reliance is a core Buddhist principle that likely helped enable the youthful Saron to step up to the role of "man in the family." Buddhism also teaches that suffering is unavoidable, a lesson that also conveys a healthy tolerance of hardships and probably helped Saron ward off self-pity during the tough times of separation from his mother. The same tenets no doubt proved helpful in adapting to life in a new country.

And so a young boy in Portland, Oregon, entered third grade speaking little English beyond the lyrics to "Jingle Bells," a tune he had mastered in a Thai refugee camp. With an arsenal of humor, determination, creativity, and intellect, the child graduated from high school with high honors, earned a degree at Portland State University (PSU), then snared jobs at FedEx and Intel.

Family New Year started as a small gathering for Portland's Southeast Asian communities. By the time this photo was taken, in 2019, the event in Glenhaven Park was attracting close to ten thousand people. Photo courtesy of Khut family archives

Saron Khut went on to open two restaurants. One of them, the Mekong Bistro, remains a vibrant presence among the Southeast Asian community in Northeast Portland. Before the social isolation brought on by the COVID-19 pandemic, the restaurant was a gathering spot where diners often danced or grabbed the microphone for karaoke sessions.

But that wasn't enough. Saron longed to bring members of the Southeast Asian community together so they could celebrate their shared heritage in a public setting. And so he organized New Year in the Park, a festive occasion that attracted thousands of participants in the five years it took place before COVID shut down such gatherings. Pandemic or no pandemic, Saron harbors grand plans to one day open a large central gathering space for the rich and varied Asian diaspora of greater Portland.

TEARS FOR THE COUNTRY HE LEFT

In a small town in the northwest part of Cambodia called Chong Kal, the five-year-old boy could not cry. His father had been taken by Khmer Rouge soldiers, bound for certain death. Now Kacrna Saron Khut was the man of the family. He must not cry.

But forty-five years later, as he leans against the counter of his Portland restaurant and tells this story, he is overcome. Sobs stop him in mid-sentence. Tears flow freely, surprising him.

"My father, he was not only a teacher, but an entertainer, a performer," Saron said of Jen da Chhoun, his father. Almost no one used his formal name. Instead, they called him Gru (or Professor) Jen.

One day in 1975, not long after the forces of Pol Pot had overtaken the country, there was a neighborhood celebration. Along with his other talents, Gru Jen was a singer and a dance instructor. Everyone in town knew him. The neighbors asked him to perform at the party.

He came home late, after dark. Saron, his two sisters and their mother were asleep. Then the soldiers came. They said they needed to take him to a re-education camp. He was an intellectual, an easy mark for the Khmer Rouge. "Re-education" was a euphemism. It meant he would likely be tortured, then put to death.

"He was a sweet guy," his son said. "He knew he wasn't coming back."

Many years later, in 2007, Saron found himself weeping as his plane circled Phnom Penh International Airport. It was his first trip back to Cambodia since 1980, when he fled with his mother and sisters to a Thai refugee camp. A year after that, the boy and his family were resettled in a distant place called Portland, Oregon. Saron entered third grade at Richmond Elementary School speaking almost no English. By high school, he was an honor student, his grade point average at 3.75. He graduated from Portland State University with a degree in art and architecture in 1996, the same year he became a US citizen.

Now, as his plane prepared to land in the Cambodian capital, "I wanted to see for myself." He wanted to see the bridge he had jumped off as a kid to swim in the river. He wanted to visit his relatives, to see his hometown. He wanted to stop wondering, "Was this where my father was killed?"

A FICTIONAL BIRTH DATE

Maybe he was born on January 28, 1970. Maybe he wasn't. In a village with no nearby hospitals, babies were born in their parents' homes. Mothers kept a record of the event, but it was more like "a Wednesday in January" than an actual account. His mother's memory that it was the Year of the Dog helped them come up with an estimate that became his birthdate.

Certain things have stuck in his mind from the years before his father was taken. He remembers the time his father lost his voice in a motorcycle accident. He remembers the time his little sister fell into the deep end of a pond and he, the big brother, managed to pull her out. Even though the Khmer Rouge had not yet taken over, the Vietnamese communist government made frequent incursions into Cambodia. Saron remembers bombings along the Ho Chi Minh Trail, and he remembers running to hide in the bunkers.

With his father teaching and his mother working as a homemaker and managing the family's small farm, their modest life was comfortable and happy. But already, war had left its mark on Cambodia. Saron's mother was young, about ten years old, when her two older brothers joined the Cambodian guerrilla militia to fight against the French in the country's struggle for independence.

Once the country fell to the Khmer Rouge in 1975, many Cambodians made plans to escape. Chong Kal was not far from the Thai border, and some of Saron's aunts, uncles and cousins were able to flee. His own family had packed their wagon to leave when his father became worried about his elderly mother. She was old, and she was alone. He decided he could not leave her.

"Everything will be okay," he told his family as they unloaded the wagon. "We will stay."

There was no way to anticipate what was about to happen, Saron said. "Nobody expected a massacre, a genocide."

Typically, he said, if the Khmer Rouge took one member of a family, they soon came back to finish the job. By now, as he told his story, Saron's voice was calm, as if he were discussing everyday behavior, not the extermination of millions, nearly a quarter of Cambodia's 1975 population.

Some estimates put the number even higher since the Khmer Rouge were less efficient at record-keeping than at slaughter.

But in a town the size of Chong Kal, "some of the Khmer soldiers, they were people we knew," Saron said. Those people watched the family, "but would not take the extra step to kill us."

Destabilization is always a hallmark of dictatorial regimes. Those who were not killed by Pol Pot's soldiers often were force-moved frequently, giving them no sense of domestic ballast and thwarting any plans to escape.

"That is what they did to my family," said Saron.

His mother was twenty-eight years old then. First, she and her three small children were crammed into a big military truck with many other families and sent to the city of Siem Reap, also in northwest Cambodia. A few weeks later, each family was sent to a different town. The strategy was as conniving as it was cold: Take the men—especially the educated men—then break down any sense of cohesion.

ON THE MOVE

In the first three years of Pol Pot's regime, Saron and his family moved four times—so often that he does not remember the names of all the towns they were sent to.

Adults were put to work, clearing forests or working in the fields. Even five-year-old children were expected to work in the fields. In fact, Saron said, the kids spent a lot of time being kids—chasing each other and playing games instead of doing the work.

Today, Saron's mother, Sarouen, lives near him in Portland. In the United States, she married another Cambodian man and had another daughter. Oregon is not noted for being tropical, but in her backyard, she planted banana trees to remind her of home.

She is known to family and friends as Mama Khut. Many years have passed, but still Saron chokes up when he recalls watching Khmer Rouge soldiers taking her away in the middle of the night. Her children were left behind with their very old grandmother, Daum.

Grandma, said Saron, "was not well, but she was strong." His grandmother would tell the children to collect their share of rice, and "whatever was left over, go and hide so it won't be taken away."

Saron was maybe five or six years old when Grandma reminded him that he was the man of the family. So it fell to him to find ways to feed his little sisters.

Months had passed when, "all of a sudden, one day, my mother showed up." Her good behavior had earned her the right to pay a brief visit to her family. But the privilege came at a price: She had to agree to go back to her work with Pol Pot's forces.

Imagine the trauma for a small boy. What six-year-old boy does not center his world around his mother? Saron pined for Sarouen. One day, he learned where she was staying. He knew that a group of travelers was headed in that direction, and he told his grandma he wanted to go, too.

But halfway on the route to the town where his mother was staying, the group abandoned Saron. The forest before him was deep and wide. He kept walking. "You think about danger," he said, "but that is not your priority." He was six years old. He wanted to find his mother.

The journey was treacherous. Saron got close, then turned back, then got close again. At last, he stumbled upon a woman who asked where he was going.

"I want to find my mother," he told her.

When Saron finally made his way to the camp where his mother had been held, she was stunned.

"What are you doing?" she asked, then wrapped her son in her arms.

Telling the story now, Saron pauses to compose himself, yet again.

"She is the strongest woman ever," he declares.

BLESSINGS—AND A NEW NAME

Saron stayed with his mother for days, or maybe it was weeks—who could keep track of time?—until his mother said she had found a safe place for him. She sent him to a temple where she knew there was a monk who would care for him. This is the monk who became "Uncle."

Saron called the monk "Uncle," not because they were related, but because the familial term at once conveyed respect and affection. As a religious man, the monk was a ripe target for Pol Pot's soldiers. When the Khmer Rouge took power in April 1975, 66,000 Buddhist monks lived in Cambodia and the country had more than four thousand temples. While a 1989 government report stated that more than 25,000 monks had been killed by the Khmer Rouge, and nearly two thousand temples were destroyed, some more recent estimates place the total number of Buddhist monks murdered by the Khmer Rouge at 50,000. Under Pol Pot, all Buddhist texts were burned.

But in his small town, the monk who Saron called Uncle stayed safe because he was beloved. "He was like a Buddha," Saron said. "The people in that town would hide him, keep him away from the soldiers."

The monk helped Saron find his sisters and grandmother. They lived with him for almost two years in a village not far from Siem Reap. On a return trip to Cambodia in 2013, Saron and his mother drove through the area. She recognized it immediately.

"This is where we lived," she said. "Thirty-something years later, my mom remembered everything about that town."

POL POT

The man who called himself Pol Pot was born as Saloth Sâr in 1925. His father was a farmer, and the family lived in relative affluence in the village of Prek Sbauv, about a hundred miles north of the Cambodian capital, Phnom Penh, in what was then French Cambodia. After high school, he was selected to study abroad, a distinction that placed him among the same narrow elite in Cambodia that he would later lash out against. While studying in Paris, he became infatuated with the Marxist-Leninist movement. Fueled with passion for the Marxist-Leninist philosophy, he returned to his country to teach history, geography, and French literature in a private school. He also became active in the growing movement toward communism in Cambodia.

By 1963, he had adopted his nom de guerre, Pol Pot. He rose steadily in the hierarchy of his country's communist guerrilla movement, and led Khmer Rouge forces as they overtook Phnom Penh in 1975 and overthrew the military government of Gen. Lon Nol. Pol Pot became Cambodia's prime minister in 1976.

As the iron-grip head of the one-party state that he renamed Democratic Kampuchea, Pol Pot closed his country's schools and required everyone to wear the same black clothing. In keeping with his plan to turn Cambodia into an agrarian utopia, cities were evacuated and factories shuttered. Currency and private property were abolished.

Along with intellectuals, such as Saron's professor father, skilled workers and those known to speak a foreign language were killed. People who wore eyeglasses or who owned symbols of decadent capitalist luxury such as wristwatches also were subject to execution. Those who were not killed were sent to the fields to serve as forced labor on Pol Pot's collective farms.

As a consequence, as they moved from place to place with their grandmother, Saron and his sisters received no formal education. Instead, he said, "Our school was life, doing whatever we could to survive."

Friction between Cambodia and neighboring Vietnam dated back at least to the thirteenth century, when Angkor, the capital of the Khmer Empire, was subjected to Vietnamese rule. But now that Vietnam's war with the United States had ended, Cambodia presented a fresh focus for the Vietnamese communists.

In late December 1978, Vietnam launched what it called the Counter-Offensive on the Southwestern Border. Cambodian nationalists called the incursion the Vietnamese Invasion of Cambodia.

As the Khmer Rouge retreated, Saron recalled, "there was a lot less tension, a lot less stress, but it was still war. There were still soldiers, still people dying." When the bullets flew or the bombs exploded, he and his family hid in trenches by the river.

When Vietnamese troops seized Phnom Penh in January 1979, Pol Pot's government toppled, and the despot fled to the jungle. Years later, in 1997, he was arrested and found guilty of genocide in what many regarded as a show trial. Although placed under house arrest, Pol Pot was never imprisoned. He died in his sleep in 1998 in Anlong Veng, near Cambodia's border with Thailand, apparently of natural causes.

The Khmer Rouge downfall meant some loosening of the rigid government control. Saron's grandfather was finally able to travel in order to locate what was left of his family. But throughout Cambodia, despondency prevailed. So many people had been killed. So many people had starved to death. So many families had been ripped apart. The standard reaction when people who had been separated greeted one another was surprise, Saron said.

"It was 'Oh, you're still alive?' Or, 'Are you for real?'" he remembers. Because, he explained, the prevailing mindset "was that everybody's dead."

HOME, BUT NOT FOR LONG

Back in Chong Kal, Saron and his mother were grateful not only that they were still alive, but that they were once again at home. Soon enough, they learned that Saron's uncle in the United States had been sending letters, trying to determine the family's fate. Once he learned that his sister and her children were alive, Saron's uncle asked some friends in Cambodia to help them leave the country. Their escape was scary, Saron said, but also, because he was just a kid, a kind of weird adventure.

They traveled by night in a group of about a hundred, making their way through woods and jungles. At one point, the group went to cross a main road in the darkness. But military cars lined the road. If they were caught, they knew they would not survive.

Among the group was a tiny baby. As the group debated how, when or whether to risk crossing the road, the baby began to wail. The noise was so loud, it was like an alarm, telling whoever was guarding the road that illicit travelers were on the move.

The group now debated a troubling moral dilemma: Should they kill the baby—because if not, everyone else would surely die? Or should they leave the infant and its family behind? They were spared a decision, because all at once, the baby fell asleep. With silence assured, they all agreed: Cross the road. Just take the risk.

But then they ran into another complication. As they began to climb the mountain that separated them from the Thai border, they ran out of food.

"We foraged. We ate leaves, plants, anything," Saron said.

As if not enough had already gone wrong, it turned out that their guide had given them bad directions, leading them to the wrong refugee camp. In the confusion, Saron and his mother were separated for a time from his sister.

"It was a wild, wild, crazy night, that night," Saron said. "In the end, we all met up in the field outside the camp."

Miraculously, some teachers had somehow managed to survive Pol Pot. As they escaped from Cambodia, some even had brought books with them. At the Lompouk refugee camp, and later at a camp named Chon Bo Ree, Saron received his first official education, mastering the Cambodian alphabet at age nine.

Indirectly, the camps were also Saron's introduction to the English language. It was December, and volunteers at the camp decided to teach the kids some traditional American holiday songs. Saron had no idea what Christmas was, and he certainly had never seen snow, but he joined in a hearty round of "Jingle Bells" with the other children.

At the camps, Saron saw his very first movies. One was a World War II movie, *A Bridge Too Far.* Another was *Spartacus,* about a Roman slave rebellion. Compared to what he had left behind in Cambodia, he said, the refugee camps were "good times."

More than once, he spied American surveillance planes flying above him. "I wish I could be on that plane now," he remembers thinking. "I want to be on that plane."

And then one day, he was on a plane.

A PLACE CALLED PORTLAND

When their immigration papers came through in 1981, Saron and his family flew from Bangkok to San Francisco. It was a long flight, on a very large plane. Several days later, a smaller airplane took them to Portland.

They arrived in winter, something else Saron had never experienced. It was cold, and so many trees had lost their leaves. He looked at the naked branches and wondered why all the trees were dead.

Saron and his family knew of just two Asian grocery stores when they arrived in Portland. Most Asian immigrants lived in one of three areas. For the Cambodians, it was North Portland. Later, as he learned to navigate the city by bus, he discovered Vietnamese stores on Northeast Sandy Boulevard. Saron's new life was disorienting at first, but it was also filled with daily adventures.

"Everything here was odd, but compared to what I had in Cambodia, it was one hundred times better," he said.

There was talk of holding him back a year in elementary school, but Saron was determined to remain with his age group. Even with the language barrier, he made friends. His secret weapon was music. He listened to the radio and did his best to sing along, even when the words meant nothing to him. One song he quickly mastered was Michael Jackson's "Beat It."

He concedes that the steady trauma of his childhood may have sharpened his sense of resilience. The fact that he had no choice but to adapt as a small child in Cambodia turned out to serve him well as a young immigrant in the United States.

"From an early time, I learned how to survive, how to fit in," he said. Even when he first arrived in Portland, speaking only fractured English, "I got along with everybody, all types, including the gangsters. I learned the value of different cultures. I don't disrespect anyone."

In fifth grade—now at Duniway Elementary School—Saron entered an ESL (English as a Second Language) program run by Jim McCall, or as Saron called him, Mr. Jim.

"He was a great man," Saron said. And as it happened, Mr. Jim used music as one of his teaching tools. In particular, Saron remembers, "He loved The Carpenters."

The sing-along teaching method worked. A few years later, Saron wrote speeches and papers while attending Cleveland High School, earning that 3.75 grade point average. He spent three years at Mt. Hood Community College before finishing up at Portland State.

The day he got his US citizenship in 1996, he remembers thinking, "This country is awesome. This country is what we as immigrants always talk about: the land of opportunity."

Saron said he has never missed a chance to vote in local, state, or federal elections.

The part-time job with FedEx Ground he held at PSU grew into full-time work as an operations manager. Four years later he was hired by Intel, also as an operations manager.

In the meantime, he married and had two kids. His son by that marriage, which ended in divorce, is sixteen, and his daughter is thirteen.

At her seventieth birthday party at the Mekong Bistro, Saron's mother, Sarouen, was honored as a kind of Portland village elder by people from throughout the Southeast Asian community. Photo by Richard Mitchell

He and his second wife, Jai, have a daughter who is four.

Saron loves sports. He also loves food. In 2009, he seized the call of the land of opportunity to leave Intel and open the city's first Asian sports bar. "Good Call," at Southeast 110th Avenue and Division Street, lasted a year and a half.

He quickly channeled his energy and his entrepreneurial spirit into the Mekong Bistro, the restaurant/karaoke-bar he owns on Northeast Siskiyou Street. The restaurant takes its name from the river that flows 2,700 miles through China, Myanmar, Laos, Thailand, Cambodia, and Vietnam. Saron offers fare from most of those countries.

At first, his mother was the Mekong Bistro's main cook. Now Saron does all the cooking, calling his mother "more of the brain—she makes everything run."

GIVING BACK

The bistro became a kind of hangout for many people, drawn by Saron's passion for music as well as good food. Some nights he offered blues or jazz. Other nights he might serve up Cuban sounds. Or Iranian. Or Ethiopian. Music from Vietnam and Cambodia is always a staple.

In non-pandemic times, people dance, and they sing, led by Saron at the mic. "We make a lot of noise," he said. His father's son, he loves to lead the room in song.

"What I wanted out of the Mekong Bistro was not just to make money, but to bring our community and our culture together," he said.

Apparently, the formula has worked. "Mekong Bistro is more than a restaurant," Saron says. "People compare it to Cheers in Boston. We connect people. We know each other by name. We call each other Brother and Sister."

Saron has spearheaded other efforts to foster community spirit among Southeast Asian immigrants in Portland. In April 2015, he organized the city's first family New Year event, attracting about three thousand people from Portland's Lao, Thai, Burmese, Hmong, and Cambodian communities to a giant picnic in Glenhaven Park. By 2019, the crowd had mushroomed to close to ten thousand people. Just as many were expected in April of 2020, but the COVID outbreak brought group gatherings to a halt.

The pandemic has not been kind to the restaurant industry. Saron says he is barely hanging on. Still, he keeps his eye on his family, his community, and his home country. Saron started working full-time as soon as he graduated from college. He made good money. But he knew not everyone had his advantages, especially those in Cambodia.

"I was always thinking back to my people in Cambodia," he said. "They are poor and they need help."

So he began raising money to send to Cambodian orphanages and also to help build water wells in that country. In Cambodia, a new tractor is a precious commodity. It didn't take long for him to raise the funds to buy a tractor for an orphanage in Siem Reap.

"It just takes somebody with a plan, or an idea to start it," Saron said. "I've been doing that. I guess my life is about serving people, helping people."

In 2007, Saron took his mother and his youngest sister to Cambodia. "I wanted to go back because it had been thirty years," he said. "Believe it or not, I missed Cambodia. I missed the country where I had spent the first nine or ten years of my life. For me, it was a mission. I wanted to check the country out, to see what was going on."

Once he got past the emotional avalanche of returning to the country he left under duress, he got to work. In Chong Kal, he was appalled by mounds of trash scattered around the Buddhist temple. When he asked his aunt why no one took care of the place, she shrugged and asked who would clean it.

So he gathered as many children as he could find and told them he would pay them to clean up the trash. Word traveled fast, and soon just about every kid in town was on the job. They smiled when Saron compensated them for their labor. Since that first visit, Saron has made four more trips to Cambodia.

THE CAMBODIAN ELVIS

One of the ways in which Saron rediscovered his Cambodian roots was through music. Specifically, he made a study of the songs of a man often called the King of Khmer music. Fans of Sinn Sisamouth in the 1960s and 1970s likened him to a cross between Elvis Presley, Frank Sinatra, and Nat King Cole. He was handsome and charismatic and is believed to have written more than one thousand songs.

"Everywhere he went, every province, every town, every fruit, every flower—all the foods he ate—he always has a song for it," Saron said. "That is how I learned about Cambodia when I came to the United States. His music painted these pictures for me. He was that good, that inspirational."

As a performer and a man with a vast popular following, Sinn Sisamouth represented a major threat to the Khmer Rouge. He disappeared, his exact fate unknown, but his death at the hands of the Khmer Rouge is almost certain. One apocryphal story holds that as he was about to be executed, he asked the Khmer Rouge soldiers for the chance to sing one last song, presumably hoping to soften the soldiers' heartstrings. They shot him anyway. Then they destroyed master copies of many of Sisamouth's recordings as symbols of Western decadence.

When Saron learned that the singer's widow was living in poverty, he was heartbroken. "His music is all over the world," he said, "but his family is poor." Once again he stepped into action.

He compiled a CD, "ordinary people singing Cambodian songs," and offered it for sale online. He charged $10 per CD, promising that all the proceeds would go to Sisamouth's widow. He raised $1,000. Delivering the money was the occasion for his second trip back to Cambodia in 2008.

"We drove for eight hours, along bumpy roads, past water buffaloes," he said. "I didn't know exactly where she lived."

Finally, they came to the house. The widow was napping in a hammock when Saron, his mother and their driver arrived. When she awoke, she was overjoyed. A strong friendship developed, and Saron went back to visit her again in 2012. With an American filmmaker, Chris Parkhurst, he is working on a movie about Sinn Sisamouth.

THE NEXT BIG THING—OR THINGS

Usually, when he has what he calls a big idea, Saron Khut knows how to make it happen. His next goal is to establish a multicultural community center for Portland's Southeast Asian immigrants. He wants a space where culturally appropriate meals could be served to as many as a thousand people.

"This is what we are missing," he said. "This is what we need in Portland."

And he has another rather grand ambition.

Whether it was soccer as a kid, kickball or pickup basketball—any sport, really—Saron has always been an avid athlete. But after he ripped both ACLs (anterior cruciate ligaments) and had to have his knees repaired, his wife banned him from playing contact sports. Try something more sedate, she advised, like golf.

In the ensuing dozen or so years, it is safe to say that he has become a fanatic golfer. He has won many town titles and describes himself as "probably the No. 1 ranked Cambodian golfer in Oregon"—not that he has legions of competitors for that title. At one point on his home course, Glendoveer, his handicap was as low as 1.5. So now the title he really wants is: "From the Killing Fields to the US Open."

"This would be a dream come true for me," he said. He smiled. The fact that he is fifty years old does not seem much of a deterrence. "I'm pretty close to it," he went on. "If I keep working hard, there might be a chance."

Rama Yousef. Photo by Sankar Raman

CHAPTER 12

A Crisis That Shocks the Conscience

Rama Yousef (Syria)

On the first day of January 2022, three civilians were killed by a Russian airstrike in the countryside near Idlib, in northwest Syria. Day after day in 2022, according to a grim timeline of civilian deaths assembled by sources that include the Syrian Observatory for Human Rights, men, women and children in Syria succumbed to violence associated with the conflict that has wracked that country since 2011.

By the third decade of the twenty-first century, civil war in Syria was such a frequent event that citizens of that Mideastern country had learned to expect violent conflict. After ten full years of fighting, the once-proud cities of Damascus and Aleppo stood dotted with bombed-out buildings. Skeletons of houses, apartment buildings, and businesses formed the cityscape of Homs, Syria's third-largest city. Throughout the country, entire neighborhoods lay in ruins.

Hospitals were destroyed. Cultural heritage sites—temples, tombs, statues, churches—were reduced to rubble. Poor sanitation brought a surge in contagious and potentially fatal diseases such as typhoid, measles, and diphtheria. A refugee crisis of unimaginable proportions arose: according to the United Nations, more than 6.6 million Syrians have fled the country.

Those who remain continue to suffer. Out of a total population of about 16 million, more than 12 million Syrians suffer from food insecurity, according to Human Rights Watch and the World Food Programme. More than 600,000 Syrian children are chronically malnourished, Human Rights Watch reports.

Human Rights Watch also concluded that "Syrian security forces continue to arbitrarily detain, disappear and mistreat people across the country, including children, people with disabilities and the elderly. The Syrian Network for Human Rights, a group based in the United Kingdom, says that nearly 15,000 Syrians have died due to torture since 2011.

Precise casualty figures for a conflict that arose on March 15, 2011, are difficult to ascertain. The UN estimates that 400,000 people have died in the civil war. The Syrian Observatory for Human Rights (also based in the United Kingdom) contends that more than 500,000 have been killed. Other organizations put the number of dead even higher.

Though the Syrian government, led by President Bashar al-Assad, continues to deny using chemical weapons during the conflict—he has blamed the attacks on his opponents—a task force led by the Organization for the Prohibition of Chemical Weapons concluded that the regime had dumped sarin gas on two towns in 2013, causing thousands of deaths.

"It is impossible to fully fathom the extent of the devastation in Syria, but its people have endured some of the greatest crimes the world has witnessed this century," UN Secretary-General António Guterres said at a 2021 briefing at UN headquarters to mark the tenth anniversary of Syria's civil war. "The scale of the atrocities shocks the conscience."

The hostilities in Syria erupted at the tail end of clashes in 2011 that rippled through the Mideast in what became known as the Arab Spring. Tension in Syria had simmered for years, as an autocratic father-son dynasty imposed tight restrictions on free assembly, criticism of the regime, and other civil liberties. Even the possibility of political opposition was squashed for many years by Hafez al-Assad and his son and successor, Bashar.

The elder al-Assad declared himself president in 1971, eight years after a 1963 coup that placed control of the country in the hands of the secular Ba'ath party. As his grasp on Syria's government tightened, his health declined. His first choice as a successor was his brother Rifaat, who later eliminated himself from consideration by staging a thwarted coup. When Hafez's oldest son Bassel was killed in a car accident, Bashar moved from second runner-up to de facto replacement.

In May 2021, Bashar al-Assad was elected to a fourth term as president. According to the Syrian government, more than 95 percent of voters supported him.

Before the civil war broke out, unemployment in Syria was high. Corruption was widespread. One way that the Assads, father and son, retained control was by rewarding friends of the regime. That was fine for the wealthy and influential citizens who curried presidential favor. Those on the lower end of the economic scale did not fare so well.

Bashar al-Assad did introduce some changes that benefited all rungs on the Syrian social ladder when he made mobile telephones more available, as well as the Internet and Facebook. Still, resentment of the repressive Assad regime festered, helping to fuel the pro-democratic protests in Syria.

Early in March 2011, an agricultural town near the border with Jordan called Daraa became the public face of the protests when a group of youths spray-painted some graffiti on the wall of a school. The Assads were so unpopular in Daraa that the local nickname for the elder leader, Hafez al-Assad, had been Abdel Ghader, or "worshiper of the treacherous."

The Daraa schoolboys could not have known what they were unleashing when they wrote: "Ash-shab yurid isqat an-nizam" on their school wall. This phrase is often translated as: "The people want the fall of the regime." Almost immediately, the local secret police swooped in and arrested fifteen boys, ages ten to fifteen. The children were detained under the cruel and watchful eye of Gen. Atef Najib, a cousin of President Bashar al-Assad. Outrage over the children's arrest exploded into sit-ins and noisy protests. The four people shot and killed by the government during a March 18 protest in Daraa are considered the first deaths in the Syrian uprising.

The government took harsh and swift retribution in Daraa, sending in tanks and security forces armed with guns and tear gas. Water and electricity were shut off. The people of Daraa continued to protest, seizing the theme of dignity that had been a pillar of the Arab Spring. Around the country, people gathered in support of the children of Daraa.

When the boys were released two weeks after their arrest, they bore the signs of torture, inciting further fury among many citizens in Daraa. Anti-government demonstrations continued, as did government crackdowns. After more than a hundred protesters around the country were killed by the regime, thousands in Daraa took to the streets in a protest dubbed "Day of Rage." In the course of ten days of protests, more than 240 protesters were killed as government troops laid siege to Daraa. Sometimes, the protesters were shot as they marched in silence, carrying olive branches. Most reports say that at least a thousand people were arrested. By early May, with many people in Daraa afraid to leave their homes, a United Nations humanitarian assessment team was barred from entering the town.

But still, the protests proliferated in Damascus, Aleppo, and elsewhere. In July 2011, a group of defectors from Assad's military announced the formation of the Free Syrian Army (FSA). This new band of soldiers was intent on tearing down the regime. The FSA was among several opposition forces that were splintered into many factions. The groups were poorly organized, and there was little coordination. In some parts of Syria, this disorder gave al-Qaeda militants the opportunity to step in. The country was in mass disarray.

A United Nations resolution in 2014 sought to assure safe routes for deliveries of humanitarian aid. The Assad regime agreed to permit the UN convoys to deliver supplies to government-held areas but not to areas occupied by the rebels.

Foreign governments stepped in to lend support to rival parties. Russia sided with Assad, deploying its air force to Syria in 2015. Iran joined Russia in backing the regime. Qatar, Saudi Arabia, and Turkey aligned with the United States in aiding the rebel groups. After years of fighting in Aleppo, the regime captured Syria's second largest city in December 2016.

"Tyranny has won," an activist in Aleppo told *The New York Times*. Another activist in Aleppo told *The Times*: "My heart is burning."

In the fall of 2019, US president Donald Trump removed a thousand US soldiers from the Turkish-Syrian border.

As the civil war in Syria continues, the human costs have become almost immeasurable. But the struggle has also decimated the Syrian economy. Theft, looting, murders, and kidnapping abound. Bashar al-Assad continues to retain power. The cities of Damascus, Aleppo, and Homs remain in apocalyptic disorder.

That state of disarray was dramatically worsened at 4:17 a.m. on Feb. 6, 2023, when a magnitude 7.8 earthquake struck southern Turkey, near the northern border of Syria. Nine hours later, a second quake hit the region, this one measuring magnitude 7.5. The quakes were the deadliest to hit Syria since 1822.

At the time, in northwest Syria, 4.1 million people were dependent on humanitarian aid, according to the nonprofit Center for Disaster Philanthropy. World Vision, another global nonprofit organization, said delivering aid to the region had already been difficult due to the twelve-year conflict in Syria and the associated ongoing refugee crisis. In March 2023, a Red Cross statement said it was believed that more than five thousand people had died in Syria as a result of the quakes.

Weeks after the quakes, Mark Kaye, director of policy, advocacy, and communication for the Middle East and Africa at the nonprofit International Rescue Committee, said, "Anywhere else in the world, this would be an emergency. What we have in Syria is an emergency within an emergency."

THROUGH THE EYES OF A CHILD

He would not even look at the child. Basem Yousef was so furious, so deeply disappointed, when his wife, Najwa, gave birth to their fourth daughter that he stomped out of her hospital room in Damascus, cursing the fates that had failed to send the son he longed for.

In the lobby, an ancient, white-bearded imam saw Basem crying. The man was so bereft that the Muslim holy man concluded he must have just lost someone he loved very much. But no, Basem said through his sobs. His wife, he explained, had just given birth to yet another baby girl.

Wearing his turban and his long white thawb—or tunic—the imam sat next to Basem to offer comfort. "Daughters are a blessing from God," he began. "They're our greatest gift from Allah. Wipe your tears, my brother, and go hold your daughter. God sent her to bless your life. The culture does not matter, my brother, your daughter will bless you."

Basem returned to his wife's bedside and asked to hold his newest daughter. He told his wife: "We will call her Rama." The name describes the holy floor of the Kaaba, the building at the center of Islam's most important mosque in Mecca, Saudi Arabia.

Then, rocking the tiny child, he said: "I feel like someone opened my heart, put Rama inside it, locked it and threw away the key."

THE CIVIL WAR

Basem and Najwa are not the actual names of Rama Yousef's parents. She chooses not to disclose their real names out of fear for their safety. Similarly, she prefers to remain vague about the name or precise location of the village in Syria where her father still lives. Rama makes no secret of her own views, but she does not want to jeopardize those she loves.

Speaking out can be risky in an autocratic society, and Syria, to put it bluntly, is a hot political mess. More than a decade of civil war has left the country battered and shattered.

Rama Yousef, a twenty-one-year-old college student in the United States at the time of our interview, remembers the exact moment that her science class in Syria was disrupted when a car blew up nearby. It was eight o'clock in the morning, and she was twelve years old. The school shook, and Yousef and her classmates assumed their building had been hit.

"About two minutes later, another bomb goes off," she said. "Same thing, same vibrations." The science teacher shouted at her students to take cover under their desks. "Me and my friends fell on each other," she said. "Then we heard the principal yelling, telling us not to leave the school." Less than half a mile away, the principal said, two cars parked under a bridge had just blown up.

As her father's favorite, Rama got a cell phone at a younger age than any of her sisters. Students at her school were strictly forbidden from bringing mobile phones to class. But what pre-teenager actually pays attention to rules and regulations? Like many of her all-female classmates, Rama had tucked her phone into her bra—for emergency purposes, she rationalized, just in case she had to contact her mom or something. This was a definite emergency, and she quickly called her mother.

Najwa told her daughter that she had been driving to work when she heard the explosions. She told Rama she had turned around and was already on her way to the school to pick her up. On their way out of the schoolyard, Rama saw something disturbing.

"When we left the school, it was the first time I had seen a tank," Rama said.

Rama stresses that she can only provide the perspective of a child when she talks about the war in Syria. Her world, like that of most children, was her family and her friends. Her only exposure to politics was being released from school to wave flags and cheer for the president at rallies and parades.

Wearing hats decorated with the Syrian flag, the students would stand on city streets, bellowing, "Yes! I love my president!" On the nightly news shows, the students loved seeing themselves on TV.

"You'd hear people say, 'Look at those little kids, they just love their president,'" she said.

In truth, their participation in these rallies was anything but political. Waving flags and shouting in support of the regime was just way more fun than being cooped up in school.

"It was so fun. We would walk for miles," Rama said. "We were having a good time. It was better than being in class."

Several months after the explosions near her school, Rama lost a close friend in another bombing incident. That tragic event prompted Najwa to begin making plans to move her youngest child to someplace safe.

A FRACTURED FAMILY

Her parents had always lived separately: Basem, in a village about twenty-five miles from Damascus where he owned clothing shops; and Najwa in Damascus, where she held a government job. Throughout their childhoods, Rama and her sisters spent the school week in Damascus and weekends and school holidays with their father.

The city-life/country-life dichotomy caused tension within the family.

"God knows why [my parents] married," Rama said. "She hated village life. He hated the city."

Rama said her mother's city-life family looked down on Basem because he was a villager—in their minds, little more than a hick. In the countryside, Basem's family despised Najwa because she preferred the city and held a full-time government job. They thought she was uppity and also inadequate because she had not given Basem a son.

"Having a son in Syria is life-changing," Rama writes in a memoir she hopes one day to publish. "If you have a son, then you're considered a perfect woman, and the ones who can't are considered to have 'something wrong with their eggs.' This concept encourages many men to practice polygamy and since Syria acknowledges the Islamic law, they are allowed by law to have up to four wives at a time."

Rama said her father's family urged him to seek a second wife, but he refused. Though her parents' marriage was rocky, Rama said the couple never considered splitting up. Divorce could only bring shame on the family, potentially rendering the four daughters unmarriageable. For a woman in Syria, Rama quickly learned, marriage was all but inescapable.

"In Syria," she said, "a girl's only way out was to be married."

In her memoir, she describes grasping this reality when she told her aunt about the perfect score she received on a writing quiz.

"Congratulations!" her aunt replied. "Inshallah, I'll see you as a beautiful bride one day."

Rama writes, "That's what I saw and that's what I was told, and I was waiting on my turn to marry. When my male cousins did well in school, their congratulations would consist of 'Can't wait to see you as a doctor.'"

Rama said that from her paternal grandmother, in particular, she and her sisters received "constant reminders that we are less, that we were four girls. We would not carry on his name. We would bring shame."

Her father worried endlessly that one of his daughters would further dishonor him by consorting, unmarried, with a male. This behavior, Najwa told her daughters, was labeled *haram*, or "sinful." Her father's family concurred. "His entire side of the family—my uncles, cousins and even my grandmother—regularly reminded him, 'You have four beautiful girls. They need a man quickly. They might bring shame to the family.'"

Marriages in Syria are usually arranged, typically as business transactions between families, according to Rama. One by one, her sisters were introduced to possible husbands. Lulu, the eldest sister, met the first prospect when she was just sixteen. To her parents' dismay, she rejected the young man. Appearing too picky, Basem and Najwa reminded their girls, could also crimp their chances at marriage.

Just to emphasize this point, when the second daughter, Zeina, refused a suitor, Basem beat her so badly that she ended up in the emergency room. Zeina told the medical staff that she had fallen down the stairs. She soon married a cousin. Rose, the third sister, saw what Zeina had gone through and married the first prospect she was presented with. She was seventeen.

Taking matters into her own hands, Lulu met a man she wanted to marry. Six months after the wedding, the family learned that their rich, Egyptian son-in-law had a wife and children at home in Egypt. By nineteen, Lulu was divorced.

Lulu later brought home the charming, handsome Hassan, a dual citizen of Syria and the United States. He told Lulu he owned a gas station in California as well as a lovely home. Both statements were lies.

One by one, her sisters married and left the home, until only Rama remained. "All I did when I was growing up was watch my sisters get married and leave the house." Her own future in Syria seemed predestined. "I knew that was going to be me next. Just marry someone."

DADDY'S GIRL

From the beginning, Rama had known she was her father's favorite, "Daddy's girl," as she playfully describes herself.

"I did everything with him that a son would do," she said.

She loved working with him in his village clothing stores. When his family would cluck that it was a shame she wasn't a son so Basem could pass the businesses on to her, Basem would shoot back: "Rama is all the son I need." In turn, Rama relished her role as the family tomboy. Ignoring her country's cultural mores, she played in the streets with boys—and she played rough. If someone menaced her, she menaced right back.

"I wasn't just sitting down and drawing like every good female in Syria," she said.

Around sixth grade, she and her best friend Isra secretly adopted male identities. Rama was Hassan, an easy choice because Hassan Sabi meant "tomboy." The move had nothing to do with actually wanting to be a boy,

Rama said. "It wasn't like I was gay or transgender. I just wanted to matter in the society."

All the other girls in her class talked about boys or makeup, she remembered. "We talked about what we wanted to do when we grew up."

Isra said she planned to be a pharmacist. Rama's plan was to be an English teacher who was also fluent in French. Today, studying at Cal Lutheran University in Southern California, her English is so good she could pass as a Valley Girl. She said she is still working on the French-speaking part.

Headstrong and confident, Rama chafed under the strict expectations of the society around her. "I was a female, and I was expected to act in a certain way," she said. "That pissed me off so much."

Though her father was not an observant Muslim, he did once ask Rama to wear the hijab. She said she wanted to wait a year, and then maybe come back to the topic. He never asked again. Nine years have passed since she last saw her father, yet Rama still speaks with him at least every other day.

"My dad loves me so much," she said. "If a bug bites me and I cry, he cries, too."

ESCAPE ROUTE

Understandably—considering the number of sisters, their various engagements and at least one divorce—the marital history of the elder Yousef girls can be confusing. By the time the car bombings near Rama's school took place, the older sisters and their spouses were scattered. One sister and her husband were living in Saudi Arabia. Another married sister lived in Egypt. And Lulu, Rama's eldest sister, had married a Syrian American and was living in San Diego, California.

Najwa quickly ruled out traveling to Egypt or Saudi Arabia with Rama. Neither country could offer her daughter a better future than she might find in Syria, she believed. But California—that was another story.

The US embassy in Damascus was shuttered by then, so early in the summer of 2012, Rama and Najwa drove to Aman, Jordan, to secure visas to travel to the United States. Najwa assured Rama that this was only a summer sojourn, "just 'til things cool down."

In reality, everyone but Rama was in on a plan for her to leave Syria permanently. "Behind the scenes, they all knew I was not going back," she said. "But I did not (know that)."

There were other deceptions. Rama's brother-in-law told Najwa that he needed $5,000 to "adopt" Rama so she could remain in the United States. He also told Najwa that if he and Lulu were to represent Rama as guardians in the United States, Najwa would have to leave the country.

Later, Rama's brother-in-law told her that the adoption effort had failed. However, he said, she could remain in the United States under what is known as Temporary Protected Status, or TPS.

As stated on the website of the US Citizenship and Immigration Services (USCIS), this category of visa is available to individuals who are in the United States "due to conditions in the country that temporarily prevent its nationals from returning safely." Along with Syria, countries whose refugees may be granted TPS status include Burma (Myanmar), Somalia, Venezuela, Yemen, Nicaragua, and Sudan.

Rama received Temporary Protected Status, the same immigration status she holds today. But, she said, "there was no lawyer." There was also no $5,000 fee. Her brother-in-law pocketed the money.

Najwa flew from San Diego to Egypt to stay with her daughter Zeina. Eventually she fled Egypt by boat and made her way first to Sweden and then to Germany. Living in separate countries, Najwa and Basem finally divorced. Rama said that in Germany, Najwa remarried.

SUNNY CALIFORNIA

For Rama, however, what was presented to her as a summer holiday in sunny California suddenly turned into a seismic life shift. A strange language, English, swirled around her like a furious spinning top. That was not all that was different.

"I saw things I never imagined I'd see," Rama writes in her memoir. "I saw a couple kissing, two men holding hands, and girls showing their skin without four men following them around."

That first summer, Rama spent most of her time indoors—in part because she did not know her way around, and in part because her brother-in-law, Hassan, forbade her to leave.

From watching American movies, Rama knew that American school kids had lockers. She wanted one, and when it came time to enroll in school, she made sure she got one. But she had no clue how to open it. At her new school, the principal handed her a class schedule. She had no idea what it said.

American school kids did not have to wear uniforms, and instead dressed in all manner of outlandish attire, Rama thought. She saw girls with pink hair, others with pierced noses. What kind of parents would allow their daughters to go out looking like that? she wondered.

In her ESL (English as a Second Language) class, hands shot up as the teacher rattled off a list of which students spoke which native languages: Spanish! French! Korean! Finally, when he got to Arabic, Rama raised her hand and looked gingerly around the room. At last, she saw one other hand. It belonged to a girl from Morocco named Hayat. Rama was elated. The two became instant friends.

Otherwise, the San Diego public school where she was enrolled as a seventh grader might as well have been the moon. In the cafeteria, kids ate different food than she had ever seen, and made fun—"EW!"—of the Syrian food in her lunch bag. Mostly, the other students ignored her.

"I often felt invisible to American kids," she confesses in her memoir. "No one talked to me or even approached me."

But they did bully her. Rama and Hayat got used to hearing their accents mocked or to be taunted as "terrorists."

"Hayat and I were being made fun of, simply because of our ethnicities," she says in her memoir.

THINGS FALL APART

Exchanging regular text messages with her father, she learned that things were getting worse in Syria. By late 2012, Rama learned that Basem had closed down all his stores, because there were no longer any customers. People had become afraid to leave their homes.

Communication with Basem became sporadic. "Sometimes, he'd lose cell service for weeks, and we would not know if he was still alive," Rama notes in her memoir. "Protests, bombs, snipers, different militias and even ISIS got inside Syria. Syria fell apart."

In California, her own life was marked by unsteadiness as well. By now the parents of a baby girl, Lulu and Hassan argued a lot. Rama felt she was watching a rerun of her parents' unhappy marriage. The arguments between Hassan and Lulu sometimes turned physical. Rama was afraid for her sister, and for herself. Hayat's mother, already embracing Rama as a member of their family, offered to take Rama in. Hassan was furious at this show of family disloyalty.

Toward the end of the summer of 2013, Hassan announced that the family would move to a cheaper apartment in the Mission Valley section of San Diego. He told Rama the garage would be her new bedroom. The move meant Rama would have to attend a new school. She was heartbroken. How could she face yet another adjustment to yet another new setting?

Luckily for Rama, Hassan and Lulu failed to register her correctly. When she got to the new school, the administrators could find no record of her as a student. Rama hastily texted Hayat and learned she was still on the roster at her old school. She hopped on a bus, and soon she and Hayat were back at the same lunch table.

One day Hayat handed her a small package. "Open it," she told her friend. Rama gasped when she found that Hayat's mother—who had already taken her shopping for clothes and supplies—had bought her a smartphone. Not only that, Hayat smiled as she told her friend, but her mom had added Rama to the family's monthly phone plan.

The gesture infuriated Hassan, who resented Rama's growing closeness to another family. Her school was a long bus ride from Mission Valley, and Hassan also became angry when Rama began spending nights with Hayat's family in order to be closer to school. In the process, Hayat's older sister Mai became a sort of surrogate big sister to Rama.

Mai encouraged Rama to "fight for herself." With this admonition, Rama found it easier either to ignore Hassan or to argue back at him. But tensions continued to mount in the house. Finally the hostility level became so high that Rama accepted Mai's invitation to move in with her and her husband.

From four regions of the globe—Germany, Syria, Egypt, and California—Rama's family waged a campaign to force her to move back with Lulu and Hassan. They accused Mai of brainwashing Rama. They threatened Rama with what amounted to banishment from the family.

But Rama held her ground. She was sleeping better. She was more relaxed than she had ever been since she arrived in the United States. She was happy. Then one day, Lulu called and said Hassan had gotten a new job and they were moving to Oregon. Rama said words to the effect of fine, hope you like it there. Lulu made it clear that Rama was expected to move with them. Rama made it just as clear that she intended to stay where she was.

"If you don't come with me to Oregon, then I am no longer your sister," Lulu said.

Rama replied, "I'm sorry. I won't."

But the decision was removed from Rama's hands because she needed to renew her TPS visa. The social worker who interviewed her could not understand why Rama was not living with her sister and brother-in-law. Who was this Mai she was living with, and why was she not with her US guardians, Hassan and Lulu?

The social worker took a hard line. "Either get deported or go back to your sister," she told Rama.

ANOTHER NEW START

On the flight to Portland, Rama was miserable.

"I was like, here we go again," she remembered. "I didn't want to go to Oregon. I didn't want to go to another new school. I didn't want to get bullied all over again."

But as she had been discovering through experience, adversity can sometimes breed opportunity. Pulling herself together after she landed, Rama summoned the self-confidence that had been brewing in her since her heart-to-heart talks with Mai.

She had just turned sixteen. By the standards of her former life, this would be the moment that she would be served up as marriage material. In her new world, Rama was teetering on the brink of young adulthood.

She was in a new state, a new city where she knew no one. Her relationship with Hassan and Lulu was strained. What she needed, Rama decided, was some independence. What she needed was a job. She marched into a Subway sandwich store in North Portland and announced that she wanted a job. Fine, said the manager: Just leave your resume.

"I had no idea what a resume was, so I went on Google and YouTube and wrote one," she said. Lacking any previous paid employment experience, Rama wrote that she had often helped her father out in his clothing stores. The Subway manager told her she was hired. "That was a boost in my confidence," Rama said. "I never thought I would get the job. I never thought I would get anything."

That summer, Rama worked every shift she could get. She rewarded herself with the totems of teenage girlhood: clothes and makeup. As they slapped together sandwiches and scrubbed the shop after closing, Rama's manager confided that her own earnings were going into an account to pay for her daughter's tuition at a private high school in Portland.

Rama listened carefully and decided that was what she wanted, too: a private-school education. Then she reminded herself: Oh, right, she was a refugee from Syria. She had almost no money. Her English was faulty. She had no private school legacy, no one to promise generous donations to the school, and no one to write glowing letters of recommendation for her.

But the manager told her about a different school in Portland. De La Salle North Catholic High School was a college-preparatory high school that catered to underserved students in Portland. It was among the most diverse high schools in the country, and one of the first to incorporate a corporate work-study program that enabled students to work one day each week, both as a way to defray tuition expenses and as a way to gain professional experience.

"They have scholarships," Rama's manager at Subway told her.

Rama made her way over to the big brick building on North Fenwick Avenue in Portland. She skipped up the steps, looked around and spotted a sign that said, "President's Office." Rama had never heard of a high school with a president, but she figured that was who she wanted to see.

"Do you have an appointment?" the president's assistant asked. Rama said no. Then she added it was really important that she see him.

The president opened his door, escorted her in, "and then I sobbed my eyes out, telling him my story," Rama said. This is how she began: "My mom and I fled the war when I was twelve years old, and I was left behind to have a better future."

Technically, admissions for the fall semester were closed. Technically, the school did not admit juniors as new students. But after the president heard Rama's saga, he said, "You're in." Grabbing a tissue to dry her eyes, Rama said she had no idea how she would pay the tuition. The president told her not to worry because the school had a strong work-study program.

Luckily, not all her Subway money had gone to clothes and makeup. Orientation was the following day, and Rama hurried out to purchase the blue-and-white plaid skirt and polo shirt that was the uniform for girls at De La Salle North.

FAST-FORWARD

At this point, Rama's story warps into fast-forward mode. High school had its usual share of drama, usually centered around boys or bullying. But Rama managed to score two terrific work-study slots, the first with the *Willamette Week* newspaper and the next with a division of Nike. She got her driver's license and a friend's parents gave her their ancient, rattletrap Toyota Camry. The engine was so noisy that everyone knew when Rama was driving up.

Rama fretted about how she would finance a US college education. She watched many, many YouTube videos on how to apply for scholarships. But so many of the scholarships or financial aid packages she investigated required US citizenship or a green card, and there she was, still under Temporary Protected Status.

Then she learned she had qualified for a full-tuition International Leaders grant at Cal Lutheran University in Thousand Oaks, California. After she realized that she was bored senseless by biology, she abandoned plans to become a dentist. She shifted gears and decided to aim for law school, and as of this writing, she is furiously studying for the Law School Admission Test (LSAT). She hopes to add a master's degree in public policy because, not surprisingly, she has big plans to change some of the ways government does business.

"I want to change the system that really wasn't there for me when I needed it," she explained.

Rama is twenty-one, and as of fall 2021, is just starting her senior year at college. Attaining US citizenship is a top priority for her. And while a part of her will always be "a Syrian girl," she said there is no way she would return to Syria to live.

In some weird and ironic way, she said, the war in Syria inadvertently brought peace to her, "because it turned my life upside down in a good way." While the frequent moves and disruptions upset her at the time, the forced adjustments and exposure to new environments "made me become more open-minded," Rama went on, "I got used to it. Every time I went to a new place, I found new people and new things to do."

In a phone conversation in the summer of 2021, Rama asked her father a blunt question. "Are you proud of me?" she demanded, knowing she had flouted just about every expectation that a Syrian father could have for his daughter.

"And he said, 'Absolutely. I am so proud of you, that you decided to go against everyone, me included, and find your own way.'"

It was just the answer she was hoping to hear. Resilience has been a hard-earned lesson, but "I would not want my life to be in any way different. I want everything to be what happened, nothing more, nothing less." Or as Rama writes in her memoir, "My life continues to bloom."

Rama Youssef was the first in her family to graduate from college, earning a bachelor's degree in political science and government from California Lutheran University. Photo courtesy of Youssef family archives

Nour Al Ghussein. Photo by Sankar Raman

CHAPTER 13

A Long History of Occupation and Oppression

Nour Al Ghussein (Gaza)

The array of occupants of the land now known as Gaza is truly dizzying. Among those who have laid claim to the area over many, many centuries are:

The Canaanites
The ancient Egyptians
The Philistines
The Assyrians
Alexander the Great and his army
Hellenistic philosophers
Bedouins
The Seleucids of Syria
Ptolemies of Egypt
The Hasmoneans
The Romans, who rebuilt the place under Gen. Pompey Magnus
Herod the Great
The Ottoman Empire
The Palestinians

Christians, Muslims, and Jews have inhabited the region over at least the last four millennia. Gaza earns the distinction in the Hebrew Bible of being mentioned as the place where Samson was imprisoned and died. In Jesus's day, the area later called Palestine was part of the Roman Empire.

The long roster of conquerors and visitors in the narrow sliver of Palestinian land that is now known as Gaza—currently governed by Hamas—has resulted in a collision of cultures that today is marked by a near-constant state of strife.

The Palestinian Ministry of Health said at least forty-three Palestinians were killed in mid-August 2022, when Israel launched air strikes on the territory that it said were in response to threats from Palestinian Islamic Jihad. The victims included fifteen Palestinian children, the Health Ministry said. Also among the fatalities was Khaled Mansour, a leader of Islamic Jihad's operations in Gaza. The attacks, halted after Egypt brokered a ceasefire, represented the most serious violence in the region since more than 250 people died after Israel launched an eleven-day bombing campaign against Gaza. A ceasefire authorized by both parties on May 21, 2021, ended the assaults. In Gaza, however, the word "ceasefire" is more likely to translate to a temporary break in fighting than a lasting truce.

For four hundred years, from 1517 to 1917, Palestine was part of the Ottoman Empire. But Ottoman rule ended with World War I, and in 1918, Great Britain took control of the region. The move was part of a broader agenda on the part of the British government, which in 1917 had issued the Balfour Declaration, calling for "the establishment in Palestine of a national home for the Jewish people."

But tensions continued to flare. Thousands of Jews sought refuge in the area following the Russian Revolution, and the Jewish exodus exploded as many European Jews fled their own countries as a result of the Nazi Holocaust. For their parts, many Arabs and Christians opposed the idea of a Jewish state in the area.

Seeking a peaceful compromise, the United Nations (successor organization to the League of Nations) in 1947 recommended dividing Palestine into two states—one Arab, and the other Jewish. The vote on UN Resolution 181 took place on November 29, 1947. Thirty-three countries, including the United States, voted for the measure. Egypt, Iraq, Iran, Yemen, Syria, Saudi Arabia, and Lebanon were among the thirteen countries that opposed the resolution—in short, the entire Middle

Eastern delegation. Great Britain, sponsor of the Balfour Declaration, joined nine other nations in abstaining from the vote. After the vote, the representatives of six Arab states staged a walkout in protest. In Tel Aviv, some cafes poured free champagne for their customers.

Opponents of the move to divide the region and give Jews their own state wasted little time in foreseeing doom. Jamal al-Husayni, co-founder of the Palestine Arab Party, predicted that "the blood will flow like rivers in the Middle East." Iraqi Prime Minister Nuri al-Said said, "We will smash the country with our guns and obliterate every place the Jews seek shelter in." Mohammed Hussein Heikal Pasha, head of Egypt's delegation to the UN at the time, warned: "If the UN decide to amputate a part of Palestine in order to establish a Jewish state, no force on earth could prevent the blood from flowing there."

The UN plan giving the town of Gaza and a small area around it to the Arabs was set to take effect at midnight on May 15, 1948, marking the official end of British rule. The timing was set to coordinate with the UN's recognition of Israel as a Jewish state on May 14, 1948.

Just one day later, war broke out between Israel and five Arab countries—Jordan, Iraq, Syria, Egypt, and Lebanon. At the end of this conflict, known as the 1948 Arab-Israeli War, Egypt was given control of the Gaza strip.

With the establishment of the new state of Israel, hundreds of thousands of Palestinians left their homes there. Many settled in the Gaza strip, a slice of land approximately twice the size of the District of Columbia in the United States.

In the modern era, violent conflict has raged in the area for upwards of seventy years. In the view of the late Edward Said, a Columbia University professor who was a founder of the academic field of postcolonial studies, the near-constant state of upheaval was an all-but-unavoidable result of the decision made in 1917 by then foreign secretary of Great Britain, Arthur Balfour.

The Balfour Declaration, Said asserted in 1979, was "made (a) by a European power, (b) about a non-European territory, (c) in a flat disregard of both the presence and the wishes of the native majority resident in that territory, and (d) it took the form of a promise about this same territory to another foreign group, so that this foreign group might, quite literally, make this territory a national home for the Jewish people."

But, Said continued, "There is not much use today in lamenting such a statement as the Balfour Declaration. It seems more valuable to see it as part of a history, of a style and set of characteristics centrally constituting the question of Palestine as it can be discussed even today."

In 1987, Palestinians in Gaza rioted against Israeli occupation of both the West Bank and Gaza. The uprising became known as the "Intifada," a word that translates roughly as "shaking off" in Arabic. On December 10, 1987, just after the beginning of the first Intifada, a rebel group called Hamas emerged as a growing force among Palestinians. The name "Hamas" is an acronym for the Arabic phrase "Harakat al-Muqāwamah al-'Islāmiyyah," or "Islamic Resistance Movement." Furthermore, the Arabic word *hamās* itself means strength, bravery, fire or zeal. As part of its original charter, Hamas called for the destruction of Israel.

Israel, the United States, the United Kingdom, and the European Union are among the governments that consider Hamas a terrorist organization. Supporters of Hamas say the organization provides services and delivers humanitarian aid to a desperately poor region.

In 2005, Israel unilaterally withdrew its troops from Gaza. A 2006 election in Gaza gave legislative control to Hamas. But Hamas is an organization, not the officially sanctioned government of an independent country. This makes Gaza unusual, in that it is an area not ruled by an actual country.

Still, Israeli oversight in Gaza remains inescapable. On three sides, Gaza is surrounded by Israel, as well as a small checkpoint entry to Egypt. Gaza's fourth border is the Mediterranean Sea. Along with controlling six out of seven land crossings out of Gaza, Israel controls Gaza's air and maritime spaces.

After another year of violence in the region, the United Nations General Assembly adopted a resolution on December 30, 2022, "deeply regretting that fifty-five years have passed since the onset of the Israeli occupation and stressing the need for efforts to reverse the negative trends on the ground." Calling for "a complete end to the Israeli occupation that began in 1967," the resolution continued by expressing grave concerns "over the tensions and the violence throughout the Occupied Palestinian Territory."

In adopting the resolution, the General Assembly stated further that it was "gravely concerned about the disastrous humanitarian situation and the critical socioeconomic and security situation" in the Gaza Strip. The resolution said that "situation" was "unsustainable" and asserted that "a durable ceasefire agreement must lead to fundamental improvement in the living conditions of the Palestinian people in the Gaza Strip."

Bluntly, the resolution—titled "Israeli Practices Affecting the Human Rights of the Palestinian People in the Occupied Palestine Territory, Including East Jerusalem—stated that the General Assembly "demands that Israel cease all its settlement activities" and "calls upon Israel, the Occupying Power, to cease its imposition of prolonged closures and economic movement restrictions."

Finally, the resolution referred several questions about Occupied Palestine to the International Court of Justice, including: "What are the legal consequences arising from the ongoing violation by Israel of the right of the Palestinian people to self-determination, from its prolonged occupation, settlement and annexation of the Palestinian territory occupied since 1967."

Israeli officials wasted little time in firing back. Zvika Fogel, a member of Israel's Knesset and a former Israeli military officer, said: "As of right now, the occupation is permanent. And as of right now, I would like to continue to apply Israeli sovereignty over all the areas that I can."

Incoming Prime Minister Benjamin Netanyahu said: "The Jewish people are not occupiers in our eternal capital, Jerusalem, and no United Nations decision can distort the historical truth." Netanyahu called the UN vote "despicable" and said his country "will not be bound by the resolution to refer the conflict to the international court."

In the meantime, 2023 got off to a violent start, with near-daily killings in the Occupied Territory by Israeli forces. With about two million people living in just 141 square miles, Gaza is one of the most densely populated spaces on earth.

"GAZA IS FULL OF DREAMS, SHATTERED IN ONE MOMENT"

Living in Gaza—one of the most dangerous places on earth—the Al Ghussein family learned years ago that where there is smoke, there are most likely bombs. And when there are bombs, the family clusters in the safest space they can find.

A basement would work. But houses in Gaza do not have basements. Often, families seek shelter under a staircase in their homes. For the Al Ghussein family, the best choice turned out to be a bathroom—tiled and enclosed. But bathrooms typically are not large, and at times of air strikes, the Al Ghussein family found that their bathroom could get quite crowded, as cousins or other relatives sometimes rushed to join them.

"Because we always say that if we die, we die together," said Nour Al Ghussein, a twenty-six-year-old Portland State University student. "You take your family, and you go and you hide."

Once, during an Israeli assault on Gaza in the summer of 2014, a bomb exploded next to her parents' bedroom.

"And parts of the house fell on our heads," she said. "Fire entered through the windows."

There is an Arabic phrase that many Muslims invoke at times of deep emotion, especially grief and fear. Outside, the Al Ghusseins could hear neighbors wailing that phrase—"Allah Akbar," meaning "God is most great"—"because they thought we were dead," Nour says.

Instead, the Al Ghusseins were crammed together in the guest bathroom. Nour kept looking around at her brother, four sisters and parents, methodically counting each one again and again to assure herself that they were all there, safe and alive.

"I would go through this multiple times a year," she said, seeking safety with her family while bombs exploded outside.

For Nour and her friends, bombings became a childhood norm.

FIFTY YEARS OF FIGHTING

Israel took control of Gaza following the Six-Day War in 1967. In 2017, Hamas—the militant Palestinian group that since 1987 has operated in opposition to Israel—unveiled a new charter that on the surface appeared to soften the group's hardline position against Israel. While the original Hamas charter had called for the destruction of Israel, the new document stated that Hamas was "not at war with the Jewish people, only with Zionism."

Moreover, the head of the Hamas political bureau, Khaled Meshal, stated at that time: "Hamas advocates the liberation of all of Palestine, but is ready to support the state on 1967 borders without recognizing Israel or ceding any of its rights."

Benjamin Netanyahu, Israel's prime minister at the time, immediately dismissed the move as a smokescreen. "Hamas is attempting to fool the world," Netanyahu said, "but it will not succeed."

Christians, Jews, and Muslims attach importance to the region, which for centuries has been marked by religious strife and conflict over land ownership. The parallel growth of Zionism and Palestinian nationalism has amplified the tension. Jews in Israel cite the area as their ancestral home. Palestinians make the same claim.

Like Nour and her family, nearly all residents of Gaza are Muslim.

Armed checkpoints at both the Israeli and Egyptian borders of Gaza prevent citizens from leaving freely or reentering once they have left. Permission to leave can take months, even years, to obtain. Often, the checkpoints are simply closed. In 2020, for instance, both the Rafah crossing into Egypt and the Erez crossing into Israel were open for just 125 days.

Inside Gaza, the blockades have meant that residents face shortages of fuel and water as well as frequent interruptions of power. In the summer of 2022, households in Gaza received an average of three to four hours of electricity per day, according to a report from the Gaza Power Generating Company. Health care is also limited, and medicine is often scarce. The border blockade by Israel and Egypt has sharply curtailed Gaza's economy.

"People are dying because there is a lack of almost everything in Gaza," Nour said. "The blockade is holding us back from advancing in the world."

Israelis counter that the blockades are necessary to protect terrorists from entering their country.

There is also a major difference of opinion about the purpose of tunnels that run beneath much of Gaza. Hamas says the tunnels are used to bring essential supplies to the territory. Israel says the tunnels are used for Hamas terrorist activities.

A LOST CHILDHOOD

For Nour, the constant aggression has had a dehumanizing effect.

"Because of this situation, I didn't know what childhood was," she said.

Once—with bombings such a commonplace event, she does not remember the year—"we got bombed inside our school." The school, run by the United Nations Relief and Works Agency (UNRWA) for Palestine, was adjacent to a government building that may or may not have been the intended target. Nour was in second, maybe third grade.

"I thought it was the end of the world. I was ready to meet God that day," she says.

Several friends perished in the incident. "I remember they (Israelis) said there was some mistake, they didn't mean to bomb the school," she said. "But how can you try to say it was a mistake? I lost my friends."

How many friends has she lost to Israeli bombings?

"Oh my God," she said. "I can't even count."

As she left for school each morning, she would kiss her parents goodbye, hoping they would still be alive at dinnertime.

The clothing factory her father owned was bombed into nothingness in 2005. Left with no livelihood, he launched a business seeking energy solutions for a region that frequently is without gas or electricity.

Nour's best friend, a journalist named Yaser Murtaya, was killed by an Israeli sniper during the 2018 Gaza border protests. Shortly before his death, Murtaya completed a video, *Between Two Crossings*, about Nour's efforts to leave Palestine and attend college in the United States.

In a Facebook posting of Between Two Crossings*, Nour is filmed and photographed as she prepares to cross the border out of Gaza. Photo courtesy of Al Ghussein family archives*

"Yaser, he was thirty years old and his dream was to travel and see the world outside," she said. "Even while wearing a 'Press' jacket, he got shot while he was doing his job."

In Portland, Nour tried talking to a psychologist about the trauma she continued to experience, even as new reports about friends who died in Gaza reached her in the United States. By mutual agreement, they ended their sessions together.

"I think she got depressed," Nour said. "The stories that I have are more than any human can handle."

But as disturbing as her own memories might be, Nour said, "there are two million people left in Gaza, people who have stories maybe even worse than the ones I have."

TRAUMA FROM AFAR

Far from Gaza, safe by comparison in her Portland apartment, Nour suffers nonetheless when her homeland comes under attack. She relives her own fraught memories and anguishes for the people she loves who remain in Gaza.

On May 10, 2021, Israel began an eleven-day bombing assault on Gaza that claimed at least 256 Palestinian lives, 66 of them children. Thirteen Israelis died in the exchanges, two of whom were children. Nour said she was unable to stop watching reports of the attacks, and that she barely slept until a ceasefire was declared. These events, she contends, are triggers for her post-traumatic stress disorder (PTSD).

"It was tragic to watch it live-streamed on my TV while being away from my family and the ones I love," she said. "I felt helpless and retraumatized because this time I was watching every bomb. Me and all my friends from Gaza were sleepless for the whole eleven days."

After a lifetime of turmoil in her homeland, Nour bristles at what she considers casual semantics—terms she says do not begin to describe what is actually taking place in Gaza. She grows particularly unhappy when the words "conflict" or "war" are attached to the situation in her homeland.

"Conflict suggests two equal powers," she said. "This is not a conflict. This is an occupation." As for the word "war," Nour rejoins, "It is an aggression, not a war."

STUDYING BY CANDLELIGHT

The youngest of six siblings, Nour—her name means "light"—was born in Gaza in 1995. Her mother, Fatima, created and ran an organization that assisted people with disabilities. Many people in Gaza lost limbs in the bombings or were paralyzed by falling rubble, so her mother had a busy job, Nour said. Her mother also ran a project aimed at raising awareness about domestic violence for young women in Gaza City, Nour said.

"She is my idol," she said.

The family lived in the northwest part of Gaza City, not far from the beach.

"It was not as crowded as the rest of the city, but it was more dangerous," Nour said. Israeli bombers often took aim at open space, she explained, such as several small farms near the family home. This meant "there were bombs going off in the field next door."

Fields or no fields, she stressed that life was far from pastoral. In Gaza, Nour says it feels as if "there's literally not even 1 percent of green space in Gaza," she said. "I really didn't see nature until I left Gaza."

Even now, five years after she left Gaza to attend college in the United States, "It's still weird for me. I get mixed feelings—feelings of, 'Oh, my God, there is nature out there, and it is charming.' We used to see pictures (of nature) and we wouldn't know if it was real or not."

Rockets fired by Israel frequently destroy Gaza's power lines. Sometimes, Gaza households receive electrical power in designated shifts. For Nour, the intermittent electrical service meant she often did homework by candlelight. But demand for candles was so high that stores often sold out. When that happened, Nour and her mother joined others who waited at the Gaza checkpoints for the next candle shipment.

During times when there was electric power, Nour and her friends often watched television. The American and British programs were more than diversion, for they helped Nour learn English. She especially loved to watch American movies and documentaries. Popular music also helped expand her English vocabulary.

There were other extracurricular lessons. After the bombings, Nour would see people lined up outside bakeries, trying to buy bread for their families. The same thing happened at shops that sold bottled water.

"I always noticed that two days after any attack, people would run out of money," she said.

Banking was not a firm part of the culture, she said. Nor was the kind of financial management that can help families to stay afloat following disaster. Before she finished high school, Nour determined that she wanted to study finance, with the goal of educating others in Gaza about financial stability.

"It's all about financial planning," she said. "People need to learn. If you have money, your kids will not starve."

Despite the ever-present tensions in Gaza, politics was never an official topic at her all-girls high school.

"We would talk about what was happening not inside class, but between us," she said. "In school we learned a lot about our history, our roots. I did not learn to hate or to talk politics in school."

STUDYING ABROAD

Twice, Nour was chosen for leadership programs outside Gaza. One was in South Africa; the other at Harvard University in the United States. But she was unable to leave because of the continuing siege in Gaza.

In 2015, Nour was selected for a five-week leadership program sponsored by the US State Department. This time, she was able to secure passage out of Gaza. She traveled to Washington, DC, where about a hundred students from the Middle East and North Africa gathered at Georgetown University and then were dispatched to six different US campuses.

"My luck was Portland State University," Nour said. She made it her business to connect with faculty members at Portland State (PSU), especially those who taught classes related to finance.

Once back in Gaza, she kept in touch with many of her professors from Portland State. She became more and more determined to fulfill her goal of bringing financial education to Gaza. She was certain that this would mean studying in the United States.

"I felt I had a responsibility, at least before I die, to try to do something," Nour said. "My main goal was education first, and to try to do something for myself, my family or my country. My plan is to bring education to an independent Palestinian economic recovery."

THE BORDER IMPASSE

By 2016, Nour had documents showing that she had been admitted to Portland State University with a full scholarship. She packed her suitcase and began the lengthy process of applying for permission to leave Gaza. The territory has had no functioning airport since Israel bombed Yasser Arafat International Airport in late 2001 and bulldozed its runway a few weeks later. In order to travel abroad, Nour would have to exit first via Egypt or Israel, and then travel through Jordan or Turkey.

But even with the necessary papers, the border crossings can bring disappointment. The scene is always chaotic, with people shouting and crowds pushing forward. Sometimes the crossing officials make arbitrary exceptions. Other times, they reject the documents and send the crossing-applicant home.

"Gaza is full of dreams that were shattered in one moment at that crossing," Nour said in *Between Two Crossings*.

Students from Gaza with hopes of studying abroad are not immune to what can seem like bureaucratic capriciousness. Pleading with the crossing officials is not always a successful strategy, Nour said.

"To be honest, there's hundreds—thousands—of students who say 'This is my last chance (to leave),' and it is true," she said. "They have had to change their plans, change their lives. They don't even know whom to blame."

When Nour was rebuffed in one attempt to leave Gaza via Egypt, "I had no choice but to keep trying. If I don't make it outside, that's it."

Between Two Crossings documents Nour's year-long attempts to leave Gaza via Egypt. At one point in the film, a woman in a headscarf tries to comfort her. The woman is Nour's mother, who tells her, "My dear, if it is meant to happen, it will happen."

Helping Nour to gather her things and return home after the thwarted effort to leave, Nour's mother sighs. "What can we do?" Fatima says in the film. "So much indignity."

A girlfriend tries to make light of their plight. "Look at Gaza," the friend tells Nour. "We're special. No one gets in, and no one gets out." The comment is laden with bittersweet irony. Nour and her friend dissolve into laughter.

Another earlier attempt did get Nour and some friends across the Israeli border. But the long delay before their names were called did not give them sufficient time to reach a scheduled interview at the US Embassy in Jerusalem. They tried anyway, but the embassy was closed by the time they arrived. Frustrated, they climbed in a taxi and headed back to the Gaza border.

"But when we came back (to the Gaza border), we were five minutes late. They wouldn't open the gates for us," she said. "They left us on the street in the dark," until finally a guard took pity on them and let them step over the border to return to Gaza.

Nour's break came in 2016 when she was asked to participate in a conference in Istanbul, Turkey. That invitation provided solid institutional backing from a non-governmental institution (NGO)—"my ticket," Nour says—for the exit papers she needed. At last, Nour's name was called, and she was waved through the border blockade to Israel. Even so, she had to manipulate the truth, telling the border agent she would return four days later when in fact she knew she might never go back.

Young women seeking to leave Gaza are well-coached by their families in safety measures, Nour said. The idea is to find one person who appears trustworthy and stick beside that person until they are safely out of Gaza. During the long wait for her papers to be processed at the Israeli checkpoint, she met a young man who was also intent on exiting. It turned out their families knew each other, so the two decided to share a taxi for the ride through Israel and on to Jordan.

As she had been instructed to do, Nour had arrived at the Israeli checkpoint at 8 a.m. It was 11 p.m. when they reached Jordan. Normally, she said, "if you do it in one shot, it's three to four hours."

Instead, she said, "checkpoints after checkpoints."

THE USA—AT LAST

At Portland State University, Nour declared a major in finance. She also found a job at a bank where she could both earn some money and hone her business skills. Her desk was near the entrance, where customers could scarcely avoid seeing her.

"Obviously, I do not look white," said Nour, a young woman with large, deep brown eyes and a mane of dark hair. One day a customer approached and asked where she was from.

"I said Palestine," she recalled. "And he said, 'Oh, I am from Israel.'"

The customer tried to engage Nour in a dialog about Israel and Palestine. Nour said she was not interested in serving as the voice of Gaza or anywhere else. But the customer, she said, pressed on.

"'Do you think you will ever be able to achieve peace?'" Nour says the man asked her. She replied, "Yes. Peace is in our hearts."

Nour said she tried to defuse what was rapidly becoming a nasty encounter. But two days later, the man came back. This time he pointed a camera at Nour, apparently with the intention of initiating another conversation and recording it. She went straight to her manager, asking for help.

"My manager, of course, he didn't do anything. I was so disappointed," she said.

Another customer who inquired about Nour's nationality suggested they go out for coffee so they could talk politics. Nour demurred. The man continued, asking her how it was that "people like you" were able to travel to the United States. Nour told the man she wanted to end their conversation.

"My identity here is always spurring uninvited conversations," she reflected. "I am a Palestinian and do not have to represent a political party. I represent my truth and what I have lived through personally and through a tragic collective punishment against innocent people who want to have a little taste of freedom."

Discussions framed as confrontation are pointless, Nour contends. For her part, she chooses her audiences carefully, aware both that she has a message to convey and that the topic is fraught with misunderstanding and fuel for conflict. So often, when she asks Americans what they know about Gaza, Nour said they reply with a single word: Hamas.

"First of all, it is completely wrong," she said. "Yes, it is a Muslim government." But unlike, say, Saudi Arabia, Muslim law in Gaza is not rigid, according to Nour. Although their mother does wear a headscarf, neither she nor any of her four sisters choose to cover their heads.

"For each family, it is a choice," she said. "You see so many girls not wearing the hijab."

She objects to what she says are one-sided media portrayals in the United States of what goes on in Gaza.

"People need to listen to people who live the situation, not from the media," she maintains. "Do not come and fight with me. I want to understand you, and I want you to understand me."

And she stresses: "I am here to share the right image of normalcy. I am a Palestinian citizen, and I am not here to talk on anyone's behalf. I am not supporting any one person. I am only supporting the innocent people of Palestine."

WHAT LIES AHEAD

In 2018, Nour applied for asylum status in the United States and was granted a permanent resident card, or green card. Soon, she hopes to apply for US citizenship. By then she also hopes to be in graduate school, pursuing a master's degree in business administration. Marriage and a family, she said, are not on her immediate agenda.

"I'm still healing from the daily trauma of the twenty years I lived in Palestine," she said. "I do wish to reach the point where I have kids who honor my homeland and history and can live a normal life in dignity.

For now, "I can't shake the imagery of all the kids suffering around the world."

A FAMILY DIASPORA

Violence between Israel and Hamas has not declined since Nour left Gaza. "I thought the war would be easier if you were not (there) in it," Nour said. "But it turns out the war was much worse if you are not with the ones you love."

With the escalating tensions in recent years, her family began leaving Gaza, one by one. One sister recently completed graduate school in New York. Nour's mother moved from Toronto not long ago to live with the sister in New York. Her father, her two other sisters and her brother are in Istanbul.

"There is no long-term accommodation for people like us in Turkey, so they've been living there on short-term, renewable visas in the hope of reuniting with my mom and sister who are now in the US," she said.

"We're scattered, each struggling on their own," she continued. "But we still try to stay tight and supportive of each other despite the distance and the burden we each deal with." Their goal, she said, is that "one day, we will all be together in one place. It could be anywhere."

Anywhere, that is, except Gaza. Without some major political shift, Nour cannot return to her home country.

So for now, living near Portland's Forest Park, the girl who had never seen nature now takes long hikes with her friends. She loves to watch the sunset and think about what may lie ahead. After all, she does have a world to save.

She smiles: "Hopefully."

Tim Tran. Photo by Sankar Raman

CHAPTER 14

The War That Changed the World— and One Man's Life

Tim Tran (Vietnam)

In the United States, it is called the Vietnam War. In the country where the conflict occurred, people today call it the American War. Tim Tran, whose story follows, just calls it "the war."

By whatever label, the long, bitter clash was a defining event of the second half of the twentieth century.

The names of more than 58,000 US armed service personnel who died in Vietnam are etched into dark polished granite on a stark memorial erected in 1982 on the National Mall in Washington, DC. Hundreds of thousands of other US troops returned with permanent physical or psychological damage—in many cases, both. The average age at death of a US soldier fighting in Vietnam was twenty-three.

On the Vietnamese side, the fatalities from both the north and south parts of the country tallied more than three million. According to official figures released by Vietnam in 1995, as many as two million civilians—also from both North and South Vietnam—died in the war that engulfed that entire country. The same government data reported that 1.1 million North Vietnamese and South Vietnamese soldiers perished.

As if the human toll were not high enough, the war in Vietnam that ended in 1975 is estimated to have cost the United States about $168 billion. In Vietnam, the environmental damage from chemical defoliants dropped by US forces persists today.

With often-brutal imagery that further polarized the nation, the Vietnam War unfolded each evening in the United States on television news—the first global conflict to be conveyed with such immediacy.

US involvement in Vietnam dates to the 1950s. In April 1954, the Geneva Conference was convened in Switzerland with the ostensible purpose of resolving matters relating to the Korean War. But the gathering of leaders from around the globe also sought to address the breakup of the French colonial empire in Southeast Asia. The region that had long been known as French Indochina now was divided into several states, including the Democratic Republic of Vietnam in the northern part of that country, and the State of Vietnam in the south. The kingdoms of Laos and Cambodia also were no longer under French rule.

In Vietnam, the split of the country followed the victory against French troops at the Battle of Dien Bien Phu by the Viet Minh, an independence movement headed by Hồ Chí Minh. Ho, as he was widely known, was a communist whose own party was nicknamed the Lao Dong, or Worker's Party. Ho's defeat of the French led US president Dwight D. Eisenhower to voice concern at a 1954 press conference of the "falling domino" principle, whereby, the president suggested, communism in North Vietnam would lead to its spread throughout the region.

While North Vietnam was under communist control, South Vietnam was run by nationalists. With assistance from the US and French navies, about 900,000 people fled from North to South Vietnam after the 1954 separation. About 52,000 people moved from the south to the north.

In 1955, seeking to provide economic and military aid for South Vietnam, Eisenhower sent a convoy called the Military Assistance Advisory Group (MAAG) to train South Vietnamese troops. In North Vietnam, Ho was receiving aid from the Soviet Union and China.

An eleven-year-old boy named Tran Manh Khiem was among thousands of Saigon school children who waved US and South Vietnamese flags along the motorcade route of US vice president Lyndon Johnson when he visited Vietnam in 1961. That was the year President John F. Kennedy began sending US Special Forces personnel—officially described as "advisers"—to train South Vietnamese military units. By 1963, the year Kennedy was assassinated, US military personnel in Vietnam numbered 17,000. Two days after his inauguration as Kennedy's successor, Johnson reiterated his determination to pursue the "battle against communism" in Southeast Asia.

On August 2, 1964, North Vietnamese patrol boats attacked the USS Maddox in the Gulf of Tonkin. A second US ship, the USS Turner Joy, also was said at that time to have been hit. Johnson immediately asked Congress to authorize an increased US military presence in the region.

"It is my duty to the American people to report that renewed hostile actions against the United States in the high seas in the Gulf of Tonkin have today required me to order the military forces of the United States to take action in reply," the president said in an address to the nation.

Congress complied, swiftly passing the Gulf of Tonkin Resolution. The bill authorized the president to "take all necessary measures to repel any armed attack against the forces of the United States and to prevent further aggression" by North Vietnam's communist government.

Most scholars consider the Gulf of Tonkin incident and the ensuing congressional resolution to mark the beginning of America's full-on engagement in the Vietnam War. But doubts about what actually had happened in the Gulf of Tonkin soon emerged. Reviews by the Navy itself showed that the Maddox had suffered little damage. The Turner Joy appeared to have been unscathed. No US military personnel were injured.

Still, a report from the office of the historian at the US State Department later concluded that the incident had provided Johnson and his administration with the justification it sought for further escalation of the war in Vietnam. Just a few months later, in March 1965, US Marines landed on South Vietnam's China Beach.

As the presence of US troops in Vietnam surged—reaching almost 200,000 by the end of 1965—the bombing attacks on North Vietnam took on names such as Operation Flaming Dart, Operation Rolling Thunder, and Operation Arc Light. Operation Barrel Roll targeted the Hồ Chí Minh Trail that ran through Laos and Cambodia.

American troops in Vietnam numbered almost 500,000 by the end of 1967. US casualties from the war topped 15,000 at that point, with more than 100,000 wounded. Each month, as many as 40,000 young men were called into service to fight the war on behalf of the United States.

Meanwhile, in the United States, antiwar demonstrations roiled the nation. Protests gripped colleges from California to Massachusetts. On October 21, 1967, 100,000 protesters gathered at the Lincoln Memorial. About half the crowd then marched across the Potomac to continue the demonstration at the Pentagon. Hundreds were arrested there.

Prominent figures from the arts, academics, entertainment, sports, and the faith communities voiced their objection to the war. In 1967, the Rev. Dr. Martin Luther King Jr. blasted the war as "a blasphemy against all that America stands for."

In the enduring tradition of American protest music, songs disparaging the war abounded. Phil Ochs recorded "What Are You Fighting For?" in 1963 and released "I Ain't Marching Any More" in 1965. Pete Seeger's "Bring 'Em Home" came out soon after. Joan Baez released "Saigon Bride" in 1967. That same year, Nina Simone took a civil rights poem by Langston Hughes and turned it into a song called "Backlash Blues" with these poignant lyrics: "You raise my taxes, freeze my wages, and send my son to Vietnam."

By 1968, an election year, President Johnson's approval rating had plummeted to 34 percent. Still, many Americans were shocked when, in a nationally televised address, he announced on March 31, 1968, that "I shall not seek, and I will not accept, the nomination of my party for another term as your president."

His Republican successor, Richard M. Nixon, campaigned on a claim that he would end the war. But he never offered specific details of how he intended to accomplish this goal, leading to speculation that he had a "secret plan." Nixon, a former California senator who served as vice president during Eisenhower's two terms, defeated Johnson's own Democratic vice president, former Minnesota senator Hubert Humphrey.

In 1969, the US began withdrawing combat troops from Vietnam. Nixon's national security adviser, Henry Kissinger, held secret meetings in Paris with top North Vietnamese officials. In Hanoi, Hồ Chí Minh died. Across the United States, waves of antiwar protests persisted.

On June 13, 1971, *The New York Times* published a front-page article with the headline "Vietnam Archive: Pentagon Study Traces 3 Decades of Growing US Involvement." The piece, which shared the front page with a story about the White House Rose Garden wedding of Nixon's daughter Tricia, was the first in a series based on a top-secret Department of Defense study called "Report of the Office of the Secretary of Defense Vietnam Task Force."

The classified documents, given to the newspaper by Daniel Ellsberg—an American economist, political activist, and former military analyst—showed a pattern of deception on the part of the Johnson administration about the extent of US involvement in Vietnam. What became known as the Pentagon Papers demonstrated that the government had misled the US Congress, as well as the American public.

By the end of 1971, just under 160,000 US troops remained in Vietnam.

Nixon secured a massive 1972 reelection victory, defeating the antiwar platform of Democratic senator George McGovern of South Dakota.

Then, a 1972 photograph from Vietnam marked an important moment in public opposition to the war. The image, captured by Associated Press photographer Nick Ut, showed a nine-year-old girl named Phan Thi Kim Phuc running naked down a muddy road. Her face is twisted into a scream and, although we can't see it, the skin on her back is falling off her body. Along with the neighbors and family members who trail her, some also with their bodies ablaze, the child had been hit by napalm dropped by the South Vietnamese Air Force onto her nearby village. Ut's photo, considered by many to be a turning point in the war, earned him the Pulitzer Prize.

The signing in Paris on January 27, 1973, of the "Agreement on Ending the War and Restoring Peace in Viet Nam" also marked a watershed moment. Representatives from the United States, North Vietnam, South Vietnam, and the Viet Cong signed the treaty, better known as the Paris Peace Accords.

The settlement included a ceasefire throughout the country. Almost immediately, those terms were violated by both North and South Vietnam. Nixon officially withdrew US troops from Vietnam, but American military and diplomatic personnel remained in the country through April 29, 1975, when they were evacuated by helicopter in a final US mission in Vietnam called Operation Frequent Wind. Many South Vietnamese refugees escaped this way as well.

One year earlier, on August 8, 1974, Nixon became the first US president to resign from office following the protracted Watergate scandal and investigations, which showed a pattern of political abuses on the part of the president and certain of his associates.

While the United States shuddered beneath its own political cloud, North Vietnam was steadily building up forces in South Vietnam. Repeated assaults by communist forces met with no resistance from the United States.

And that is where we will leave this introduction. One South Vietnamese citizen whose attempt to flee with his family on that April day was thwarted by a cruel confluence of events was a US-educated accountant named Tran Manh Khiem. Today he is an American citizen known as Tim Tran. His story follows.

A LIFE SHAPED BY WAR

Tim Tran is quite the jokester.

"Old professors never die," he told an otherwise serious meeting at Pacific University in Forest Grove, Oregon. "They just lose their faculties."

And then there is the strategy he uses in teaching his university finance classes, Tran likes to say he avoids the "burqa" method of his alma mater, the University of California, Berkeley, ("They cover everything") in favor of the "bikini" approach ("Just cover the essentials").

Or consider his report to a stockholders' meeting when asked to explain how interest rates can fluctuate: "Sometimes they fluc down, other times they fluc up."

His sense of humor is hard-earned and may also provide a key to what helped him survive a treacherous escape from his native Vietnam and prosper as an American business executive.

Tran, born in 1950 in a village on Vietnam's northern coast, did not have a lot to laugh about in a childhood marked by war and displacement. His name then was Tran Manh Khiem. Following Vietnamese tradition, the family name comes first. His given name, Khiem, was pronounced "Kim."

A FAMILY ON THE MOVE

Rather than accepting his expected role—running the family rice farm—Tran's father became one of countless young men in his country who joined up with the Việt Minh, the Vietnamese nationalist movement that was seeking independence from France. The group's leader was Hồ Chí Minh, known throughout his country as Uncle Ho, and so beloved that more than fifty years after his death in 1969, steady crowds line up to view his embalmed body in the Vietnamese capital of Hanoi.

Eventually, Tran's father became disenchanted with the Việt Minh, viewing the group as little more than a front for communism. Leaving that guerrilla group put him at personal risk, so he changed his name from Nguyen Dinh Muu to Tran Duy Tinh. The decision to quit the Việt Minh came back to haunt him in 1954, when the Geneva Accords divided Vietnam into two parts: the North, controlled by communists with support from Russia and China, and the South, backed by the French and the United States.

Still fearing retribution, his father felt he could only ensure his own safety and that of his family was by heading south. Khiem, as he was known then, was just four years old when he and his parents boarded a crowded boat in the North Vietnamese port of Haiphong. The journey was rough, and Khiem was so violently seasick that the family disembarked before their intended destination of Saigon, arriving in a fishing village in the southern half of the country called Nha Trang.

"The very first memory I have was the trauma of leaving North Vietnam to settle in South Vietnam," he said.

The family was part of an immense exodus from the north region of Vietnam. Their first home in Nha Trang was a tent in a refugee camp. Propaganda in the north had warned potential evacuees that the Americans would storm their boats, rob them of their possessions and then push them into the sea. Instead, little Khiem found himself eating from tins marked "USAID," the US Agency for International Development. He tasted cheese, something alien to traditional Vietnamese cooking, and found he liked it very much. His wealthy paternal grandfather had owned water buffalo, but in Vietnam, those beasts—along with cows—were used for labor, not milk. (And now a pause for another burst of Tim Tran humor: "In rural Vietnam, we didn't butcher a cow until the odometer read 100,000 kilometers.")

While her husband took whatever odd jobs he could find, his wife Noi rose every morning at two o'clock or three o'clock to prepare food she sold around Nha Trang. Her specialties were *che*, a sweet dessert soup, and *xoi*, a sweet rice dish. By 5 a.m., she was balancing a bamboo pole called a don ganh on her shoulders with a basket of each dish dangling from either end. A year after they arrived in Nha Trang, Tran's sister Thanh Binh was born. Her name translates to "calm and peaceful," reflecting the serenity the family felt after their hasty retreat from the north.

Like most boys in his home village, Tran's father had not gone past fifth grade. But what he lacked in formal education he made up for through voracious reading. The training he gave himself paid off when he landed a civil service job that prompted another move, this time to Tay Ninh, an inland province near the Cambodian border.

TEACH YOUR CHILDREN WELL

It was in Tay Ninh that Tran's father began rigorously drilling the boy in mathematics, writing, and reading. Tran's father set high standards, insisting that his son finish his daily homework before taking on anything else. As a result, Tran was already a year ahead of his classmates when he started school.

The following year, his father won a promotion that took the family to Saigon. By now the family also included a second sister, Xuan Thao, or "springtime shoot of grass." But their life was still spartan. It took just two suitcases to accommodate all their possessions.

Saigon, the capital city of South Vietnam (known as Hồ Chí Minh City since 1976) had a population of just over one million when the family arrived in 1958. "But everyone in South Vietnam had the same logic, viewing Saigon as the safest city," Tran said. "The population grew and grew." By 1975, Saigon had a population of 2.3 million. Today, that figure is more than nine million.

Like the city itself, the family continued to grow. Tran's brother Khoi was born in 1958. Another brother, Khoa, came along in 1959. A baby sister named Mai completed the family in 1961.

Tran's elementary school was so crowded that students attended in shifts. His school day began at dawn, and after classes each day he went home to tackle the extracurricular homework his father continued to give him. Along with reading, writing, and mathematics, his father added lessons in science and rudimentary English.

"Everybody in Vietnam at that time was studying French," Tran said. "But my dad saw that the French influence was over."

Battles, skirmishes, and incursions between north and south had been going on for years. But guerrilla attacks by the north increased markedly in 1961. In the United States, Kennedy made the decision to send helicopters and military advisers to Vietnam. The rumblings of war were everywhere in that country.

"I was 10 years old," Tran remembered. "Life became worse and worse." Terrorism was rampant, he said: "The communists put explosives inside bicycles and parked them in front of key sites, including the US Embassy."

Riding his bicycle to school every day, his parents urged him "to go fast when I went by the US Embassy."

Tran did so well on the state-sponsored public high school entrance exam that was required for admission by Vietnam's top schools that he won a spot at one of South Vietnam's two most prestigious high schools. His high score and strong record also ensured scholarship money to help pay for supplies and uniforms. By his sophomore year in the all-boys high school, he was awarded a national scholarship from the South Vietnamese Ministry of Education.

NO FUN, FEW GAMES

"The only fun we had was kicking a soccer ball in the street," Tran said. His family was large, and though his father's government salary was not meager, there was little extra for luxuries, such as the Canadian athletic shoes—a brand called Bata—that Tran coveted. So he played barefoot.

"Also for fun," he said with no trace of irony, people in South Vietnam watched government propaganda films in the city soccer stadium. These films stressed what a great job President Ngo Dinh Diem had done in kicking out the French and rebuilding the country's economy. Not only that, the films pointed out, but now the Americans had arrived to help defeat the communists. It never occurred to Tran and his pals to question this portrayal.

"We didn't know any better," he said. "We were kind of like blank sheets of paper."

In November 1963, Tran's father heard on the radio that President Kennedy had been assassinated. He sent his oldest son out to get a newspaper so he could read about what happened. Tran was shocked. But he found some small reassurance when he read the name of the man who would succeed Kennedy in the White House because of what had happened two years earlier when Tran had joined his schoolmates to greet the visiting vice president. Tran, then an eleven-year-old student, waving an American flag in one hand and a Vietnamese flag in the other, swears that Johnson looked directly at him from his open limousine, waved and smiled.

Unrest continued. In a successful coup attempt, President Diem and his younger brother Nhu were assassinated. In a year of instability marked by the formation and fall of several South Vietnamese governments, more coups followed. "The situation got worse day by day," Tran said. "The economy of South Vietnam went from bad to worse."

He was "about thirteen" when, perhaps unwittingly, he joined in a high school protest against the government. Older students had organized the demonstration, featuring a large anti-government banner. It did not go well.

"Every student was grabbed, me included, and taken to police headquarters," Tran remembered.

There, one by one, a police officer gave each student a swift smack on the face. Standing near him, Tran's friend challenged the officer. "Don't you dare slap me," Tran said his friend told the policeman. "My father works at the presidential palace."

The policeman looked at his superior officer, who shook his head: No, don't slap that one. When the officers told the boy to go home, he said he would not leave without Tran.

"So we were sent home," he said.

A FAMILY BUSINESS

Ever industrious, his mother set up a small gray-market enterprise. The Vietnamese girlfriends (and sometimes wives) of American GIs received goods that their soldier friends purchased at PXs (public exchange markets) on US military bases. Along with cases of Coca-Cola, there were cartons of Pall Mall cigarettes, cans of Dole fruit cocktail, and multipacks of Wrigley's chewing gum. Khiem's mother bought these products from her Vietnamese friends, then sold them at a comfortable profit to Saigon citizens eager for the comforts of US-made merchandise.

As her transport assistant, Khiem piled his schoolbooks on top of the Coca-Cola in his bicycle basket. Usually, officials waved him through as just another kid on a bike. One day, crossing a bridge, he was stopped.

"They checked my ID and military deferment card, then asked 'Why are you carrying all that Coca-Cola?'"

Tran thought fast and replied: "'We're having a party at my high school.' So they let me go."

It fell to his father to transport the adult beverages.

"Same deal," he said. His father was stopped by officials wondering why he had so many bottles of Johnnie Walker Black and White. Equally quick with an answer, his father explained that he worked for a very thirsty judge at the Ministry of Justice.

A STAR STUDENT

Even as the war was raging, about two hundred South Vietnamese students per year won scholarships sponsored by the United States, Great Britain, France, Australia, New Zealand, Canada, and Japan that enabled them to study abroad. Khiem had been among the top scorers on his country's national baccalaureate exams. His grades were strong, and his English was competent. He had supplemented his school work with trips to Saigon's Abraham Lincoln Library, run by the US Information Service, where he pored over US maps and periodicals such as Time magazine.

"I spent a lot of time at the Abraham Lincoln Library," he said. "The first thing I noticed about it was, wow, it was so cool." But he did not mean "cool" in the teenage or hipster sense of the word. "They ran the air conditioner 24/7," he said. "For a Vietnamese, it was very, very cold."

He also visited the British Library in Saigon. Big difference: "It was very small, like a two-bedroom apartment, and there was no air-conditioning." There was also the contrast between the hulking US Embassy in Saigon and the smaller outposts of countries such as New Zealand—"just a brownstone, really," Tran said. "So you could see no-body was as wealthy as America."

He wanted nothing more than to study in the United States and thought he had a strong shot at a USAID scholarship. "The best dream of any high school graduate is to study abroad," he said. "Preferably in the United States." Still, he checked the list of winners over and over, just to make sure he hadn't imagined that Tran Manh Khiem was among the winners.

"America," he thought. "Here I come."

He left Saigon on March 12, 1970. After an orientation in Honolulu the students were sent to different US campuses for intensive English-language training. Tran was sent to Georgetown University in Washington, DC.

At first, he had trouble falling asleep without the sound of bombs dropping nearby. The silence kept him awake. He was perplexed by US breakfast foods. Sometimes, the speed at which Americans spoke their language overwhelmed him.

Gradually he grew more bold. He explored the capital's museums and national monuments. He took in the pink floral sea that is the city's annual National Cherry Blossom Festival. He hung out in the periodical section at Georgetown's library. He discovered scrambled eggs.

One day, he was summoned to a meeting with the USAID official overseeing his scholarship. An attractive young student named Thuy Trinh, also from Saigon, caught his eye. The official told them they would both be attending a school called Pacific University in some place called Forest Grove, Oregon. Unsure just where Oregon might be, Tran pulled out a map at the university library so he could find out.

If he had been hoping for the Ivy League, he did not pause long enough to feel let down. "I didn't know enough to feel disappointed," he said. "I thought this is just another adventure, and adventure is good for me."

Thuy and Tran sat next to one another as they flew across the country. Imagine their surprise when they were greeted at the airport by Ken Meyer, then the dean of admissions at Pacific University. The two were even more impressed when this high-ranking school official drove them to his home in Portland, served them a home-cooked dinner, and installed them in separate bedrooms at either end of his large house. From their cultural standpoint, this was astounding: an important university official driving them in his own car, feeding them, and allowing them to sleep in his home?

ON CAMPUS, IN AMERICA

On campus, Tran was an instant curiosity. Fellow students asked him if he had been in the war. But no one blamed him for what was happening so far away.

"There were no problems," he said, no one assailing him about the ongoing conflict in his country. "A lot of Americans of different races took an interest in me when I introduced myself from South Vietnam."

Even one of his professors, "a wonderful, kind, mild-mannered man with shoulder-length hair" named George Evans, peppered him with questions about what was actually going on in Vietnam. Tran's first assignment from Evans was to read Philip Roth's *Goodbye, Columbus,* and write a

Khiem and his girlfriend Thuy experienced—and enjoyed!—their first snowfall on the campus of Pacific University in 1970. Photo courtesy of Tran family archives

paper on it. Slowly, holed up in the campus library and using his English-Vietnamese dictionary, he plowed his way through the novella about a summer love affair.

His lessons continued outside the classroom. For instance, he learned the rules of American football. A Black student named Cliff Wood patiently answered his questions about Black culture in America. One memorable conversation centered around lynching. Another discussion focused on busing.

Tran worked so hard at becoming a typical American college student that he joined a fraternity. With two fraternities on campus, he opted for the more academic house, Gamma Sigma, not the one whose members streaked naked across the campus. It was his fraternity brothers who taught him slang, along with swear words. They also took him to J.C. Penney, where he found that the blue jeans in the boys department fit him just fine. With his new tie-dyed T-shirt, he said, "I fit right in."

In short order, he formed three opinions about Americans: "One, they are very open and direct. We Vietnamese could not be as open as Americans. With Americans, what you see is what you get. They mean what they say, and they say what they mean.

"Number two: The overwhelming majority of Americans that I met were college-educated people. They were absolutely against the war—very opposed to American involvement in Vietnam.

"Three: America is a very free society. You can say anything you want, including (verbally) attacking the sitting US president."

The more fluent he became in English, the easier his schoolwork became. After asking one of his professors to recommend the best undergraduate business program in the country, he decided to transfer to the University of California, Berkeley.

Meanwhile, his friendship with Thuy had turned to romance. Thuy, too, felt she needed a greater challenge. When she told Tran that she was planning to transfer to the University of Oregon, they agreed that the distance between Eugene, Oregon, and Berkeley, California, would provide a good test for their relationship.

With the proceeds from a summer job teaching high school math, Tran put down $375 for a white Volkswagen Beetle decorated with flower decals. It was a model from 1967, the year of the legendary Summer of Love in San Francisco. Tran was ecstatic. Once again, he fit right in.

Sure enough, at Berkeley he found the academic challenge he had been seeking. He declared a business administration major and spent long days and nights at the cavernous campus undergraduate library. He made new friends, including a former Marine with a Vietnamese wife. Stopping by their apartment for a meal became a regular event.

In the fall of his senior year, he decided to have some fun. He and his friends headed across the Bay Bridge to see The Who perform. It was his first rock concert, memorable equally for the police presence and the clouds of marijuana smoke. The sound from dozens of giant loudspeakers rang in his ears for days. After that, deciding classical music was more his style, he used his student discount to buy a season pass to the San Francisco Symphony's concerts on the Berkeley campus.

Denizens of the twenty-first century—a generation that communicates both instantly and electronically—will find this hard to fathom, but in those early years of the 1970s, Tran stayed in touch with his parents via the post office. Sometimes it took a month for a letter to get from one country to the other. His notes home did not dwell on politics, for he knew the Vietnamese censors might block the letters from going through. But on campus, the war in Vietnam was a nonstop topic of conversation.

While his classmates were struggling over what to do if they were drafted, Tran had to decide what to do once he graduated. A stipulation of the USAID scholarship was that he would return to his home country. Tran had always dreamed of using his education to help Vietnam grow. But all around him, friends said he would be crazy to go back to a country in such disarray. Several friends even offered to let him live secretly in their parents' homes in the United States.

When Thuy finished her degree at Oregon and told Tran she was returning to Vietnam, that sealed the deal. He would go back to Saigon. But first, he decided, he would enjoy one last summer teaching math in Oregon.

All the while, the United States was going through its own domestic upheaval in the form of the Watergate scandal. As Nixon resigned and was replaced by his vice president, Gerald Ford, Tran was amazed that there were no military tanks in the streets of Washington, DC, or any other US city.

RE-ENTRY

In late summer 1974, "The culture shock began as soon as I stepped off the plane," Tran wrote in *American Dreamer: How I Escaped Communist Vietnam and Built a Successful Life in America*, the memoir he authored with Tom Fields-Meyer. He had forgotten about how heavily the humid air could weigh in Saigon. He had become so Americanized that he was shocked to see armed soldiers all around him. He was appalled when the official who examined his passport retained it to send to the Ministry of the Interior "for safekeeping." (In other words, there would be no future travel abroad without government approval.)

He and Thuy began meeting each other's families. Thuy started with a job in the Saigon office of USAID, and soon switched to a position as a financial analyst for Esso, Standard Oil's outfit in Vietnam. Tran pounded the pavement, sending resumes and seeking contacts before landing a job as an auditor at one of South Vietnam's largest companies, Shell Oil.

The couple's professional good fortune took place against a backdrop of rising political tension. North Vietnamese troops were moving steadily into the southern part of the country. Communist forces claimed Hue, South Vietnam's second largest city. South Vietnamese president Nguyễn Văn Thiệu resigned and found exile in Taiwan. In late April of that same year, North Vietnamese soldiers surrounded Saigon.

As the North Vietnamese presence grew more ominous, Tran and Thuy explored options to leave the country to which they had so hopefully returned. He had focused his early life on attaining an education abroad. Now his American university degree branded him as an enemy of the communists. Not only was he an intellectual, but he wore eyeglasses, a sure badge of elitism in the North Vietnamese playbook.

His goal was to evacuate with his entire family, as well as with Thuy. In case that was not possible, he gave each member of his family the name of his boss and friend at Pacific University. If any one of them made it to the United States, he told them to contact "Paul Hebb, Pacific University, Forest Grove, Oregon."

On April 29, 1975, Tran and his two brothers left their house before dawn and walked to the US Embassy. Tran was certain he could find some means of escape once they got there. But he was not alone in this opinion. The crowds around the embassy had grown impenetrable.

Nearby, Tran spotted a US Army bus crammed with passengers. The driver was American, and Tran asked in English if he and his brothers could board. The bus was headed to the Saigon airport. Tran believed they could find a spot on a US military plane if only they could get to the airport. But halfway there, the driver received a message that the airport had come under rocket attack. The bus stopped abruptly and turned back to downtown Saigon.

Feeling more hopeless than ever, Tran and his brothers walked home. That evening, South Vietnam's government issued an unconditional surrender as the North Vietnamese took control of Saigon.

AFTER THE FALL

That night, as communist victory speeches blared over the radio, Tran methodically destroyed any evidence that he had lived in the United States. Document by document, he set fire to every paper he had saved. Into the flames he threw all correspondence and then, most sadly of all, his treasured diploma from UC Berkeley. As a souvenir, he had brought home a small American flag given to him by a Berkeley friend who was active in the Berkeley Young Republicans and who had encouraged him to return to Vietnam. He burned the flag, too.

Into the backyard conflagration went letters of recommendation, admissions documents from US graduate programs he had never pursued, and the USAID certificate that marked completion of his study abroad.

"The communists believed that having spent four years in America, I must be some kind of spy for America, or I got some kind of espionage training, or I was pro-American and anti-communist," he said. "All of these were reasons to arrest me. Every day, I worried that they would imprison me."

If his arrest was not imminent, he knew it would happen soon. The communists, he understood, had their priorities for elimination.

"First they had to take care of the South Vietnamese army, then the South Vietnamese journalists, then the heads of the South Vietnamese political parties," Tran said. "I was only 24 years old. The only thing they had against me was that I had studied at an American university. I knew when my time comes, they would come for me."

He also knew that once the communists took over an essential corporation such as Shell Oil, he would be fired. Sure enough, that's exactly what happened. He managed to piece together some accounting jobs. He stayed silent, knowing that "In a communist country, if you are wise, you keep your mouth shut." Quietly, he focused his attention on a single goal: "Every waking moment, I tried to get out."

An air of desperation overtook the city. People—such as Tran's own father—who had ties to the South Vietnamese government were terrified. With that kind of anguish comes a sense of urgency. Tran and Thuy decided that if they were ever going to get married, the time was now. There was no formal wedding, just a small gathering where everyone present recognized the couple's union.

Tran became more and more intent on finding a way out of South Vietnam. Through a former Shell Oil colleague, he connected with a former Air Vietnam pilot who was secretly building a boat. He wanted to sail to Malaysia, but he needed a map to get there. Tran remembered his afternoons at the Abraham Lincoln Library when he was a teenager. He also remembered the maps he had pored over in back issues of National Geographic.

The library was closed to the public, but a librarian he knew still worked there. He arranged to have coffee with her and asked if she could find him a map of Southeast Asia that included the Gulf of Thailand. He offered to pay her 50 dong, more than she made in a month.

The next time they met for coffee, she was beaming. As agreed, Tran handed her the newspaper he had been reading. Politely, she excused herself and stepped into the restroom. When she returned, she handed Tran the folded newspaper that concealed the map.

"She hid it in her underwear," Tran said. As he told this story many decades later, he still sounded gleeful at the deception.

Months passed. The ex-pilot kept demanding more and more gold in exchange for safe passage. Finally, Tran realized he had been duped. There was no boat. When he tried to confront the former pilot one last time, he had disappeared.

A second route brokered by a friend of Thuy's brother also brought disappointment, not to mention further loss of funds. "Everyone was bribed," said Tran.

The next attempt had Tran posing as a Filipino in order to obtain fake citizenship papers. Even when Tran grew his hair and slicked it back to change his appearance, that did not end well, either.

Escape effort No. 4 put Tran in touch with a tough guy in his twenties named Song who said he represented the owner of a boat that could take them to freedom. Tran's mother refused to take part in the escape attempt, explaining that she wanted to stay behind to make sure the communists did not commandeer the family home. After much back and forth, Tran negotiated a price to transport himself, his father, and Thuy.

Under cover of darkness, the three of them rode their bikes through Saigon. They boarded a ferry across the Saigon River, then rode three kilometers more to their designated departure spot.

"It all made sense at the time," Tran wrote in *American Dreamer.* "The moonless night, the remote location, the middle of the night departure. Clearly, Song and his crew were doing everything possible to avoid attracting attention and raising the suspicions of the communist authorities."

They boarded the small boat intended to take them to the larger escape vessel. When it docked, Song told the passengers he and another smuggler would escort them to the ship, one passenger at a time. Following the Vietnamese tradition of honoring one's elders, Tran urged his father to go first.

Minutes passed. When the escorts returned, Tran saw that Song was carrying a large knife, which he dipped with blood-covered hands into the river. When Tran asked where his father was, Song said he was already on "the big boat." Shuddering, Tran understood that his father had been killed.

In a cold voice, Song told Tran and Thuy that they needed to move to a different spot on the boat. He started the motor and ordered his passengers to stand. He tied their hands. Then he shoved them into the dark water.

Suddenly, the survival skills they had learned during a swimming class in their freshman year at Pacific University came back to Thuy and Tran. They managed to loosen the knots binding their hands. They squirmed out of their pants and knotted the bottom of each leg. They blew air into the pants and waved the pants-balloons above them.

To their astonishment, they looked up to see Song's boat returning in their direction. The crew men extended their arms and lifted them back onto the small craft. Thuy and Tran wondered if they would be taken someplace to be killed, just like his father. Instead they were dropped off where they had originally boarded the boat. They retrieved their bicycles and rode home. But they knew the smugglers would be back to demand more money for not reporting Tran's and Thuy's attempted escape to authorities.

Tran achieved some small measure of justice when he reported the murderous smuggling ring to the local police. He knew Song would come back for more money; that was how the gangsters operated. He also knew he was putting himself and Thuy at risk by admitting that they had tried to leave. It was a tradeoff he was willing to make. The local police set up a sting, and Song was arrested.

"Under communism, they make sure that people understand that if you confess to your wrongdoings and help them catch the bad guys, you will be treated fairly," he said. "And that is what happened." Tran admitted to the authorities that he was wrong to have tried to escape. Song was sent to jail.

But without a body as proof, they could not be charged with murder. Song refused to tell the police and Tran where his father had been killed. To this day, Tran anguishes over the fact that he could never arrange a proper burial for his father.

A LAST-DITCH ESCAPE EFFORT

"That was the fourth attempt," Tran said. He is a slight man, and at seventy-one at the time of our interview, his hair has turned silver. As he described those days of despair and treachery, he sat in his study in his comfortable home in Camas, Washington.

"After that I almost ran out of funds," he continued. "I ran out of self-confidence. I felt guilty. Obviously it was my fault that my father was murdered."

No one else blamed Tran, least of all his mother. While she wanted to remain in Vietnam to safeguard their property, she worried daily that Khoa, her youngest son, would be drafted, then sent to fight for Vietnam against Cambodia. Through her gray-market work, Tran's mother Noi had established relationships with a number of ethnic Chinese merchants in Saigon. After the communist takeover, some of those merchants had set up side businesses of building ships to carry refugees away from Vietnam.

Officially, of course, this kind of venture was illegal. But generous payoffs persuaded Vietnamese officials to look the other way. Noi called in favors from a Chinese merchant friend, handed this friend an agreed-upon amount of money, and sent Khoa out to sea. Their own experience had taught them how dangerous this could be, and horror stories abounded about the risks of fleeing on these overcrowded vessels. Boats capsized. Pirates trolled the South China Sea, robbing passengers of food and valuables. Sometimes the bandits even caused damages to the boat's engines, leaving the passengers to drift without food or water.

Later, the family learned that Khoa had made it safely to Malaysia.

As word circulated that communist leaders intended to quash the wave of refugees leaving Vietnam, Tran's mother once again visited her Chinese merchant friend. She negotiated a price for her twenty-year-old son, Khoi, and for Mai, eighteen. Tran and Thuy paid for their own passage. Noi and Binh, Tran's oldest sister, elected to remain in Saigon to protect their home.

On the morning of March 18, 1979—five long years after they had returned to Vietnam—Tran and Thuy climbed on his moped and waved at any spies who might be watching as if they were going to work. A circuitous route took them to a truck festooned with the label "Construction Company of Southern Vietnam." As they had agreed in advance, the driver handed them papers identifying them as his employees. Mai and Khoi joined them as they slipped under a green tarp for the ride to the port.

Sometimes the world can be a disarmingly tiny place. The following day, as they waited on a dock for the next phase of their getaway, Tran spotted Quang, a Vietnamese friend from UC Berkeley. At Cal, Quang had earned a PhD in mathematics. His wife was a pharmacist. Now, with their two children, they were making the same attempt to leave as Tran and Thuy. It was too dangerous to speak. So as they passed each other, they made eye contact but said nothing.

A short boat ride took them to the home of a Chinese family, part of the network that helped people leave Vietnam. Tran, Thuy, Khoi, and Mai slept in a thatched-roof lean-to in the family's backyard. Weeks passed before they were escorted to a rickety fishing boat designed for perhaps fifty passengers. Hundreds of men, women and children of all ages crammed their way onto the deck.

"We must have been 350 people," Tran said, "packed like sardines."

The boat lurched its way into the choppy waters of the open sea.

"I thought about all I had endured over the past five years," Tran wrote in *American Dreamer.* "I had lost my career, lost my father, lost my hope and nearly lost my life. But at this moment, I felt optimistic." For the first time in many months, Tran wrote, he allowed himself a smile.

That glimmer of hope was short-lived. As predicted, bands of pirates attacked the boat. First they confiscated gold, jewelry, and foreign currencies from the passengers. They took Tran's eyeglasses, even his Levi's. Then, seeking possible hidden loot, they slit open the boat's bags of rice and used their sharp knives to pierce water jugs. After she was raped by a pirate, a teenage girl threw herself into the sea to die.

The May sun in the Gulf of Thailand was brutal—and unrelenting. The boat drifted, seemingly without destination. The passengers sat in numb silence, until finally someone said, "I see a mountain! I see land!"

REFUGEE ISLAND

They suspected they had landed in Malaysia, though at first, no one knew for sure. When they spotted a large SUV emblazoned with the letters UNHCR—for United Nations High Commissioner for Refugees—the bedraggled group heaved a collective sigh of relief. An official-looking man emerged and asked if anyone spoke English.

Tran's was among several hands that shot up. Pointing at Tran, he asked "What are your credentials?" Without hesitation, Tran answered, "Khiem Tran. University of California, Berkeley. Class of 1974."

The treacherous, eight-day voyage had taken them to the island of Pulau Bidong. The tiny land mass, less than one square kilometer, lay about seventeen miles off the coast of Malaysia. The refugee camp run by the United Nations housed about 30,000 people. Astonishingly—but again, proof of just how small this vast world can be—Tran's brother Khoa was among them. On a tiny speck of an island, the siblings were reunited.

It took no time for Tran and Thuy to be drafted as interpreters. "Half a year in the refugee camp, I made myself useful, interpreting for the English-speaking delegation: America, Great Britain, Canada, Australia," Tran said.

His accounting skills also proved valuable. New refugees arrived daily. Each family group had to be interviewed and classified according to, among other qualities, their desired destination for immigration. Each country had different entry requirements and preferences. Tran helped keep track of the various categories.

To the enjoyment of the officials for whom he was translating, Tran also displayed his sense of humor. After an interview with a Vietnamese man who said he had no living relatives anywhere, but wanted to settle in the United States, one of the American team leaders remarked that the poor man must be very lonely.

"He's even lonelier than J. Edgar Hoover," Tran joked. "At least Hoover has his mother." The team leader laughed hard.

As a graduate of a major US university and a former Shell executive, Tran enjoyed a status that extended beyond his language skills. Along with interpreting, he became the camp's unofficial press secretary. This meant he met with dignitaries who came on inspection missions, such as a New York Democratic Congressman Stephen Solarz. After Tran briefed him and walked him through the crowded, makeshift housing at Pulau Bidong, Solarz told Tran he thought conditions were dreadful. But Tran protested, explaining that after what they had all been through, residents of the refugee camp were happy to be there.

Tran also met journalists from around the world. His picture appeared in *Life* magazine. The Canadian Broadcasting Corporation taped an interview with him. A reporter from the German magazine *Der Spiegel* interviewed Tran in English and was impressed when Tran concluded the interview by saying "Auf Wiedersehen"—German for "farewell."

His work as camp press secretary also brought him in contact with journalists from *Time* magazine, *Newsweek*, the *Los Angeles Times*, and *The Washington Post.*

There were side trips, too. With English as their common language, he served as the translator for a French surgeon from Medecins San Frontieres (Doctors Without Borders) during an operation on an offshore medical ship. For Tran, the highlight of the experience was the croissant and café au lait he savored in the ship's mess hall after the procedure.

"Fantastic!" Tran said as he described the buttery pastry and steaming coffee so many years later.

On another occasion, he translated for a Malaysian court trying a Vietnamese man for sea piracy. This time, the standout features involved sleeping in a cushy hotel bed and relishing a beer with lunch.

Finally it came time for Tran and his family to be interviewed for resettlement. Tran was stunned to discover that his friends in Oregon had organized a campaign on his behalf. His file bulged with letters from the state's two US senators at that time, Robert Packwood and Mark Hatfield, both Republicans. The file also contained a letter from then Rep. Les AuCoin, noting that Tran had worked on his campaign while attending Pacific University. His friends from California had contacted then Sen. Alan Cranston, a Democrat, who also wrote on Tran's behalf.

And so they set forth to the life they had longed for. A UNHCR boat took them to the Malaysian coast. From Kuala Lumpur they flew to

Tokyo. Next came a nonstop flight to Seattle, then a puddle-jumper to Portland. The war felt far behind and so did the horrors of their escape.

BACK IN THE US OF A

"Part of my life was that boat trip," Tran said. "The better part was looking forward, making things better."

Once they learned that Tran and his family would actually be coming to Portland, the same friends from Pacific University who had lobbied on his behalf sprang into action. They found the couple an apartment and furnished it from garage sales. They got him a job as a math tutor, the best thing they could find in the sluggish American economy of late 1979.

With characteristic determination, Tran set about finding more suitable employment. He sent out resumes, and without fail received responses informing "Ms. Tran" that no positions were available. So now, on top of the war, on top of the boat trip, on top of the murder of his father—there was gender discrimination, as potential employers falsely assumed he was female because of his first name, Khiem.

He revised his resume, adopting the name Timothy Tran. He sent the new resumes to the six companies who had rejected him as Khiem. All six invited him for interviews.

Thuy, for her part, had preceded her husband in this renaming effort. In high school in Saigon, her first English teacher had given her the name Cathy. Cathy Tran quickly found a job as an accountant at US Bank. Rising through the ranks, she stayed at the bank until 1990, then moved to an insurance company.

For the newly christened Tim Tran, the best offer came from Johnstone Supply, an international distributor of heating, vacuuming, air-conditioning, and refrigeration products that has its roots in Portland. Tran started at Johnstone as an accountant. Twenty-three years later, he retired as a chief finance officer (CFO) and vice president of finance, the number two person in a multibillion-dollar company.

Since they had never had an official marriage ceremony, Cathy and Tim decided to renew their vows before a Multnomah County judge. At the party afterward, a friend playfully asked if Tim had married for love or for money.

Here comes Tim the comedian, as recorded in *American Dreamer*: "When we married the first time, Cathy did not have a lot of money, so I call that marrying for love," he said. "This time, Cathy has a job that pays well, so it must be marrying for money. I'm looking forward to using that money to buy a lot of love!"

Tran took up golf. Once again, his wit served him well. In his golf club's locker room, a player glanced at an Asian man and assumed he was the attendant. The player told Tran to get him more towels. Tran's golf partner started to object, but Tran shot a crafty smile and said, "Right away, sir."

GIVING BACK

"Being accepted as a refugee in America, it is never a right, but it is a privilege," Tran said. "The privilege creates indebtedness."

As he retired from Johnstone and started teaching at the University of Phoenix, Tran took a long look at his net worth. From a refugee who arrived in the United States with scarcely a penny, he had become a wealthy man. It was time, he decided, to give back.

Starting with the day he discovered the air-conditioned sanctuary of the Abraham Lincoln Library in Saigon, Tran had always loved libraries. He and Cathy also felt a special tie to Pacific University. It was where, after they met in Washington, they launched their American education, and it was where their romance first took hold. They decided to create an endowment that would support the library in perpetuity. In return, Pacific University gave its library a new name: The Tim & Cathy Tran Library.

The Trans are inveterate travelers. They have visited most of America's national parks and nearly all the presidential libraries. They have made many trips to Europe, cruised the Amazon, and admired the art at the Hermitage Museum in St. Petersburg, Russia. By careful design, they have not returned to Vietnam.

"Too many sad memories," he said.

With great pride, he explains: "I am from Vietnam. My country is the United States of America."

Afterword

Lessons of Survival

Over the five-plus years of The Immigrant Story's existence, more than 225 people from seventy-two different countries have shared their stories with us. Among them, more than fifty are survivors of genocide, Holocaust, or the atrocities of war. Collectively, they represent sixteen different conflicts in nineteen countries. Uniformly modest, these brave men and women have also been stunningly devoid of bitterness. As my colleagues and I at The Immigrant Story set out to present the stories that make up this book, we recognized other common traits—qualities these survivors shared despite vast differences in geography, in geopolitics, in their age or in their gender. These attributes, we realized, offer important lessons to all of us as we face our own challenges.

And now for a highly personal digression. For the three years that this book was in progress, its working title was "To Bear Witness." The name was a paean to the late Holocaust scholar and survivor Elie Wiesel, a Nobel Prize winner who was also my Boston University colleague. We viewed this title as a way to honor our book's subjects, all of whom had borne witness to terrible cruelties wrought by other humans. Then, after approving our manuscript, our editor at Oregon State University Press said we needed a new title because "To Bear Witness" had been used by too many other authors.

Changing a book's title after three years is a bit like renaming your son or daughter as the child prepares to enter preschool. At The Immigrant Story, we wracked our collective brains, searching for something that would encompass our book's scope and purpose. As I read and re-read the chapters, I kept flashing back to the day I first interviewed Emmanuel Turaturanye. When I asked why he believed he had survived the massacres in Rwanda that claimed nearly everyone else in his large family, he told me, "I think I lived in order to tell the world."

That thought—that quote—was so powerful and profound that it became (with some small tightening) the name of this volume.

But that is not where this personal digression ends. In a sense, it is where it begins. Two days after our editor agreed to this new title, I was felled by a terrifying medical event. "Spinal epidural hematoma" is so rare that it prompts many physicians to furrow their brows and murmur something to the effect of, "hmm, I remember reading about that in medical school." "Idiopathic" is medical-speak for "we have no idea," which remains the causal description of what happened to me one Saturday evening as I stood up from my desk, pondering what I would cook for dinner.

Skipping over the gory medical details, following eight and a half hours of emergency spinal surgery, my initial diagnosis was "incomplete quadriplegia." Only much later did my neurosurgeon tell me that she feared I would never walk again and would likely breathe only with the assistance of a respirator.

So this is where the connection to this afterword comes into play. Immobile at first, I found sleep elusive. Though my body felt like concrete, my brain was racing nonstop. I kept thinking about the hardships that the subjects of this book had endured. In my sleepless head, I replayed the words of hard-earned wisdom they had proffered—in other words, what it was that enabled them to move forward. These lessons became a kind of silent mantra for me.

I was still in the Intensive Care Unit when two unscheduled visitors entered my room. I could not turn my head to greet them, so I asked them to please stand close to my hospital bed so I could see who they were. A very tall man, Emmanuel Turaturanye, stood beside Sankar Raman, founder of The Immigrant Story. They gave me big whoops of encouragement, foreseeing optimistically that—diagnosis be damned—I would soon be entering ballroom dance contests or jogging backward up Mt. Hood. Laughing together felt great, and then I surprised myself by asking Emmanuel if he would please take my still-limp hand and say a prayer with me. I knew how important Emmanuel's Christian faith was to him, and I selfishly figured that if anyone might have connections with higher authorities, it was him.

Though my body was immobile, I am certain that a wave of warmth swept through me as Emmanuel voiced his prayer.

I did not hear him say this, but Sankar said later that as they left my hospital room, Emmanuel tossed him a confident smile and said, "She's going to walk again."

And he was right.

I am grateful to each of the subjects of this book for providing inspiration that has helped me navigate this frightening phase of my life. Without intending to appear didactic, I hope these lessons will be of value to other readers as well.

FORTITUDE—THE STRENGTH TO KEEP GOING

These survivors reached deep inside themselves to find the courage to hang on, even when keeping going seemed futile—maybe even crazy. They taught us to accept that you can't know what's ahead—but to believe in your bones that whatever does lie ahead, it's got to be better than the present. And so you keep going forward. As one example, at just seven years old, a survivor from Sudan named Peter Magai Bul told us he said goodbye to his mother and told himself he could do it; he could take care of himself and walk to a safe place away from the war. Sleeping by day and walking by night, avoiding wild animals and enemy soldiers, Peter walked more than a thousand miles with the other Lost Boys and Girls from Sudan to safety in a refugee camp in Kenya. As they set out each evening he made that same decision again and again: to get up and keep walking. This is the same sense of determination we heard from Sivheng Ung, who endured five years in Cambodia's Killing Fields; from Les and Eva Aigner, prisoners first of Nazi tyranny and then of communist despotry; from Dijana Ihas, who with her fellow musicians kept performing in Sarajevo while the city was under siege by Serbia for more than three years. Ultimately, we heard this message—or a variation thereof—from every survivor we interviewed.

ABSENCE OF SELF-PITY

What every one of these survivors showed us was that feeling sorry for themselves was a luxury they could not afford. Also, as long as they were breathing, they knew they were probably better off than the friends and family members who had perished in the crises they were enduring or had survived.

FAITH—BELIEF IN A FORCE GREATER THAN ONESELF

Genuine faith transcends any one religion or creed. This is not to say that faith based in a specific religion is not sometimes what bolsters a survivor in the darkest moments. In her story, Hatidza Polovina, a devout Muslim, described riding a bus into a combat zone to become a bride in wartime Sarajevo. As she heard the bombs exploding around her, she sustained herself by remembering, "God knows what is good for you; you don't have to worry about deciding what to do." Emmanuel Turaturanye, a Christian, swears that he heard a heavenly voice telling him to straighten his life out. After she lost her pregnancy and her husband, Sivheng Ung considered killing herself, but chose not to, because the Buddha did not condone suicide. Virtually all the survivors described something like this, a certain existential confidence that there was a larger future worth fighting for, and that some guardian force would ensure that future.

FEARLESSNESS—WILLINGNESS TO TAKE BOLD RISKS

It was a kind of chorus, what these survivors told us: When death is the certain alternative, what is there to fear? Thus they recounted audacious steps they took in the face of peril that eventually proved to be what saved them. "Risk" becomes an inevitable part of the journey to safety, they explained, and so any danger associated with that risk loses its potency. When death seemed almost inevitable, Emmanuel Turaturanye, a Tutsi teenager with his baby sister in his arms, knocked on the door of a Hutu neighbor, not knowing if she would take them in or kill them. She not only took them in but confronted her own son, a member of the Hutu militia, warning him that if he harmed their guests, she would take her own life. In the United States at his age, Saron Khut would have been in kindergarten. In Cambodia, he set out on his own, walking for days as a child alone, with the sole goal of finding his mother.

A SENSE OF PERSPECTIVE

Tim Tran was floating in the ocean on a crowded boat filled with men, women, and children seeking refuge from the horrors of war and political upheaval in their native Vietnam. Food and fresh water were scarce. The harsh heat and blazing sun were unrelenting. Pirates had already struck, stealing anything of even dubious value. Tran had lost his father in an earlier, thwarted attempt to escape. He had lost his career. He had come close to losing his life. He certainly had reason to have lost all hope. And yet, squeezed onto that boat and uncertain just where, when or whether the vessel would reach safe harbor, Tran felt optimistic. How much worse could things get? Wherever they were headed, it had to be better than what they had left behind.

In story after story, this sense of perspective helped survivors to move forward with their lives. Or as Sivheng Ung's father counseled: no matter how bad she might have it, someone else had it worse.

RESILIENCE—THE ABILITY TO BOUNCE BACK

Building a new life and repeatedly getting up to try again is commonly associated with the immigrant experience. These qualities are frequently listed as part of "the American story" of a land of newcomers, even by those who know few recent immigrants personally. We are in no way trying to foment the tired stereotype of "the good immigrant." But we did find that overcoming trauma was a shared experience for many of our interview subjects. Obviously no magic emotional eraser can eliminate horrific memories. No delete button can make terrifying recurring images disappear. But research shows that resilient people—people who can adapt well in the face of trauma or tragedy—tend to share three common traits. These are: acceptance, purpose, and flexibility. In Rama Yousef, we saw these characteristics carry her through obstacle after obstacle. A teenager in a new country without either of her parents, Rama found her own safe havens, couch surfing with friends, talking her way into a private high school, connecting with another like-minded immigrant family, and finding a scholarship that gave her a full ride to college. Today, Rama is on her way to law school.

PAY IT FORWARD

Gratitude comes in many packages, many shapes and sizes. Often, gratitude accompanies recovery or even respite from trauma. Again, we are not trying to paint these survivors as saints or to feed into the trope of the good immigrant. Certainly they all have tempers. They've all lost their patience in traffice jams. They've probably all said unkind things, at one time or another, to their spouses or others. But though our sample is small, our percentage of men and women determined to give back is high. Arriving in the United States, escaping terror and trachery, these survivors have committed time and personal energy to the goal of improving the quality of life within their adopted communities. Here are some examples: Dijana Ihas launched the Pacific University String Project, enabling hundreds of boys and girls in Oregon—many of them from disadvantaged backgrounds—to learn to play stringed instruments. Iraqi psychiatrist Dr. Baher Butti became a counselor for Catholic Charities, focusing much of his attention on new immigrants. After the COVID-19 pandemic shut down the immense outdoor gatherings he had organized each year for Portland's pan-Asian and Pacific Island communities, he set to planning a permanent venue for such events. The plans for this facility are posted in his restaurant. Khut is certain it will come to pass. Meantime, his seven-year-old daughter has started a nonprofit of her own, raising money to build a school in Laos, her mother's home country.

AN OCCASIONAL LAUGH

So what's funny about tragedy? Absolutely nothing. But in the face of the worst of circumstances, our subjects did sometimes yield to whacky humor. Maybe it was the absurdity of what was happening around her that made Sivengh Ung laugh as her mother-in-law insisted on hauling her television set and Sivheng's fancy wedding shoes on their forced march out of Pnomh Penh as Pol Pot's troops took control of the Cambodian capital. It's a bittersweet laugh—but it's a laugh, nonetheless—when Baher Butti remarks that every time he corresponds with friends in Iraq and talks about how much he would like to return to his country to help with its rebuilding, they say, "Fine. Come over here and get killed." Or Tim Tran, cracking jokes about J. Edgar Hoover while guiding US officials through a crowded refugee camp.

Gallows humor exists for a reason, and sometimes even a small, ironic laugh can relieve unbearable tension.

Although our daily challenges can never close to matching the perils these survivors confronted, every one of us faces large and small hurdles in the course of our lives. Every one of us gets discouraged at times. When that happens, it is our hope that we can remember these stories of courage and withstand our own adversities with a measure of fortitude, faith, fearlessness, resilience, an occasional laugh, and a healthy sense of perspective.

A Brief Glossary

CRIME AGAINST HUMANITY: A deliberate act, typically part of a systematic campaign, that causes human suffering or death on a large scale.

DEPORTATION: The formal removal of a foreign national from the United States for violating US immigration law. More broadly: expulsion of a person or a group of people from a place or a country.

ETHNIC CLEANSING: A purposeful policy designed by one ethnic or religious group to remove by violent and terror-inducing means the civilian population of another ethnic or religious group. Coercive tactics used in ethnic cleansing include: murder, torture, rape or other sexual assault, arbitrary arrest and detention, severe physical injury to civilians, and confinement of a civilian population in a ghetto area.

FOREIGN NATIONAL: A person who is not a naturalized citizen of the country in which they are living.

GENOCIDE: A crime committed with the intent to harm or destroy a national, ethnic or religious group, as a whole or in part.

GREEN CARD: An identity document issued by the US Citizen and Immigration Services that shows a person has permanent residency in the United States. Known officially as a permanent resident card. A Green Card allows a foreign national to live and work permanently in the United States. Green Card holders do not have the right to vote.

IMMIGRANT: A person who comes to live permanently in a foreign country.

IMMIGRATION: The process through which individuals become residents or citizens of another country.

LAWFUL PERMANENT RESIDENT (LPR): Someone who has permission to live and work in the United States, but is not eligible for certain benefits, such as voting and some social services; someone with a Green Card.

POLITICAL ASYLUM: Protection granted by a nation to someone who has left their native country as a political refugee.

POLITICAL REFUGEE: A person who has fled their homeland because of political persecution.

REFUGEE: A person who flees for refuge or safety, especially to a foreign country, typically at times of upheaval and/or war.

SPONSOR: A person who has helped an immigrant become a lawful, permanent resident.

TEMPORARY PROTECTED STATUS (TPS): Temporary immigration status extended to individuals from countries undergoing difficulties that make it unsafe for those individuals to be deported to those countries.

UNDOCUMENTED IMMIGRANT: Someone who does not have permission to live or work in the United States and is at risk of deportation.

VISA: An official document or stamp on a passport that allows a person to enter or leave a particular country.

WAR CRIME: An action carried out during the conduct of a war that violates accepted international rules of war.

Acknowledgments

This book would not have been possible without a cadre of remarkable individuals and dedicated partner institutions. Leading the list of exceptional people who helped us are the survivors who shared their experiences with us. Their courage is matched only by the generosity they displayed in opening up about their suffering and hardships.

We must also thank the phalanx of friends of The Immigrant Story who assisted us in locating these survivors. We are grateful to Judy Margles, executive director of the Oregon Jewish Museum and Center for Holocaust Education, who helped connect our team with Holocaust survivors living in Oregon. We also want to thank the staff of OJMCHE for assisting us in our research and for providing us access to their collection of archival images and oral histories.

We also extend our gratitude to Lauren Fortgang, director of Portland's Never Again Coalition, who has been instrumental in linking us to the region's Rohingya and Sudanese communities.

We also owe thanks to Imam Abdullah Polovina and Hadija Polovina of Portland's Bosniak Educational and Cultural Organization. Not only did they take the time to talk to us about their wartime experience, but they also put us in contact with others in their community.

Chanly Bob, chairman of the Cambodian American Community of Oregon (CACO), graciously introduced us to community elders, ensuring that we would hear strong and powerful voices belonging to those who have endured tremendous adversity. Chanly, himself a survivor of the Cambodian Killing Fields, wanted to be sure that "the right stories" from his community were told.

As an activist in his home country of Iraq, Dr. Baher Butti of Catholic Charities of Oregon has also been an advocate for immigrants in Oregon, especially those from the Middle East. Among other acts, Dr. Butti, a psychiatrist, showed his sensitivity and kindness by acting as our translator.

Thanks also are due to Felix Ruhiri of the Pacific Northwest Rwandan Association; Tim DuRoche, director of programs at WorldOregon; and Sam Gaty, executive director of NW Documentary.

Now comes the part where we pat ourselves on our own collective back. The Immigrant Story is an all-volunteer organization. The talent and experience among this wildly divergent group cannot be exaggerated. We work on this project because we care deeply about its mission: "To document, narrate and curate stories about immigrants in order to produce empathy and advance an inclusive community."

Along with this book, The Immigrant Story team has in only a few short years produced live storytelling events, podcasts, videos, museum exhibits and the ongoing series of profiles of immigrants that appears on our website, www.theimmigrantstory.org. None of this would have existed without a former Intel engineer named Sankar Raman, who arose one day with a fully formed vision of a platform that would help to normalize the increasingly strident conversation around immigration. Sankar, a native of Madras, India, who earned two master's degrees and a doctorate after he came to the United States, had first-hand experience with the kind of bias against immigrants that, sadly, sometimes still surfaces in the United States. Under Sankar's masterful guidance, The Immigrant Story has evolved into a premier multimedia storytelling platform in the Pacific Northwest. All of us who work with Sankar agree that being part of The Immigrant Story is an ongoing privilege.

Over the last five years, The Immigrant Story has gathered the stories of more than fifty survivors of war and genocides. To produce these stories—stories the world needs to hear—Sankar worked diligently with his contacts and networks to find suitable subjects who were willing to participate.

Among our roster of dedicated volunteers, acclaimed photographer Jim Lommasson has been a true partner, sharing the material from his "What We Carried" project and acting as a key advisor during this book's three-year gestation.

Another brave lensman, John Rudoff, can often be found shooting photos in conflict zones around the globe. His insights have greatly enriched this effort.

Longtime television producer David Lipoff also added expertise and helped direct us to certain subjects.

Every word in this book, every punctuation mark, has been examined and considered by our masterful and godsent editor, Matt George Moore. Matt lets no sloppy statistic or dubious fact slide by him. His deft hand has improved each paragraph; his keen eye has spotted inadvertent errors—and he has done this all while serving as the father of two energetic young children. We are so fortunate to count Matt as a colleague.

Author and educator Nancy E. Dollahite also signed on as an early member of the editorial team at The Immigrant Story. She has lived and worked in China, Mexico, Brazil, Scotland and the United States and authored or co-authored four books. She currently edits for TIS, both contributes stories to our website and plays a vital role in shaping the work of our corps of student writers. True to form, Nancy also graciously helped to smooth out some of the rough edges in the manuscript that became this book.

We also are grateful for the assistance of TIS volunteer Julietta Bekker, who weighed in with valuable suggestions. As the book progressed through its wordy gestation, Julietta brought new life of her own, a beautiful baby daughter, into the world.

At The Immigrant Story, we approach storytelling in a collaborative way. While it is impossible to thank each of our volunteers individually, we acknowledge the contribution of every single volunteer and staff. They all enrich our projects with their skills, expertise, and experience. They all make us whole. We thank everyone in our community for making this happen.

One final, very important acknowledgment needs to go to the subjects of the first chapter in this book, Les and Eva Aigner. Our first "Survivors" (as we came to think of them) interview took place in their living room in Tualatin, outside Portland. They served us a home-baked cake as they opened their hearts, souls, and memories to us.

The passing of Les Aigner on August 18, 2021, reminded us anew of the importance of documenting these remarkable, first-person stories.

Les died at home with his family after a long and fruitful life. This fact alone defies the evil plan that Adolf Hitler and his Nazi followers made to eliminate anyone who, like Les Aigner, happened to be born Jewish. The Nazis tried their best to work Les to death in four different concentration camps. Instead, he survived and thrived.

Not long before his death from a heart attack, Les agreed to sit for a video shoot with Immigrant Story founder Sankar Raman. Les promised Sankar that he would bake bread for the occasion, a tradition dating back to his childhood. We are so sorry that we will not break bread together again.

It was such an honor to spend time with Les Aigner. As if we needed no other proof, his courage and resilience demonstrate the reason we must continue to preserve and honor these remarkable stories.

Bibliography and Suggested Reading

Barnett, Michael. *Eyewitness to Genocide: The United Nations and Rwanda.* Ithaca: Cornell University Press, 2002.

Bartop, Paul R., ed. *Cambodian Genocide: The Essential Reference Guide.* ABC-CLIO publisher, 2022.

Bashir, Halima, and Damien Lewis. *Tears of the Desert: A Memoir of Survival in Darfur.* London: One World, 2009.

Belton, David. *When the Hills Ask for Your Blood: A Personal Story of Genocide in Rwanda.* New York: Doubleday, 2014.

Bezdrob, Anne Marie du Preez. *Sarajevo Roses: War Memoir of a Peacekeeper.* Cape Town: Struik Publisher, 2006.

Braham, Randolph L., and Scott Miller. *The Nazis' Last Victims: The Holocaust in Hungary.* Washington, DC: U.S. Holocaust Memorial Museum, 2002.

Brinkley, Joel. *Cambodia's Curse: The Modern History of a Troubled Land.* New York: Public Affairs, 2012.

Buergenthal, Thomas. A *Lucky Child: A Memoir of Surviving Auschwitz as a Young Boy.* Back Bay Books, 2010.

Carmichael, Robert. *When the Clouds Fell from the Sky: A Daughter's Search for Her Father in the Killing Fields of Cambodia.* London: Robinson, 2019.

Chandler, David. *Voices from S21: Terror and History in Pol Pot's Secret Prison.* Berkeley: University of California Press, 2000.

Cockett, Richard. *Sudan: Darfur, Islamism and the Modern World.* New Haven: Yale University Press, 2010.

Coghlan, Nicholas. *Collapse of a Country: A Diplomat's Memoir.* Montreal: McGill-Queen's University Press, 2017.

Coker, Margaret. *The Spymaster of Baghdad: A True Story of Bravery, Family and Patriotism in the Battle Against ISIS.* New York: Dey Street Books, 2021.

Collins, Robert O. *A History of Modern Sudan.* Cambridge University Press, 2008

Dallaire, Romeo. *Shake Hands with the Devil: The Failure of Humanity in Rwanda*. Toronto: Random House Canada, 2003.

Deng, Alephonsion, Benson Deng, Benjamin Ajak, and Judy A. Bernstein. *They Poured Fire on Us from the Sky: The True Story of the Lost Boys from Sudan*. New York: Public Affairs, 2015.

Filkins, Dexter. *The Forever War*. New York: Vintage, 2009.

Galloway, Joseph L. *We Were Soldiers Once, and Young: Ia Drang—The Battle That Changed the War in Vietnam*. Novato, CA: Presidio Press, 2004.

Gourevitch, Philip. *We Wish to Inform You That Tomorrow We Will Be Killed with Our Families*. London: Picador, 1999.

Habiburahman, with Sophie Ansel. *First, They Erased Our Name: A Rohingya Speaks*. Pontiac, MI: Scribe US, 2019.

Hatzfeld, Jean. *Machete Season: The Killers in Rwanda Speak*. London: Picador, 2006.

Hin, Chanrithy. *When Broken Glass Floats*. New York: W.W. Norton & Co., 2001.

Ibrahim, Azeem. *The Rohingyas: Inside Myanmar's Hidden Genocide*. London: New St. Martin's Press, 2009.

Jai, Emmanuel. War Child: *A Child Soldier's Story*. New York: St. Martin's Press, 2009.

Jong, Chanty. R*unning toward the Guns: A Memoir of Escape from Cambodia*. Jefferson, NC: McFarland, 2021.

Karnow, Stanley, Edward Holland, et. al. *Vietnam: A History*. New York: Viking, 1983.

Kayihura, Edouard, with Kerry Zukus. I*nside the Hotel Rwanda: The Surprising True Story . . . And Why It Matters Today*. Dallas: Ben Bella Books, 2014.

Keat, Nawuth. *Alive in the Killing Fields: Surviving the Khmer Rouge Genocide*. Washington, DC: National Geographic Books, 2009.

Keo, Patrick. *Khmer Rise: How I Escaped the Genocide*. Independently published, 2019.

Lakin, Jeanne Celeste, and Paul Lakin. *A Voice in the Darkness: Memoir of a Rwanda Genocide Survivor*. Independently published, 2018.

Lee, Ronan. Myanmar's Rohingya *Genocide: Identity, History and Hate Speech*. London: I.B. Tauris, 2021.

Lewis, Tim. *Land of Second Chances: The Impossible Rise of Rwanda's Cycling Team*. Boulder, CO: Velo Press, 2013.

Longman, Timothy. *Memory and Justice in Post-Genocide Rwanda*. Cambridge, UK: Cambridge University Press, 2017.

Lowry, Lois. *Number the Stars.* New York: Houghton Mifflin Harcourt, 1989.
Lyons, Robert, and Scott Strauss. *Intimate Enemy: Images and Voices of the Rwandan Genocide.* London: Zone Books, 2016.
Maas, Peter. *Love Thy Neighbor: A Story of War.* New York: Vintage, 1997.
Mamdami, Mahmood. *When Victims Become Killers.* Princeton: Princeton University Press, 2002.
Mamdami, Mahmood. *Saviors and Survivors: Darfur, Politics and the War on Terror.* New York: Crown, 2010.
Martell, Peter. *First Raise a Flag: How South Sudan Won the Longest War but Lost the Peace.* Oxford, U.K.: Oxford University Press, 2018.
McCormick, Patricia. *Never Fall Down.* New York: Balzer and Bray, 2013.
Melvern, Linda. *A People Betrayed: The Role of the West in Rwanda's Genocide.* London: Zed Books, 2019.
Myint-U, Thant. *The Hidden History of Burma: Race, Capitalism and Democracy in the 21st Century.* New York: W.W. Norton & Co., 2021.
Ngor, Haing. *Survival in the Killing Fields.* New York: Carroll & Graf, 2003.
O'Brien, Tim. *The Things They Carried.* New York: HarperCollins, 1991.
Offenberger, Ilana Fritz. *The Jews of Nazi Vienna 1938–1945: Rescue and Destruction.* New York: Palgrave MacMillan, 2017.
Oun, Leth, and Joe Samuel Starnes. *A Refugee's American Dream: From the Killing Fields of Cambodia to the U.S. Secret Service.* Philadelphia: Temple University Press, 2023.
Packer, George. *The Assassins' Gate: America in Iraq.* New York: Farrar, Straus & Giroux, 2005.
Pran, Dith. *Children of Cambodia's Killing Fields: Memoirs of Survivors.* New Haven: Yale University Press, 1997.
Prunier, Gerard. *The Rwanda Crisis: History of a Genocide.* New York: Columbia University Press, 1996.
Rees, Lawrence. *The Holocaust: A New History.* New York: Public Affairs, 2018.
Rever, Judi. In *Praise of Blood: The Crimes of the Rwandan Patriotic Front.* Toronto: Vintage Canada, 2020.
Sanders, Dr. Julia. *Rwandan Genocide: The Unspeakable Evils of Ethnic Cleansing and Genocide in Rwanda.* Independently published, 2017.
Sheehan, Neil, Hedrick Smith,, E. W. Kenworthy, Fox Butterfield, and James L. Greenfield. *The Pentagon Papers: The Secret History of the Vietnam War.* New York: The New York Times, 1971.
Strauss, Scott. *The Order of Genocide.* Ithaca: Cornell University Press, 2008.
Thomson, Susan. *Rwanda: From Genocide to Precarious Peace.* New Haven: Yale University Press, 2018.

Tran, Tim (Tran Manh Khiem), with Tom Fields-Mayer. *American Dreamer: How I Escaped Communist Vietnam.* Forest Grove, OR: Pacific University Press, 2020.

Ty, Seng. *The Years of Zero: Coming of Age Under the Khmer Rouge.* Independently published, 2014.

Ung, Luong. *Lucky Child.* New York: HarperCollins, 2005.

Ung, Luong. *First They Killed My Father: A Daughter in Cambodia Remembers.* New York: Harper Perennial, 2006.

Vertin, Zach. *A Rope from the Sky: The Making and Unmaking of the World's Newest State.* New York: Pegasus Books, 2020.

Wade, Francis. *Myanmar's Enemy Within: Buddhist Violence and the Making of a Muslim 'Other.'* London: Zed Books, 2019.

Ward, Geoffrey, and Ken Burns. *The Vietnam War: An Intimate History.* New York: Alfred A. Knopf, 2017.

Warrick, Joby. *Red Line: The Unraveling of Syria and America's Race to Destroy the Most Dangerous Arsenal in the World.* New York: Doubleday, 2021.

Whitlock, Craig. *The Afghanistan Papers: A Secret History of the War.* New York: Simon & Schuster, 2021.

Wiesel, Elie. *Night.* New York: Farrar, Straus & Giroux, 200.

Yathay, Pin. *Stay Alive, My Son.* New York: Touchstone, 198